Variance in Approach Toward a 'Sustainable' Coffee Industry in Costa Rica: Perspectives from Within; Lessons and Insights

Melissa Vogt

]u[

ubiquity press
London

Published by
Ubiquity Press Ltd.
Unit 322-323
Whitechapel Technology Centre
75 Whitechapel Road
London E1 1DU
www.ubiquitypress.com

Text © Melissa Vogt 2019

First published 2019

Cover design by Amber MacKay
This cover has been designed using resources from Freepik.com. Cover image by CHAIWATPHOTOS, used under license from Shutterstock.com.

Print and digital versions typeset by Siliconchips Services Ltd.

ISBN (Paperback): 978-1-911529-76-7
ISBN (PDF): 978-1-911529-77-4
ISBN (EPUB): 978-1-911529-78-1
ISBN (Mobi): 978-1-911529-79-8

DOI: https://doi.org/10.5334/bce

This work is licensed under the Creative Commons Attribution 4.0 International License (unless stated otherwise within the content of the work). To view a copy of this license, visit http://creativecommons.org/licenses/by/4.0/ or send a letter to Creative Commons, 444 Castro Street, Suite 900, Mountain View, California, 94041, USA. This license allows for copying any part of the work for personal and commercial use, providing author attribution is clearly stated.

The full text of this book has been peer-reviewed to ensure high academic standards. For full review policies, see http://www.ubiquitypress.com/

Suggested citation:
Vogt, M. 2019. *Variance in Approach Toward a 'Sustainable' Coffee Industry in Costa Rica: Perspectives from Within; Lessons and Insights.* London: Ubiquity Press. DOI: https://doi.org/10.5334/bce. License: CC-BY 4.0

To read the free, open access version of this book online, visit https://doi.org/10.5334/bce or scan this QR code with your mobile device:

Author and contributor information

Melissa Vogt, MA, MPH, completed her PhD early 2019 developing a concept for human natural environment interactions, ecological sensitivity within human realities (ESHR). She completed fieldwork in Costa Rica and Cuba and has worked in the Great Lakes Region of Africa. Her interest in sustainability certifications as a method for adjusting trade practices and mentality commenced in 2006.

Competing interests

The author(s) declare that they have no competing interests in publishing this title.

Acknowledgements

The monograph is based on my MA dissertation completed in 2010 and acknowledgements for extensive fieldwork and during the writing of the dissertation are included in that work.

I would like to thank the people who agreed to fund the monograph, allowing me to allocate partially paid time to update and complete the writing, formatting and proof reading of the manuscript, and to address reviewer comments. Funding was sought through www.pozible.com.au in 2016 and ten people pledged funds to support the project.

Leonardo Astoria Sanchez provided research and writing support for the extended Costa Rica history chapter between September 2016 – February 2017. He worked with the Costa Rica history chapter from my dissertation. His input was considered valuable to ensure adequate scholarly representation from a Costa Rican historian. It was provided in Spanish and then translated to English. At the time, he was completing his masters dissertation and is now a professor of history at the University of Costa Rica. He was paid for his contribution to the book.

Thanks is also extended to the publishers for agreeing to support a manuscript based on what could be considered historic fieldwork, and accepting it as an academic contribution for learning about Costa Rica and the sustainability certification effort. Thanks are also extended to the peer reviewers, Anna Snider, Eva Kraus and Ana Afonso Gallegos, who provided constructive and valuable comments that led to improvements within the content of this publication. All errors remain my own.

Table of Contents

List of Figures	xiii
List of Tables	xv
Acronyms	xvii

Introduction: Aim and Scope — 1

Background — 7

Chapter 1 Historic account of Costa Rican development: the creation of an identity — 13

Introduction	13
PART I: The Costa Rican colonial experience (1540–1821)	13
PART II: History of independence in Costa Rica (1800–2000)	18
The Central American political experience	18
The Costa Rican political experience	18
Land tenure in Costa Rica and a rural democracy	21
Costa Rica and Coffee	22
Social stratum associated with the Costa Rican coffee industry	23
Expansion of coffee farming (1886–1948)	25
Softening dependency and insecurity for small and medium coffee farmers (1900–1936)	27
Increasing intensive coffee farming and mono-export (1950–1970)	28
Resolving the influence of intensive farming and economic crisis (1970–2000)	30
Summary	30

Chapter 2 Trade's influence in development — 33

Introduction	33
Paradigm and praxis cycles counterbalancing created imbalance	34
'Sustainability': meaning and efficacy	37
Summary	38

Chapter 3 The international coffee industry — 39

Introduction — 39
Brief history of coffee — 40
Botanic background of coffee — 41
The Bean Belt: who wears the pants? — 43
Collapse of the International Coffee Agreement — 47
   Market Saturation — 49
The contrast of a coffee crisis — 52
Summary — 53

Chapter 4 Sustainability Certifications — 55

Introduction — 55
Sustainability certifications — 55
Sustainability certifications and coffee — 56
History of Rainforest Alliance (RA) and Fairtrade coffee sustainability certifications — 57
Costa Rica and sustainably certified coffee — 58
Organisational structure of certifications — 58
Basic differences between Fairtrade and RA premise and standards — 60
Approaches to verifying compliance — 64
Compliance requirements for use of label — 64
Summary — 65

Chapter 5 Overview of the contemporary Costa Rican coffee industry — 67

Introduction — 67
Costa Rica compared to regional indicators of development and happiness — 68
Land distribution nurturing cultural and social significance — 70
Costa Rica: Coffee, sustainability and poverty reduction — 70
Conservation and sustainable development efforts during intensification — 70
Physical suitability of coffee farming locations — 73
Coffee farming in Costa Rica (from the 2000s) — 74
Coffee Industry structure — 77
Lowering popularity of *cooperativismo* — 78
Farming coffee: complications and implications — 79
   Disease and pest epidemics — 79

Environmental impact	79
Environmental and health (in)security	80
South-South Labour Migration: Destination Costa Rican coffee farms	80
Summary	81

Perspectives from within Costa Rica 83

Chapter 6 Methodology and Methods 85

Introduction	85
Rainforest Alliance (RA) and Fairtrade	86
Poverty as a guiding theme within sustainability for fieldwork considerations	87
Ethics	88
Methods	88
Fieldwork	88
Cooperatives included in fieldwork visits in 2009	93
Triangulation of fieldwork information	93
Presenting common opinions, quotes and results	95
Addressing subjectivity and representation of fieldwork presented in results	96
Quantified summary and assessment according to poverty reduction indicators	96
Qualifying how findings should be used and understood	98

Findings 99

Chapter 7 The subtler advantages of 'sustainability' certifications 101

Introduction	101
Orientation in the international market and redistributing national power dynamics	101
Law and certification standards: correlation, causality and influence	103
Access to credit	105
Summary	106

Chapter 8 The cost of 'sustainability' certifications: intention versus outcome 107

Introduction	107
A minimum price	107

The Fairtrade premium 110
Auditing 111
Summary 112

Chapter 9 Standards for producers: variance in objective and approach 115

Introduction 115
Standard development: politics of change and a top down approach 115
   Standard development according to certification 116
   Producer involvement in standard setting 117
   Inappropriate Standards 118
Summary 123

Chapter 10 Increasing the number of certifications and associated benefits or disadvantages 125

Introduction 125
Top down demand 125
Symptom of a supply chain power imbalance? 127
Limited capability for market access 127
Certifications as a market movement 128
The producer perspective: observed and understood difference between certifications 129
The influences of a top down, market demand-based approach 131

Chapter 11 Reputation beyond intention and influence 133

Introduction 133
Subsistence farming, and regulated and reduced chemical use 133
The producer perspective: the difficulty of assigning influence of change to certifications 136
Frustration with Fairtrade 137
   Certifying existing practices? 138
   Scope for improvement: more recent changes 139
   Requirements for implementation: Minimal support or building capacity? 140
Summary 141

Chapter 12 Reinforcing international trade power dynamics? 143

Introduction 143

Increasing certified markets and resulting compromises	143
Voluntary regulation and vulnerability to power dynamics Interdependence between corporation and certification	144
Power dynamics between producers and certifications	146
Monitoring producers more than traders and roasters	147
Summary	147

Chapter 13 Summative discussion   149

Introduction	149
Considerations and concerns identified	150
Outcomes associated with RA and Fairtrade	151
An economic loss	152
The cost of becoming certified for small producers compared to benefit	153
Producer voice in Fairtrade organisational processes	154
The challenge of adequately involving producer groups for Fairtrade	155
Hired labour standards	155
Formalised land title	156
Certifications: labels and market-based reputation	156
Quantified summary of key topics against poverty reduction indicators	157
A whim of the market	162
Reinforcing international trade dynamics	163
The role of the 'developed' world: from Green Revolution to a Sustainable Revolution?	164
Positive outcomes and pressure points for influence	165
Summary	166

Opportunities for Improvement   167

Chapter 14 Alternatives to and complements for sustainability certifications in Costa Rica   169

Introduction	169
Structured education programs for premium investment	169
Certifying direct trade compared to international sourcing chains	171
Examples of Fairtrade certified and directly traded coffee in Costa Rica	173
Learning from experimental precedents in Costa Rica	174
Reducing the cost of compliance	174
Vertical integration of the sourcing chain	175

Locally developed standards 177
Limiting international certification schemes to specific situations 179
Summary 180

Conclusion — 183

Chapter 15 Summarising comments and recent developments — 185

Introduction 185
Quantified summary according to poverty reduction indicators 186
Recognising in-country frustration with international sustainability certification process 186
The difference between RA and Fairtrade in Costa Rica 187
Overview of achieved intentions 188
Identified benefits 188
   Producer participation 189
   Price and poverty reduction 189
   Considering the benefit of certifications over time 190
Sustainability standards and legal requirements 191
Demand for multiple certifications 191
Summary 192
Recent developments 193

Epilogue — 195

Coffee: Whose Sustainability? — 197

Introduction 197
Social and cultural significance of coffee in Costa Rica 198
Reducing intensive coffee farming 200
Summary 200

Bibliography 203
Recommended Reading for Recent Developments 217
Glossary 221
Appendix A: Themes for fieldwork discussion and interviews 223

List of Figures

Figure 1:	Classification of coffee: species and varieties	41
Figure 2:	The bean belt	44
Figure 3:	Periphery of coffee belt: coffee consumption by country (60kg bags/year)	44
Figure 4:	Basic In-country coffee sourcing chain	45
Figure 5:	Example of variance in country specific sourcing chains	46
Figure 6:	Coffee export price per pound (1969–2015)	49
Figure 7:	Coffee export price per pound (2009–2018)	50
Figure 8:	International coffee production during two coffee crises (1990–2003)	51
Figure 9:	International coffee prices during two coffee crises (1983–2008)	51
Figure 10:	RA organisational structure 2017	59
Figure 11:	Fairtrade International organisational structure	60
Figure 12:	Costa Rican export of coffee green by quantity and value	75
Figure 13:	Costa Rica: major agricultural exports	75
Figure 14:	International coffee production yield per hectare	76
Figure 15:	Four horizontal and vertical tiers of coffee industry structure	77
Figure 16:	Ten coffee farming communities and three cooperative visited in 2009	94
Figure 17:	Two coffee farming communities farm visited in 2014	95
Figure 18:	Basic comparison: direct trade and certifications	172
Figure 19:	Costa Rican green coffee imports by quantity and value	177

List of Tables

Table 1:	Major traders in coffee industry	47
Table 2:	Comparing RA and Fairtrade hired labour standards	62
Table 3:	Regional indicators	69
Table 4:	Export trade matrix, coffee, green	76
Table 5:	Interview schedule 2009	89
Table 6:	Information about cooperatives visited in 2009	92
Table 7:	Poverty reduction indicators to summarise fieldwork	97
Table 8:	Accumulated poverty reduction indicators and outcomes by identified issue	158
Table 9:	Production, supply, demand data statistics	178

Acronyms

AECID	Agencia Española de Cooperación Internacional para el Desarrollo
ASCONA	Costa Rican Association for the Conservation of Nature
CAN	Community Agroecology Network
Coocafe	Consorcio de Cooperativas de Caficultores de Guanacaste y Montes de Oro
EFTA	European Fair Trade Association
FAO	Food and Agriculture Organisation
FLAANZ	Fairtrade Labelling Association of Australia and New Zealand
GDP	Gross Domestic Product
HDI	Human Development Index
HPI	Happy Planet Index
ICAFE	Instituto de Café, Costa Rica
ICO	International Coffee Organisation
ILO	International Labour Organisation
INEC	Instituto Nacional de Estadisticas y Censos, Costa Rica
IOM	International Organisation for Migration
ECLAC	Economic Commission for Latin America
FI	Fairtrade International
GATT	General Agreement on Tariffs and Trade
INBio	Instituto Nacional de Biodiversidad
MDG	Millenium Development Goals
MNC	Multinational Corporation
NAMA	Nationally Appropriate Mitigation Actions
NEWS	Network of European World Shops
OECD	Organisation for Economic Co-operation and Development
RA	Rainforest Alliance
SAN	Sustainable Agriculture Network
SAP	Structural Adjustment Programs
SDG	Sustainable Development Goals
TNC	Transnational Corporation
WCED	World Commission on Environment and Development
WTO	World Trade Organisation
WFTO	World Fair Trade Organisation

Introduction: Aim and Scope

I was to walk two hundred metres and turn right, to find the house with a blue façade and a family waiting for me. It was a small coffee farming community in the south of Costa Rica surrounded by mountains, forest and coffee, slightly run down; the community was similar in design to a town on the Caribbean Coast, Cahuita. Walking through their house, it seemed like most houses in Costa Rica until I looked straight through the back window to a tropical forest garden. I was given a personal tour of the large variety of trees, fruits and orchids growing through the one-hectare space that used to be a small coffee farm. Practicing some ornithology, I identified approximately nine species of birds that would visit every morning to eat the bananas grown in the garden. The diverse range of fruits included some kiwi fruits introduced by an international exchange student. It was a beautiful and peaceful location to stay for a couple of days. Breakfast was served with a cup of coffee and a knowing smile, some gallo pinto[1],

---

[1] 'Spotted roaster' is a traditional Costa Rican dish of rice, beans, coriander, red capsicum and lizano sauce.

How to cite this book chapter:
Vogt, M. 2019. *Variance in Approach Toward a 'Sustainable' Coffee Industry in Costa Rica: Perspectives from Within; Lessons and Insights.* Pp. 3-5. London: Ubiquity Press. DOI: https://doi.org/10.5334/bce.a. License: CC-BY 4.0

eggs, a tortilla[2], plátano del horno[3], with some natilla[4] on the side. Most of the food was served from the garden or traded with neighbours. The barter economy is alive and well in Costa Rican rural areas. The father of the family explained why he would never grow coffee again now focusing on cultivating organic lettuce amongst other activities.[5] There was a coffee shop in town which locals rarely visit as they can make perfectly good coffee at home or, even better, agua dulce[6] or refresco.[7] In Costa Rica, all coffee exported is of first grade quality; the second grade is consumed in Costa Rica, it is 'better quality anyway'[8] ('Ronaldo', Cooperative employee 13 April 2009). The atmosphere of a coffee shop cannot compare to the smell of fresh air, forests, and the sound of birds that enrich many regions of Costa Rica. It is from this side of the coffee trade that this book develops.

Using interviews, focus groups and observations in ten coffee farming communities in Costa Rica, the influence of sustainability certifications is considered. The methodology provides perspectives from within the country and a different and more detailed way of understanding the influence of sustainability certifications. The study aims to consider the role of Rainforest Alliance and Fairtrade in the Costa Rican coffee industry context to evaluate the advantages and disadvantages for farmers, cooperatives and communities and identify opportunities for improvement.

To encourage a better understanding of the regional and international context, the history of the region and of Costa Rica and associated coffee industries is presented in three historic periods.

The influence of trade in development is considered within a poverty reduction and sustainability frame; a summary of the international coffee industry; and an explanation of sustainability certifications are provided in the following sections: Introduction; Background; Methodology and methods: perspectives from within Costa Rica; Findings: Advantages and disadvantages of sustainability certification experience; Further developments and opportunity for improvement. The epilogue considers the meaning of sustainability according to stakeholder, and how aligned the coffee industry is

---

[2] A small flat cake, similar in shape to a pancake made of corn flour and water.
[3] Plantain baked in the oven.
[4] Sour cream.
[5] He made enough money from his organic lettuce, which was sold in a new organic section of the fruit and vegetable section at the local supermarket dedicated to the tourist and expatriate market.
[6] Warm drink made from sugar cane and water.
[7] Fresh fruit juice, with pulp filtered out.
[8] The coffee berries/beans are graded by size and sorted at the mill.

with sustainability. Suggestions for adjustments in producing countries with cultural and social implication for producing communities and consumers are made to encourage a conceptual rather than a limited, and often subjectively determined sustainability.

Background

In the early mid 2000s I started volunteering with Oxfam campaigns and became involved in their shop and Fair trade products. At that time, Fairtrade products were mainly available overseas. Having completed a double degree in Management (Marketing) and Arts (International studies) I was intrigued by how to effectively integrate trade with sustainability and fairness, and how products could be certified or guaranteed as sustainable. Initially, my interest was primarily from a marketing point of view and how consumers could learn about topics and situations in producing countries through their daily consumption practices.

In 2006 Fairtrade certified products were introduced to the Australian market. I was, at that time, volunteering with the Fairtrade head office in Melbourne, Australia. Living between Adelaide and Melbourne I became involved in coordinating Fairtrade fortnights in Adelaide, a national marketing and promotion activity for newly introduced fairtrade certified products which were sold mainly in Oxfam shops and in Coles through Australia. During these promotional activities, Fairtrade organised for representatives of Fairtrade certified cooperatives to visit Australia and speak about their experiences with

How to cite this book chapter:
Vogt, M. 2019. *Variance in Approach Toward a 'Sustainable' Coffee Industry in Costa Rica: Perspectives from Within; Lessons and Insights*. Pp. 9-11. London: Ubiquity Press. DOI: https://doi.org/10.5334/bce.b. License: CC-BY 4.0

Fairtrade. I hosted cacao cooperative representatives from Ghana and a coffee cooperative representative from Costa Rica in consecutive years. Speaking with these representatives at length, their experiences as, not only representatives of cooperatives but as farmers led to an interest in what these logos were achieving in the producing country.

While I believed sustainable products needed to be available on the market and mainstreamed, it was also important that their influence in producing countries was aligning with marketing claims. At this time, and at a more political level, concerns about the fairtrade minimum price were expressed by various thinktanks which favoured liberal trade arrangements. They considered Fairtrade to be fixing prices which was not sustainable. There were therefore several discussions occurring about whether fairtrade was sustainable and what it was achieving.

I was interviewed around that time (2006.2007) about my opinions on fairtrade, and when I read it back, (see https://fairtradematters.wordpress.com/interview-with-melissa-vogt), I still agree with most of what I said but there was still so much to consider.

In 2009, as part of a MA in International Development, I went to Costa Rica to consider how Fairtrade coffee was achieving stated intentions in a producing country. I would visit coffee farming communities according to their affiliation and membership with an umbrella cooperative, Coocafe while also allowing an opportunity to visit other coffee farming communities. It was the beginning of my exploration of sustainability certifications related to in-country contexts.

Leading to the fieldwork component of my study, I worked in Sydney with an organisation that sought to improve legal and actual protections for migrant workers who worked in Australia making clothes. At that time company codes of conduct, an independent label, legal frameworks and industry reviews were developing and occurring. The garment and coffee industry; and Australia and Costa Rica are extremely different contexts and no comparison was possible in this regard. What was beneficial from the experience in Sydney was an ability to consider how the various mechanisms were necessary and how each served specific and important roles to make an industry more socially just and therefore sustainable. Of course, what sustainable meant in the context of socially just was an additional consideration.

The monograph has therefore arisen from years of considering how to make trade more sustainable, with a starting focus on the coffee industry and international trade. Fieldwork from 2009 is complemented with secondary literature and follow-up fieldwork to consider not only findings from 2009, written into a dissertation in 2011, but also how these findings resonated years later. It was a conscious decision to not publish dissertation findings in 2011 despite it being recommended by an examiner. The findings were quite controversial related to the effectiveness of Fairtrade certification and the risk of damaging what was quite a promising introduction to improving consumer awareness about where, how and who the products they consume daily were produced, sourced and traded seemed too great. Had I come to the topic from an academic background only I may have felt differently. For marketing and consumption practice benefit, I was not sure that it was the appropriate measure, instead I chose to continue studying and considering the topic. There was also, at that time, concern about how subjective the findings were. Eventually I decided the findings were complicated to a point they might confuse opinions about the bigger picture benefit of sustainability certifications. While they were not demonstrating positive, and in fact, in Costa Rica Fairtrade demonstrated to be creating situations contrary to marketing claims, there were benefits that required further consideration before introducing an idea that they do not work.

Since my study in 2001 there has only been one other based in Costa Rica that has considered the number of cooperatives that I visited and interviewed. This study has been conducted through a larger research institute, CATIE which could influence the discussions and findings. My study was more organic and informal in design and approach, and there would therefore be a difference in how participants viewed me and how they would respond to my questions and our discussion.

While the method is not necessarily superior, in-depth interviews with few participants can successfully demonstrate common perspectives, opinions and thinking across a group of similar experience related to specific topics. Combining these studies with in-depth community studies could be an effective method for future considerations. It is useful to consider an entire industry, community or organisation of farmers alongside certifications, instead of considering certifications as the focal point of all in-field studies. To say in a different way, the context within which certifications operate is extremely relevant and important to consider. In-depth interviews and discussions allow considerations inclusive of but not only specific to certifications.

Opinions related to sustainability certifications have changed over time, the marketing and promotions in 2006 and 2007 no longer exist, and an idea of their being an absolute solution for sustainable trade has diminished, slightly. How certifications are viewed by smaller roasters is not exactly or consistently positive. There have however been replacement buyers of certified produce to ensure a continuing increase in sales of certified products.

With an improved understanding of how certified products benefit producing countries, and how it varies, and knowing that most certifications are working to improve their processes, and that institutions and organisations have been founded and are developing to support these improvements, presenting the findings from 2009 and complementing them with further considerations is considered good timing.

CHAPTER I

Historic account of Costa Rican development: the creation of an identity

With research and writing assistance from Leonardo Astorga Sanchez

Introduction

A detailed history of Costa Rica provides a context for the monograph. How the Costa Rican experience differs to neighbouring countries is described to ensure an understanding of Costa Rica in the Central American region, and as compared to other coffee farming countries. Understanding the difference is important as extrapolating findings to other country's experience with certifications could be inappropriate. The first part of this chapter is based on the colonial experience (1540–1821); and the second part provides information about contemporary history.

PART I: The Costa Rican colonial experience (1540–1821)

The conquest and colonization of Costa Rica was carried out after the rest of Central America. Resources found in Costa Rica were initially below expectations and as such Costa Rica was given less importance and experienced minimal colonial administrative presence. It was well into the sixteenth century when the Spanish managed to establish permanently in the interior of Costa Rica (Quiros & Solorzano 2006). The pacification and subjugation of the country coincided with important changes in the way in which the Spanish Crown directed and controlled its colonies. Elizabeth Fonseca identifies three fundamental processes that came to differentiate the expeditions that were carried out in Costa Rica. After 1540, the Crown decided to impose effective control over the Central American territory (Fonseca 1994, 95). Despite a

---

How to cite this book chapter:
Vogt, M. 2019. *Variance in Approach Toward a 'Sustainable' Coffee Industry in Costa Rica: Perspectives from Within; Lessons and Insights*. Pp. 13–31. London: Ubiquity Press. DOI: https://doi.org/10.5334/bce.c. License: CC-BY 4.0

desire for control, it was very common that the authorities sent did not obey his orders, taking advantage of the remoteness of Costa Rica from Guatemalan colonial presence and control.

In the first instance, the *Audiencia de los Confines in El Reino de Guatemala*, a territory composed of Chiapas, Guatemala, El Salvador, Honduras, Nicaragua and Costa Rica, was created with executive, legislative and judicial functions. The creation of this institution sought to suppress the great power held by the governors (conquerors or descendants of the first conquerors) and subject them to the authority of officials appointed by the Crown, charged with overseeing respect for laws, taxing and to render direct accounts to the king and the Council of the Indies in Spain (Fonseca 1994, 96).

Secondly, the reduction of the Indigenous ('first nation') in towns was carried out, for greater control and to avoid exploitation by the Spaniards. Each *pueblo de indios* would have its own authorities, grouped in a first nation Cabildo, who would regulate the work and the taxes given to the Spanish authorities and the *encomenderos* (Fonseca 1994, 97–8). Finally, and very important, the application of the *Leyes Nuevas* (1542), the proclamation of which were a direct consequence of the denunciations made by Friar Bartolomé de las Casas before King Charles I. Slavery as a form of labour exploitation was not eliminated, but the indigenous were exempt from it and subjected to another type of forced labour, favouring the trafficking and increase of Africans towards America. As early as the fifteenth century, the first Europeans who came to the African continent saw a lucrative business in the slave trade. For that purpose, a whole legal and ideological apparatus was established and supported in the idea of ownership of some individuals over others, and the use of coercion as the foundation of the relationship between masters and slaves (Caceres 2000, 13). The Europeans were also based on the phenotype of the Africans, like legitimising elements of their condition as slaves (Caceres 2000, 14).

The *Nuevas Leyes* not only denounced and condemned the excess of the Spaniards, they fixed the tax amount according to the characteristics of the region, the age and number of the first nations of each town (Solorzano 2008) paid by each community to its *encomendero* or managers. They also determined that the first nations were subjects and therefore protected by the Spanish Crown (Fonseca 1994, 100–6). The application of the *Nuevas Leyes* was an important milestone and before this, the first nation population had experienced a strong demographic decline to be forced to work in the mines, as porters, or as happened in Nicoya, they were sent to Panama, Peru and other regions of South America (Bacci 2006, 22; Luis & Sibaja 1982, 32).

The *Audiencia of Guatemala de los Confines* commissioned Juan de Cavallón to conquer Costa Rica, due to the demographic decline of the native population and the depletion of gold deposits in the rest of the Reino, especially in Nicaragua. Cavallón oversaw laying the first bases for the colonization of the Costa Rican territory, establishing populations for whom the land was secured, and the castle of Garcimuñóz (1561) in the western sector of the Central Valley. It was the first stable settlement in Costa Rican soil. Juan Vázquez de Coronado, after being appointed mayor of Nueva Cartago and Costa Rica in 1562, pacified the eastern part of the Central Valley, moved the population of Garcimuñoz and founded Cartago by 1563 (Quiros & Solorzan, 2006, 197–8).

By 1570–1575, much of Costa Rica's territory was under virtual domain of the Spanish authorities, with an important exception being the Caribbean coast, specifically the Talamanca mountainous and forested region that served as a refuge and resistance to the first nations fleeing the Central Valley (Solorzano 2008, 52–3). During colonization, the encomienda laid the foundations for the economic development of society and allowed a group of Spaniards to settle permanently in the country. An encomienda was a group of first nation people or a town that remained under the care of a Spaniard, or Spaniards who in exchange for work and taxes gave them "protection and education" (Quiros 2001, 42–4). The *encomenderos* were the dominant social group in colonial Costa Rica, thanks to the control and monopolization of first nation labour through tribute. The process of economic development in Costa Rica was by the 1570s based on the exploitation of about 70,000 first nations grouped in *pueblos de indios* located in the Central Valley and on the Pacific coast (Solorzano 2008, 21). The economy pre-independence relied on the sporadic export of cacao, cattle migration, tobacco, leather and various other commodities, including the export of indigenous groups as labour from Nicoya and Nicaragua in the 16th Century (Molina & Palmer 2008, 20).

During the first decades of the seventeenth century, the economic and social model of the *encomienda* went into crisis due to disappearance of the majority of the first nation tributary population and a strong process of *mestizaje*, one in ten individuals were *mestizos (*Molina 2003, 60). At the end of the seventeenth century a large part of the Spanish population was dedicated to production for self-consumption. The most impoverished and landless population sectors were in the majority Spanish and first nation, or black and mulatto. At the beginning of the eighteenth century the *mestizaje* provoked a strong demographic increase in the Costa Rican population (Molina 2003, 63–65). The trade of cattle, mules and other derived products, such as *sebo*, animal fat to make candles, an important product of commercial exchange (Fonseca et al. 2001, 309–15; Molina 2003, 79–80), were important activities with Nicaragua and Panama.

In the mid-seventeenth century another economic alternative emerged on the Caribbean coast in the Matina region, the cultivation and exploitation of cocoa. Eventually it was exported to Jamaica, Curacao, Portobelo and Cartagena (Molina 2003, 37). As early as 1670 a large group of plantation owners residing in Cartago who moved to their properties at the time of harvesting the fruit had consolidated (Madrigal 2007, 181–9). Parallel to the sowing and commercialization of the cocoa, contraband appeared mainly with the English and Dutch, the main buyers of the cocoa produced in Matina (Fonseca et al. 2001, 326–7). Along with the work of the first nations, the trade of cattle and mules with Nicaragua and Panama and cocoa, tobacco played an important role in the Costa Rican economy (Acuna 1978, 279–392) and between 1787 and 1792 it was an effective driver of the Costa Rican economy. The tobacco industry allowed the regular contracting of transport services for products to Leon, Nicaragua, strengthening the leather industry as *petacas*, bags in which the product was transported, were necessary. Guatemala granted Costa Rica a monopoly on the supply for the region (Molina 2003, 113), monetizing the economy. With the profits, those involved managed to develop a business of import and marketing of textiles, luxury goods and tools for the initial internal market of Costa Rica (Molina 2003, 90–2).

By 1800, 21 years before Costa Rica's independence, the country was exporting cocoa, livestock, tobacco, timber and subsistence products such as basic grains. Agricultural activity occurred in the *chacras*, very diverse productive units of small and medium size (Molina 2003, 23; Montero 2014, 294) which allowed the farmer[9] to survive and whose surplus was commercialized. The Costa Rican peasantry was characterized by its heterogeneity; there was an impoverished sector with reduced access to land, a medium sector with more land and better conditions both in labour, tools, technologies and livestock possession, and well-off farmers, many of which were descendants of the conquerors and *encomenderos*, with extensive areas of land dedicated to the cattle ranch that combined subsistence agriculture with commercial. The well-off also owned warehouses where sugar cane was ground and milled (Montero 2014, 295; Molina 2005, 3). Commercial activity, used by many of the descendants of rich conquerors and peasants, using products such as tobacco, livestock and sugar cane for alcohol production allowed primary capital accumulation (Gudmundson 2010, 61–3). The accumulated capital was used in other activities, among them coffee, from 1820. The Costa Rican merchants were characterized by a constant accumulation of movable and immovable goods, they managed to control tobacconists through a monopoly of alcohol and tobacco

---

[9] Farmer and producer are used interchangeably through the monograph. Producer is often referred to by Fairtrade, and Costa Rican cooperatives. They include farmers and processors organised into a cooperative, or can also refer only to farmers. RA refers most to plantations and farm managers. Farmers and producers are referred to more generally through the monograph, particularly in the history chapter. Farmers are individuals who directly manage a farm. Producer implies farming and/or processing but not roasting. In Costa Rica processing occurs at a community level *beneficio* or on a plantation.

sales, the purchase of public offices and the monopolization of money and control of merchandise export and import (Molina 2003, 126–39). Thus, as the social relations within Costa Rica were characterized by an important disparity, inequality was reflected in unequal exchange (Molina 2003, 161). The merchant appropriated the peasant surplus by giving him money or products with a value less than that of the crop sown. In Costa Rica, small and medium property was the norm, but they were not the only forms of land tenure. They coexisted with extensive cattle ranches and sugar plantations, located mainly in the region of Alajuela-San Ramón, the Valley of Reventazón and Turrialba (Montero 2014, 285).

Large land distributions of the sixteenth century, close to the Central Valley were dominated by cacao and tobacco but were not agriculturally intensified due to varying topography, poor infrastructure for transport and a limited pool of labour due to low first nation population rates, a financial inability to pay for labour, and a regulatory barrier to imported labour from Africa (Alfaro 1980; Hall 1985).

Between 1750 and 1821 the peasantry combined subsistence agriculture with the commercialization of agricultural surplus. With coffee it was increasingly common for peasants and their families to rent their labour force during harvest. Likewise, the demographic increase of the population made it difficult to equitably share the family inheritance. The more children, the more difficult it was to inherit a fair share of the land. When a farm was divided among numerous children. many of them received nothing, and so they had to choose between colonizing lands on the agricultural frontier or being employed as laborers on the farms and coffee plantations of the Central Valley. Alongside this commodification of peasant labour, coffee favoured privatization of land. The Government, including the municipalities (Montero 2014, 280), decreed a series of laws that promoted the privatization of communal lands, belonging to *pueblos de indios* and wastelands in order to promote coffee production and encourage peasants to grow. As the historian Mario Samper points out, the expansion of coffee was based on a strong accumulation of capital by the rich merchants and exporters. Unlike the rest of Central America, it was not based on an excessive exploitation of the peasantry. As an important sector it managed to preserve its property or obtained it at the agricultural frontier (Samper 1989, 114). Héctor Pérez acknowledges that in Costa Rica the coffee economic dynamics, in the absence of an important first nation population that was subjected to forced and servile labour (Perez 1981, 6–9), favoured the employment of wage labour, hired seasonally during harvest or permanent planting and tending of coffee plantations.

These factors all heavily influenced Costa Rica's export activities pre-independence, which were minimal in comparison to neighbouring countries. Many of these limitations were compounded by the lack of colonial activity and support available.

PART II: History of independence in Costa Rica (1800–2000)

The Central American political experience

Notions charged with strong positivism favoured the creation of nations in the Central American region where citizenship and the right to vote were granted, following patterns of exclusion that affected women, first nations, illiterate and black. The first nations, where they were the majority, for example in El Salvador and Guatemala, as the main subordinate group, experienced unequal relations to the international market and their citizen duties. Their communities were stripped of property rights or subjected to forced labour on coffee plantations (Torres-Riva 2011, 63). Following the political and economic consolidation of the liberal elite, the oligarchy and parallel to coffee activity in Central America, it is possible to establish three different types of state, or liberal reform projects.

1) The radical liberalism of Guatemala and El Salvador, based on the massive expropriation of first nation communities and forced labour, and as a productive and control centre, the great hacienda. Radical liberalism produces states with powerful repressive and coercive apparatus
2) Reformist liberalism, typical of Costa Rica, where the small and medium property characterized the coffee activity, with a concentration of power in the *beneficiado* for the preparation of grain for export. The development of a militarized state was not necessary, coercion gave way to consensus, and
3) Abortive liberalism present in Honduras and Nicaragua, the coffee-growing activity was delayed, and the state could not be fully consolidated by the presence of strong foreign interests and military intervention, Nicaragua's case is exemplary. (Mahoney 2001, 230–31; Torres-Riva 2011, 65)

In summary, political experience in Central America was characterized by military dictatorship in El Salvador and Guatemala, liberal democracy in Costa Rica and traditional dictatorships in Honduras and Nicaragua. For each of these experiences the economic elite depended on the State and the law granting an abundant source of labour. Achieving demands and improvements to their standard of living and exercise of citizenship was according to the degree of violence and control mobilized and faced. In Costa Rica the degree of violence was minimal compared to neighbouring countries, and control was maintained.

The Costa Rican political experience

In Costa Rica, liberal reformism (Mahoney 2001) was not based on a militarized state, nor propitiated a strong polarization of social class (Mahoney 2001, 241).

The concentration of Costa Rican land was smaller in comparison with the rest of Central America. While in Guatemala and El Salvador, coffee production revolved around the hacienda, the large property, in Costa Rica, coffee was planted in small and medium-sized land. Despite the social stratification that came from the colony, small and medium property was the rule in Costa Rica. An elite linked to coffee activity was not therefore like the great Guatemalan proprietors who relied on forced first nation labour. Nor the Salvadoran expropriating first nation communal lands, making of these a peasant without semi-proletarian land.

The army played a secondary and limited role in maintaining the country's social order. After independence (1821), a process began to consolidate a centralized, non-militarized state. This process was facilitated because Costa Rica escaped the conflicts faced by liberals and conservatives, although not completely. The low level of conflict involved in the Ochomogo War of 1823 and the War of the League in 1835 allowed a much faster modernization of the productive apparatus inherited from the colony and a link with the International Market (Edelman 2005, 84). The basic institutions of conservative power such as the Church, colonial authorities and the traditional elite as large landowners were weak. This was owing to Costa Rica's remoteness from centres of power, lack of precious metals and an important first nation component (Mahoney 2001, 241). Faced with this weakness, they were unable to oppose the liberal project, or share views on the need for modernization that sought Costa Rica's "order and progress."

Costa Rican governments, especially liberal ones, favoured and encouraged the privatization of communal lands and wastelands. The central government and the municipalities promoted the use and appropriation of land through small properties, rather than the development of large tracts of land (Mahoney 2001, 242). Privatization was without significant coercion. Decrees and laws on land tenure tended to favour those who could afford the legal procedures to present documentation that credited them as owners. A situation that was taken advantage of by the economic elite to gain the best land and consolidate itself against the medium and small peasant. Unlike Guatemala and El Salvador, where elites formed a united front opposed to peasants and their manifestations, in Costa Rica it was divided into family factions, like the Montealegre family (Stone 1982). These factions used mechanisms such as voting, to resolve conflicts resulting from the exercise and control of power (Mahoney 2001, 243).

During much of the nineteenth century the Costa Rican oligarchy used coups to seize power. Juan Rafael Mora Porras president of Costa Rica between 1849 and 1860 was deposed by a coup organized by the Montealegre family, Mora's main political rivals. While the army was instrumental in resolving elite political rivalries, it was not used to control the peasantry or to protect coffee activity in Costa Rica, militarization of the countryside was not necessary as was the case in Guatemala and El Salvador (Mahoney 2001, 244). Beginning in

1870, a year of the consolidation of the liberal republic in Costa Rica (Salazar 2003), a professionalization of the army began as an institution at the service of the State and not as an instrument at the service of the oligarchy. By becoming professionalized, the army became depoliticized, it had autonomy and ceased to be an extension of the ruling class.

The centralization of government administration and the professionalization of the army prevented Costa Rica from following militarism typical of the rest of Central America. The military was never a key player in coffee activity (Mahoney 2001, 245). By the middle of 1880, the national budget dedicated to defense was diminishing. The abolition of the army in 1948 was the result of a long process of decay and loss of protagonist military. In Costa Rica the armed forces were a marginal actor and cohesion was more important than coercion. The depoliticization of the armed forces left the oligarchy without the traditional mechanism to resolve their conflicts, because of that void, the vote and electoral competition were strengthened. Costa Rican elections should not be idealized, many of them characterized by fraud. As from 1889 the presidential succession was made based on electoral results. Political stability of the late nineteenth century reflected growth in institutionalization of elections as a mechanism for resolving conflict.

Even if one party lost the presidency they were ensured, by the number of votes, to obtain a position in the Legislative Assembly. The incentives to take power violently decreased in the first two decades of the twentieth century and as electoral guarantees were consolidated (Edelman 2005, 84). The institutionalization of suffrage within the Costa Rican political culture laid the foundation for its democratization. During the decades of 1920 and 1930, with the appearance of new social subjects including an urban proletariat, the workers of the banana enclave, the effort of the Costa Rican Communist Party/ Block of Workers and Peasants (1931) to represent these groups, the Costa Rican political elite sought to address their demands (Mahoney 2001, 246).

It was during the 1940s in order to gain support and institutionally channel the claims of the subordinate sectors, that an alliance was established between the government of Rafael Ángel Calderón Guardia and the communist party. This resulted in the enactment of social legislation elevated to constitutional rank in 1942 (Molina 2008). During the twentieth century, the popular sectors became an important political force, their support provided legitimacy to the government. Therefore, voting in Costa Rica became the instrument par excellence for the resolution of conflicts. Their disrespect and violation of the rules of electoral competition served as an excuse and justification for the Civil War of 1948. This was the most violent armed conflict in Costa Rican history. Rather than ensuring respect for the vote, confrontation aimed at new power groups led by José Figueres Ferrer and the *Ejército de Liberación Nacional,* which became one of the main political parties in Costa Rica's recent history, toward a new political and economic project.

Between 1950 and 1970 we witnessed the evolution and consolidation of a Costa Rican welfare state. This would be characterized by growing participation of the State in the economic and social policy and by a series of mechanisms, including voting, that were refined to meet the needs and respond to the demands of subordinate groups (Edelman 2005, 100). Through these mechanisms the State legitimized itself to the population as an entity capable of resolving conflicts. The channeling of the demands through the state apparatus was made through a giant network of institutions that consolidated State presence throughout the Costa Rican territory (Edelman 2005, 111). The State managed to permeate practically all aspects of the lives of its citizens, through a social safety net and the universalization of medical insurance. By 1978, 86 percent of the population was covered, and high levels of life quality were assured. In education, the State guaranteed quality education from primary to university, and in labour the Government and its institutions were the main employers of Costa Ricans (Edelman 2005, 108). At that time, the rest of Central America viewed the State as a threat to the population by the implementation of State Terrorism, violence and social exclusion. In Costa Rica, the State represented the interests of the population, it was inclusive, and benefits were shared by the wealthy elite, the middle class and the poor.

A series of new policies were implemented during the 1980s and 1990s and to date, in response to the economic crisis of 1978 and 1982. The most visible features have been an increase in the levels of inequality, the reduction and reorientation of the size and functions of the State according to the logic of the market, and the liberalization of the economy that has benefited the private banking sectors, the exporters of non-traditional agriculture and foreign investors (Edelman 2005, 136–7). Thus, Costa Rican democratic tradition and peaceful resolution of conflicts should be understood as a long-lasting process. A process of perfecting a system of electoral competition that could manage a population more than take power in their hands through an armed revolution. The electoral system was thus refined and profiled as the main instrument for resolving conflicts. The State was a legitimate entity with the capacity to solve problems, provide solutions and maintain peaceful coexistence for the social fabric.

Land tenure in Costa Rica and a rural democracy

For Lowell Gudmundson, pre-coffee Costa Rica was characterized by a series of hamlets and settlements with a nucleated pattern of dwellings, removed from the idea of dispersed and isolated populations (Gudmundson 2010, 43). Alongside, the variety of properties ranging from small subsistence agriculture to the extensive exploitation of crops and products more oriented to export reflect the different experiences of land tenure in Costa Rica. Where there were expropriations of land, processes of appropriation of ejidos and communal lands and combination of estates and plots also occurred (Gudmundson 2010, 11–23). It was a different experience to small peasants', poor and isolated in their plot of land, dedicated only to subsistence agriculture depicted by harmonious and peaceful relationships, and later to the planting of coffee, from which emerged the 'rural democracy' referred by Carlos Monge Alfaro in 1937. He claimed that in Costa Rica in the eighteenth century, lack of trade and widespread poverty prevented social differentiation, small peasants being the centre of economic life (Molina 2008, 65). Conflict that arose from the exploitation of large capital represented by large landowners (Molina 2008, 74) in neighbouring countries was avoided through the correct performance of the public function. The administration of the Government according to scientific parameters recovered harmonious relations in the field.

Costa Rica although not economically dynamic compared to El Salvador and Guatemala had commercial activity, economic differentiation and social mobility between the towns and cities, where most of the population resided for the eighteenth century (Edelman 2005, 83–84). As Marc Edelman points out, Costa Rica was not characterized by peaceful relations between its inhabitants, nor by a rural landscape dotted with homogeneously poor, dispersed and subsistence farming households. It did however experience less violent conflict compared to other countries in the colony. So, what some consider an idealization that responded to a political and ideological project that Alfaro was part, from a utopian past, an ideal future led by a specialized technocracy was hoped for.

The idea of 'rural democracy' was also used by small farmers to define themselves and their farms, as the origin of democracy in Costa Rica, and thereby gave strength and legitimacy to their demands and struggles in moments of conflict and crisis. Even political parties such as *Liberación Nacional*, after the 1950s, defined part of their political ideology according to that ideal of 'rural democracy', the recovery of the Costa Rican peasant past.

Costa Rica and Coffee

The influence of coffee on Central American political development was significant and favoured the tendency to concentrate power in the hands of an elite oligarchy, supported by a repressive apparatus army, and a bureaucratization of the government apparatus (Torres-Riva 2011, 62). Through coffee, liberal minded governments promoted and exploited their success via specific projects based on the idea of order and progress. By comparison, in Costa Rica, coffee is considered to have broken a trend of poverty and agrarian reform contributing to an egalitarian approach. The distribution of land not only influenced patterns of conflict as argued by Williams but also the eventual and accidental cultural and social significance of farming coffee through the country. Alongside the 'rural democracy' idea, Marc Edelman's proposes that Costa Ricans possess a feeling of common destiny, linking peasants with elite groups (Edelman 2005, 86) and that coffee was the product that best represented that feeling. Coffee is understood as generating wealth and prosperity for all, as the essence of being 'Costa Rican'. Together with this sense of common destiny Costa Rican political culture also supported, as Iván Molina explains, an inclusive citizenry which was facilitated by a mestizo relatively homogenous population that shared the same worldview (Molina 2003, 163). The inclusive citizenship contrasted with ethnic differences, violent labour mobilizations, great extremes of wealth and poverty (Edelman 2005, 86), and colonial legacies which have been the cause and consequence of the problems confronting countries such as Guatemala, El Salvador, Honduras, and Nicaragua.

Williams (in Pendergast 1999) argues that the way coffee land was divided and labour available in the late nineteenth century not only influenced the shape of Central American governments but also set patterns related particularly to conflict that continue to this day. Central American patterns of conflict were mistakenly perceived to be episodes of the Cold War when:

> They were in fact deeply rooted in the social and economic structures of the region. These structures in turn were shaped by a single commodity that has dominated these small export economies from the nineteenth century to the present – coffee. (Paige 1997, 3)

Between 1800 and 1840, Costa Rica experienced a series of economic booms before the consolidation of coffee as the vehicle of economic advance. Coffee successfully linked Costa Rica to the World Market. Mining, in the mountains of Aguacate between 1821 and 1843 also allowed the economy to monetize, in 1828 the mint was created. Limited technology and the demand for increased capital resources slowed down any boost to the internal market (Molina 2005, 13). The *Palo de Brasil*, a luxury wood produced and extracted in the Guanacaste region, was another important activity that had its moments of splendor between 1827 and 1835, before being exploited without control, causing its disappearance (Molina 2005, 14). These activities allowed the accumulation of resources that were later used in the sowing, production and commercialization of coffee.

Between 1821 and 1914 there was a boom through consolidation of an agri-export model, supported by one or two crops linking the country to the international market and the ups and downs resulting from strengthening dependence. The development of Costa Rican agrarian capitalism went through three key periods after independence (Montero 2014, 282). From 1821 to 1850: a transition to the new economic and social system was based on activities developed as a colonial legacy. Between 1850 and 1890: the consolidation of this system with coffee as a main economic activity; and finally, 1890 and 1914: system diversification.

Social stratum associated with the Costa Rican coffee industry

Coffee production in Costa Rica from 1820 caused a series of important changes, not only economic but also social and political. Since 1840 coffee was the main export product of the country. The economic and social structure of coffee production was characterized in the Central Valley by the primacy of small and medium sized properties. Harvest fell into the hands of small and medium farmers, processing and marketing for the farmers and large coffee growing land holdings, *hacendados*, was carried out by the oligarchy. The elite coffee oligarchy was not dedicated to growing coffee on their properties but to the *beneficiado*, financing and marketing of the product. In this context, the division of labour established a relationship of exploitation between producer and *beneficiador* and in turn they exploited an important sector of peasants with access to no or little land who worked temporarily or permanently on the coffee farms. This generated a strong social stratification within Costa Rican society, away from the idea of a poor and homogeneous peasantry the 'rural democracy' suggested.

The societal stratum can be understood within categories (1a) British and/or foreign capital, (1b) agro-export bourgeoisie merchants and wealthy *hacendados*; (2) small and medium coffee farmers; and (3) labourers and peons. A hierarchical power dynamic between the societal stratum did not however maintain, see 1900–1936 with the second stratum ensuring equity. The 'rural democracy' was supported in that instance despite the social stratum.

The agro-export bourgeoisie merchants and wealthy *hacendados* controlled the *beneficiado*, financing and marketing of coffee (Gudmundson 2010, 93–100). They established contacts with British capital, the first market par excellence of Costa Rican coffee and were part of the first societal stratum. The British capital paid for coffee in advance which, in turn, financed the small and medium-sized producers, who in exchange for the money lent committed to deliver their crop to the merchant. The merchant subsequently controlled the *beneficiado* business. This advanced financing is known as *habilitation* (Molina 2003, 258–9), in exchange for money, merchandise and agricultural inputs the coffee producer undertook to cancel with its harvest the commitment acquired. Again, there was an unequal exchange between the coffee producer and the *Beneficiador*/Merchant, and this inequality was also reflected in the relationship between the agri-exporting bourgeoisie and British capital that financed and established the terms of purchase and sale of coffee, as well as supplies of manufactured and other import products.

After 1850, the formation of companies of British capital with Costa Rican *beneficiadores* became more common, facilitating greater access to money to finance the small and medium farmers. One of the most prolific foreign companies related to the coffee business was William Le Lacheur and Son (Leon 2002, 230), and at the national level the companies Tinoco and Cía, J. Knohr and Hno, Joy and von Schroter and Le Quellec Tournon & Inc. (Leon 2002, 228).

In the second instance, small and medium farmers of coffee, were peasants with access to land, but not money and credit, nor possessors of a profit. This second societal stratum was subject to the *beneficiadores* and was the contractor of waged labour, and impoverished farmers, and empowered small farmers to capture labourers. This type of coffee producer dominated the landscape of the Central Valley (Montero 2014, 286), taking care of the transport of the product by means of carts to the port of Puntarenas and small-scale commerce. Finally, in the lower strata, the laborers and peons, were peasants who often had lost their farm because they could not fulfill their obligations to the exporter (indebted), and they had no choice but to offer their labour force.

In the middle of the nineteenth century, in Europe a country like Holland had consumption per capita between 3 and 4 kg/year which grew to 8 kgs by 1880 (Leon 2002, 87). The English market was, throughout the nineteenth and early twentieth centuries, the main purchaser of Costa Rican coffee. During that long period the percentage of coffee shipped very rarely fell below 50 percent (Leon 2002, 87). Credit and transport were essential to the coffee industry and many Costa Rican coffee farmers had limited financial resources. English purchasers became at times the sole source of credit for coffee farmers and processors and a financial dependence on London import houses developed through loans for future harvests (Leon 2002, 106). The second market was the United States which, by 1900, consumed 340000 tons of coffee. Even between 1850 and 1900 growth in demand came to match Holland, Germany, Belgium, France and Austria-Hungary, adding to the number of countries demanding coffee (Leon 2002, 87). Economic development in Costa Rica due to the expanding coffee industry was significant and stimulated infrastructural development as a necessity, including the postal service, paving of streets in San José and Cartago, the National Theatre, the University of Santo Tomas, and the reconstruction of Cartago after an earthquake.

Along with the growth of coffee cultivation and trade were 'coffee tickets' as a form of small currency. These tickets were illegal but were used with the secret permission of the government, influenced by political connections of the large coffee farm owners (Museos Banco Central de Costa Rica 2019). Import taxes contributed to national wealth and created a stronger market for merchants. The issue of credit was a prime focus for establishing and maintaining the coffee trees prior to the first harvest of coffee, four years after planting. The relationship established with the British market facilitated contacts with commercial firms and traders in Europe for coffee marketing and provision of credit. As coffee was exported, the returning ships would complementarily be full of different products to sell in the country.

Expansion of coffee farming (1886–1948)

Demand for coffee depended on the international context of the time. During the American Civil War, 1860–1865, a rise in prices resulted whereas the

European depression and crisis of 1873–1896 depressed the general prices (Leon 2002, 91). In 1886, different varieties of *Coffea Arabica* (arabica) travelled from West Africa through Jamaica to Costa Rica and were trialed when growers struggled with the *Typica* variety of arabica. In 1908, *Coffea Canephora* (robusta) was experimented with in the Caribbean lowlands and Northern plains. This would expand the spread of coffee even further through the country into the lowlands; however, once the issue of low quality was highlighted and prices were lowered, the variety was destroyed. The only coffee varietal that was seen to guarantee high quality coffee was *Typica*, which can only grow at high altitudes. Between 1914 and 1948, coffee without losing importance, remaining an economic and cultural reference point for Costa Rica gave way to other products that came to complement the agricultural export model. This included bananas, harvested on the Caribbean coast of the country since the end of the 19th century and on some of the southern Pacific coast. During this period, the crisis of 1929 and the depression of 1930 the First and Second World War affected the demand for coffee, causing a constant fluctuation in prices. Pre-World War Two coffee exports from Costa Rica went to Europe and the United States. When the European market closed during World War Two, the US was the only destination for coffee exports in Latin America and this bestowed them a significant amount of power.

The twentieth century witnessed the expansion of coffee outside the Central Valley. By 1935 coffee was grown from the West in San Ramón to the East in Turrialba. There were also coffee plantations in Tilarán, high parts of Nicoya, the valley of Sarapiquí and San Carlos, the area of Los Santos, Tarrazú and Dota, and the valley of the General and San Vito. Outside the Central Valley coffee cultivation was combined with other activities such as the production of sugar cane, cocoa, bananas and livestock (Botey 2005,4–12). In the 1940s, *Bourbon* coffees were classified to be at the same quality level as *Typica* with a tendency for higher yield production and the Costa Rican coffee board planted large seedbeds. Once ready for transport the variety was distributed widely. Shortly afterward in Villa Sarchi, an area in the Central Valley, a mutation of *Bourbon* with a dwarfing gene was found.

This dwarf variety, which facilitated the picking of the cherries at harvest, was named *Villa Sarchi*, a type of *Caturra* and more commercial seedbeds were established. Smaller and more productive, *Villa Sarchi* was suitable for high-density cultivation with little or no shade and large amounts of fertiliser and uniform pruning were necessary. After 1948, modernizing projects for economic and productive diversification were led in Costa Rica mostly by the *Partido Liberación Nacional*, which after triumphing in the Civil War that year prompted a political process that sought the development of new social groups, different from the traditional coffee exporters. The modernization policies were based on the developmentalist theses promoted by the Economic Commission for Latin America (ECLAC). This proposed the need for industrial development (Vargas 2003, 1213).

Softening dependency and insecurity for small and medium coffee farmers (1900–1936)

Exploitation and dependence did cause disputes over the fixing of coffee prices (Acuna 1986, 114). Between 1900 and 1936 conflict was common due to the absence of mechanisms to fix the price, by the decision of the *beneficiadores*. As early as 1930, the goal for coffee farmers was to achieve a solution to the problem of prices, demanding that the State establish mechanisms of fixation and control through regulatory legislation. It was during these conflicts, during the first decades of the twentieth century, that small and medium farmers used the thesis of 'rural democracy' to present itself as the essence of *being Costa Rican*. As Victor H. Acuña points out, there was a clear difference between farmers and the *beneficiadores*, presenting them as a group or trust that monopolized and exploited the peasantry leading to impoverishment and ruin of the Costa Rican economy (Acuna 1987, 150–2). Within the discourse of coffee farmers, which Carlos Monge Alfaro would support, values such as equity, distributive justice and harmony were ideal, and the fate of Costa Rican democracy was associated with the fate and survival of the coffee grower. Thus, establishing that coffee farmers were the foundation of Costa Rican society. With this social imaginary and faced with a situation of inequality, the farmers defined themselves as exploited.

One of the organizational strategies of coffee farmers was to associate themselves in cooperatives as practiced since 1902, to finance the crops so to no longer depend on the credit provided by the *beneficiadores;* and to acquire a profit centre for the *beneficiado* and break with the dependence of exporters (Acuna 1986, 116). It would not be until the creation of the Coffee Institute (1933) and a greater intervention and control of the State that levels of discontent diminished (Botey 2005, 83).

In the 1930s, Paige (1997) considered two central elements of small farm holder ideologies in Costa Rica. One was the firm conviction that small coffee farmers were the bulwark of Costa Rican democracy and therefore the nation. A clash between small farmers and *beneficiadores* in 1933 reflected dissatisfaction but was not as revolutionary as experienced by neighbouring countries such as El Salvador. It was instead a social movement against the elite with moderate tactics and goals from the small farmers (Paige 1997). The conflict was resolved democratically and in favour of small and medium sized coffee farmers (Pendergast 1999).

The success of small farmers in regulating the price paid by the *beneficio* owners could be understood as a demonstration of strength of the middle class in Costa Rica, a 'rural democracy' at work. It proved to be a turning point in regulation of the coffee industry in Costa Rica. Rodrigo Facio, a well-known Costa Rican intellectual, stated:

> In a country such as ours, social justice can only be achieved by the double path of social legislation that guarantees juridical to the

less-fortunate classes their right to live, and by economic organisation which guarantees, materially, in terms of an augmented and diversified production, that the lower classes will be able to effectively exercise that right. (Facio 1948 cited in Mitchell & Pentzer 2008, 101)

An ideological parallel and understanding between acceptance of position between small farmers and large processors, and democracy through negotiations with a responsive government are both attributed to the resolution of these conflicts without violence. Additionally, the introduction of state intervention and price regulations also forced processors to pay a decent price for the berries (Pendergast 2001, 150).

Increasing intensive coffee farming and mono-export (1950–1970)

The signing of the ICA and the freeze on America's import price for coffee in the 1950s stimulated a global movement toward intense cultivation of high yielding hybrid arabica varieties through the Green Revolution. Coffee production was intensively and extensively strengthened, seed sowing spread throughout the Central Valley which had optimum topographic and climatic conditions.

Subsistence agriculture and livestock was subsequently displaced; the primacy of coffee was indisputable. Coffee favoured mono export (Molina 2005, 33–6), dependence on a single product and this in turn favoured the agricultural exporting bourgeoisie which was consolidated as the main political and economic class of the country, the so-called coffee oligarchy. Although coffee became the central axis of capital accumulation this also left the country in a position of vulnerability to price fluctuations, during an international coffee crisis, poor pay and expensive access to the international market was a common problem (Botey 2005, 52).

To support intensive coffee production and export, the state, as the main agent of change, promoted an industrial model of import substitution, producing consumer goods that were previously imported light goods such as footwear, canned food, personal hygiene products. It aimed at supplying demand for a growing domestic market, which was strengthened by the emergence of the middle class (Vargas 2003, 22–3). Along with this industrial development and supported by a nationalized bank, coffee activity received strong support. The former Coffee Defense Institute became the Coffee Office and handled the management of coffee credit and encouraged the creation of Cooperatives (Rovira 2000, 52).

Costa Rica continued to expand coffee production by settling new land into the 1950s. After this time, coffee farming began to intensify production within already settled coffee lands (Samper 2000, 146–48; Naranjo 1997, 94-104). During the first administration of José Figueres Ferrer (1953–1958) increasing coffee productivity relied on fertilizers, application of new cultivation techniques and the implementation of better coffee varieties (Rovira 2000, 67). *Villa Sarchi*, *Caturra* and *Catuaí*, a hybrid of *Mundo Novo*, a hybrid of *Typica* and *Bourbon* (Mitchell & Pentzer 2008, 102), began to dominate Costa Rican coffee farms (Samper 2000, 146–48; Naranjo 1997, 94–104). The government subsidised transition to the hybrid tree as well as subsidising fertiliser and herbicide purchase, which was necessary for maintenance (Mitchell & Pentzer 2008, 103). This was the beginning of the green revolution. Although appearing as perfect economic sense, in 1952 a Costa Rican agronomist stated:

> Coffee production in Costa Rica is in a state of complete exploitation. There is no technology. The agriculturalists are not concerned with conservation. They cultivate coffee like a mine, taking out and never returning anything to the land. (in Winson 1989, 107–10)

From 1950 to 1970, there was a 170 per cent increase in the average yield per hectare of coffee (Mitchell & Pentzer 2008, 102). In the 1960s, there was a strong fight at the international level to maintain high prices and at the national level to continue modernizing production with the use of fertilizers. This gave support to the small and medium farmers through state credit programs. By 1970, Costa Rica was the third most productive coffee exporter in the world and the most productive in Latin America (Winson 1989, 107–10). This was an astounding statistic considering the size of the country. Costa Rica experienced the highest rates of deforestation and population growth in the world (Rosero-Bixby & Palloni 1998, 2). From 1970, the United States Agency for International Development (USAID) directed $AUD 111.20 million, "much of it funneled through a Costa Rica- based program called the Programa de Mejoramiento del Café (PROMECAFE)" (Rice & Ward 1996), to the Central American region to industrialise the coffee industry. Mono-cropping increased and so too did dependency on the international market. The increase in price however was not to last.

Waters were contaminated from an increase and mass use of fertilisers and herbicides, and the health of farmers and their children using the fertiliser and herbicides was compromised (Mitchell & Pentzer 2008, 103). The benefits and downfalls of the green revolution became evident; not only did the country become more dependent on one crop that relied on the international market, but farmers had to source the fertilisers and herbicides necessary to maintain the hybrid variety from international companies. From 1976 to 1985, Costa Rica's public debt rose more than six-fold from $889.60 million to $5.28 billion (Carriere 1991, 186). This has been detrimental to livelihoods and the environment at varying scales across the country. A cycle of poverty in coffee farming regions emerged as the fluctuant nature of the coffee market became evident.

*Resolving the influence of intensive farming and
economic crisis (1970–2000)*

In the 1980s and 90s, following a severe economic crisis between 1978 and 1982, efforts to change Costa Rica's export profile without abandoning coffee production were witnessed. As an exporter of non-traditional products (Vargas 2003, 40), agriculture of change favoured the production of pineapple, cardamom, flowers, squash, among other products (Honey 1994, 171). In 1982, it was forbidden to farm *Robusta* by law in Costa Rica, from that year arabica is the only coffee species grown across the country which reduced expansion of intensive sun grown Robusta farming across the country. In addition, tourism began to shape as a lucrative economic activity, going hand in hand with the protectionist measures of the various governments to protect part of the country's natural resources. Despite these efforts, the centralised power dynamic increased and entrenched the dependency that coffee farmers had on international markets and consumers.

Many new coffee cooperatives were established from the early 1960s and 1970s. The National Council for Cooperatives (CONACOOP) were created in 1973 and works between government and the public to represent Costa Rican Cooperatives. INFOCOOP works to promote new cooperatives and capacitate existing cooperatives through technical assistance, finance and investigation.

Through these public mechanisms the cooperative movement and support in Costa Rica strengthened. Cooperatives in the Costa Rican coffee industry were increasing in number between 1970 and 2000, particularly as land distribution patterns maintained and the coffee price demonstrated particularly volatile in the 1970s and 1990s which can often reinforce reliance on a cooperative rather than selling direct to the market.

Summary

The current day coffee industry in Costa Rica is different to other coffee producing countries. Continuing dependence on colonial powers through trade relations was offered to Costa Rica as much as other countries of the region post-independence. Costa Rica, the government and their citizens, including farmers did however manage independence in a different way. The sheer population of coffee farmers in Costa Rica due to small farm holding presence, distinct from the number of labourers, certainly offered opportunity for a united movement against a hierarchy of beneficios and foreign traders in one of the more significant agricultural exports of the country.

Providing a detailed history of Costa Rica is an important basis for this monograph. How Costa Rica has developed as a country and how it has handled the coffee industry and coffee farmers demonstrates similarities and difference with other coffee farming countries, and with neighbouring countries. It has been considered the country of peace in the region. While experiencing conflict through the centuries the experience has not been as severe or complicated as those experienced by other countries in the region. These differences and similarities emphasise how findings presented in chapter 5–13 should be understood within a country context only.

The following background chapters provide an overview of considerations related to how trade influences development, and of the international coffee industry as a precursor to introducing and explaining sustainability certifications for the coffee industry. Bringing understanding from these chapters together with the findings chapters, chapter 6–13, contributes to and strengthens understanding specific to the Costa Rican context. A contemporary history of Costa Rica related to coffee is provided in chapter 6 which combines fieldwork quotes and findings with secondary literature.

CHAPTER 2

Trade's influence in development

Introduction

The geographically distanced approach of Multinational Corporations (MNCs)[10] and Transnational Corporations (TNCs)[11] only increases trade's negative influence on the environment, individuals and society with little ability to regulate or ensure accountability (Vogt 2019a). The dominant paradigm of a time and ideas of acceptable outcomes, and/or an ability to fulfill trade priority above other development indicators are also influential. Development indicators have come to be understood in different ways, with attention previously going to Gross Domestic Product (GDP) then shifting to address and recognise human development indicators, such as the Human Development Index (HDI), used since 1990 by the UNDP and developed by Manhbub al Haq. In addition, sustainability indicators, such as the Millennium Development Goals (UN Millennium Project 2005) and the Sustainable Development Goals (UN 2018) (MDGs and SDGs) which include environmental indicators and outcomes, are more recently used. Often, sustainability and human development definitions influence how development indicators are included and considered as positive. This chapter discusses how paradigms and praxis cycles influence how outcomes are understood as positive; and how poverty reduction and sustainability became an integrated consideration for development. The definitions of poverty reduction and sustainability have changed over time and as such they are explained in more detail.

---

[10] Multinational Corporations are worldwide enterprises which own or control production of goods or services in more than one country (as well as) home country operations.
[11] Transnational Corporations operate substantial facilities and do business in more than one country without a home country of operations.

How to cite this book chapter:
Vogt, M. 2019. *Variance in Approach Toward a 'Sustainable' Coffee Industry in Costa Rica: Perspectives from Within; Lessons and Insights.* Pp. 33–38. London: Ubiquity Press. DOI: https://doi.org/10.5334/bce.d. License: CC-BY 4.0

Paradigm and praxis cycles counterbalancing created imbalance

The influence of corporate, non-governmental or governmental action limits or works within the scope of categorised ideas of progress and development, with inevitable influence on the culture in country (Vogt 2019b). The cultural influence of varying approaches on the 'subject' community, that is the community that is to be developed, rely on implementation of these ideas. Watts (2005) explores the idea that development itself is inevitably a manipulation of culture, in a search for things that 'work.' There is, within this idea, the underlying assumption that what exists now in 'subject' communities does not work. A cultural shift resulting from any development process is then inevitable; it is only a question of the 'direction' and whether local culture will also be influential. A corporate prerogative to shape culture to complement profit driven strategies and activities can result without consideration of benefit for local population or culture, for example.

The influence of corporate investment and activity has been noticed in Costa Rica. In 1953, the President of Costa Rica, Jose Figueres Ferrer stated:

> The notion of business as private is an illusion. In practice, we accept every kind of social regulation, from the moment at which a company is founded and organised passing then to control of quality and characteristics of their products, until the moment at which the benefits are distributed. All life in society implies the renunciation of certain liberties in exchange for certain guarantees. (Martz 1959)

Since that time, Figueres recognised the inevitable influence that foreign business can have on the Costa Rican people and how it can shape social conditions of the country. The comment foreshadowed developments in the 1980s when structural adjustment programs (SAPs) allowed a foreign owned fruit industry to develop in Costa Rica (Amanor 2013). The development of the Costa Rican coffee industry examples how an industry and resulting practice can transform culture.

Indeed, the expansion of coffee farming landscapes across the world represent an accumulated cultural shift, as practices, routines and mentalities align and change by industry or national priority.

Development as poverty reduction understanding and approach

Approximately three quarters of the world's poor live in rural areas and most are dependent in some way on agriculture (Castaneda et al. 2016). A focus on agriculture is necessary for reducing poverty as a basis of economic livelihoods for the poorest people (IFAD 2006, 4). The Millennium Development Goals (MDG) sought to increase and unify effort to reduce poverty (UN Millennium Project 2005). The first of these goals was to halve the proportion of hungry and extremely poor people by 2015 (UN 2019). Mchumo (2017) stated at an official pre-UNCTAD XII meetings that:

> We believe that it is impossible to eliminate poverty and hunger, [to] achieve sustainable development and attain the targets of the MDGs without addressing the commodity *problematique* and improve the conditions and prospects of commodity producers. (Mchumo 2007)

The approach to eliminating poverty and hunger to achieve sustainable development is important. Also important is how poverty is defined and understood. Ludi and Bird (2007, 2) argue that a monetary approach to measuring poverty is the most commonly used by government and international institutions. Decades ago, Townsend (1980) considered the multi-dimensionality of poverty, moving beyond income to relative societal position. Sen contributed a broader understanding of poverty considerations beyond income and economic indicators with his theory of poverty as a deprivation of basic capabilities (Sen 1999). This was influenced by and influenced many situations including but not limited to low income.

Poverty can be sensibly identified in terms of capability deprivation; the approach concentrates on deprivations that are intrinsically important, unlike low income which is only instrumentally significant (1999, 87). Sen recognised that there is a reciprocal relationship between income and a person's capability, describing it as a "connection going from capability improvement to greater earning power and not only the other way around" (Sen 1990, 90). The capabilities approach expands the evaluation of poverty to consider not only "opulence, utilities, primary goods or rights but functionings (doings and beings) – [as] a measure that encompasses these other units of evaluation" (Comin 2001, 4). He proposed that we evaluate development in terms of "the expansion of the capabilities of people to lead the kinds of lives they value – and have reason to value" (Evans 2002, 55). This connects with ideas of freedom, development and wellbeing, complementing Townsend's (Evans 2002, 55) societal position theory. Sen (1992) discusses the links between capabilities and functionings where functionings determine the nature of a person's being. A person's capability to achieve the functionings they choose will determine that "person's freedom – the real opportunities – to have well-being" (Sen 1992, 40). Achieved well-being is dependent on the capability to function. It is argued that there is a link between well-being, democracy and freedom stating that in a freedom-orientated approach the participatory freedoms cannot but be central to public policy analysis (Sen 1999, 110). Hence, he stresses the importance of social choice in democracy that involves "a thick, sense of messy and continuous involvement of the citizenry" (Evans 2002, 55) which goes beyond electing leadership in government.

The World Bank's approach to development shifted as of 2000/2001 to a focus on poverty reduction. It began to consider the multi-dimensionality of poverty inclusive of and beyond economics. Despite a deeper understanding of poverty, the international approach of the time was shaped by market deregulation and a focus on economic development exemplified by the 'De Soto' (2000) approach.[12] Hints of De Soto's approach to development could be found in IFAD's report on supporting small land holders in agriculture to reduce poverty (IFAD 2013; Ravallion 2016). Dr Lorenzo Cotula, a senior researcher at the International Institute for Environment and Development (IIED) wrote:

> Agricultural investment can bring benefits to developing nations, but large land deals carry big risks as local people may lose access to the land and resources, they have used for generations. The more promising investments are those that involve supporting local smallholders, rather than large plantations. (IFAD 2010)

The World Bank's exploration and report on what poverty meant for the poor (Kanbur et al. 2000, 7) supported the multi-dimensionality of poverty, demonstrating tones of Sen's capability approach.

Poverty, according to the World Development Report 2000/01 is related to material well-being lacking to the point of physical deprivation. It is also a psychological experience related to a lack of empowerment and exclusion from decision-making which leaves the poor vulnerable and exploited. A lack of social and community relations, infrastructure such as water, roads, health and assets are perceived to be directly related to vulnerability and risk. These poverty indicators complement Sen's considerations of poverty in the realm of capability and functioning, leading to freedom by the elimination of oppression, improved community relations and access to education and health and social security provisions. Poverty is subjective and personal according to gender and the country or region where it is experienced. Increasing the 'sustainability' of coffee is central to efforts to reduce poverty and protect the environment. This is usually assumed achievable within a market-based economic development approach. Evans (2002, 59) suggests that ideas of development as freedom be

---

[12] Hernando de Soto, Chief Executive Officer of one of the largest European engineering firms and governor of Peru's Central Reserve Bank is also the President and founder of the Institute of Liberty and Democracy (ILD). This institute takes practical implementation measures to bring the poor into the economic mainstream.

extended further than initially introduced. Evaluators must correspondingly focus more closely on how to prevent market-based power inequalities from undermining development as freedom (Sen 1999).

'Sustainability': meaning and efficacy

The most common definition of sustainable development is based on an idea of Our Common Future:

> Sustainable development is development that meets the needs of the present without compromising the ability of future generations to meet their own needs. It contains within it two key concepts: the concept of needs, in particular the essential needs of the world's poor, to which overriding priority should be given; and the idea of limitations imposed by the state of technology and social organization on the environment's ability to meet present and future needs. (WCED 1983, written into a report in 1987)

In this context, coffee grown and traded in a 'sustainable' way seems a contradiction. Peak oil and global targets to reduce carbon emissions are only contributed to through the international trade of coffee. It is suggested that how sustainability is understood and used will influence how outcomes are understood and subsequently the strength and effectiveness of the sustainability discussed. In an international trade context greenwashing is commonly referred to where sustainability is the claimed intention or activity but does not align with actual outcomes or activities.

Sustainable development concepts and goals are considered to have moved from a concern of pollution control and availability of natural resources to a more balanced position that puts human development at the centre (Quentel et al. 2009). Sustainability within international trade seeks to manage myriad interests where commercial production can dominate. Where broad definitions and multiple goals guide negotiation, the interests of trade can outweigh those of the environment and society. The 2030 Agenda for Sustainable Development outline areas of critical importance for humanity and the planet understood as people, planet, prosperity, peace and partnership (UN 2015) based on the SDGs. The SDGs allow for seventeen goals and 169 targets. Negotiating with trade interests and existing structures may limit ambitious outcomes for society and the environment where definitions of sustainability are not specific enough. Within the SDG goals and targets, while detail is provided, interpretations can allow a range of activities within sustainability intentions. Where interpretations are misaligned, contradictory practices to purpose emerge.

Summary

As understandings of acceptability in approach and outcomes within international trade continually change, including how different interests are prioritised, the contribution of paradigms and praxis cycles are important for and influential to producing countries. Underlying this importance is how such definitions are understood and the detail they allow to truly address the intention of a concept. Poverty reduction and sustainability are two leading paradigms or concepts that seek to counter the imbalance caused through international and local trade practices. Sustainability certifications are one of the complementary institutional efforts developed for the sustainability paradigm and complement poverty reduction intentions. For the context of this monograph, the following background sections explain the international coffee industry and sustainability certifications for the coffee industry.

CHAPTER 3

The international coffee industry

Introduction

Coffee is one of the most popular and legal psychoactive drugs in the world. It stimulates the central nervous system and metabolism. It is commonly believed that coffee is the second most valuable exported legal commodity on earth (to oil) (Pendergast 1999; Avery 2006; National Geographic 1999). Further investigation reveals that coffee is the second most valuable commodity exported by developing countries, the first is oil (Pendergast 2009). The international coffee industry was worth $20 billion (ICO 2017) in 2017. When compared to oil, income from coffee is directly and more evenly distributed in producing countries according to the number of people involved, and the dominant farm size. There are approximately 125 million people directly reliant on coffee for income (O'Brien & Kinniard 2003, 237; Leonard et al. 2012[13]). Considering the number of undocumented and under recorded transitory and seasonal migrant populations that work during the coffee harvest, this would be an underestimated figure. Amongst farmers, most hold 10 hectares or less of coffee (Gresser & Tickell 2002). A farmer's experience in the coffee industry will be influenced by the size of the farm, established networks for sale and distribution, and access to credit to name a few. It is important to recognise the difference between a small coffee farm and a larger centrally owned and managed plantation. The difference is not only by number of people involved in managing the farm but also by the explicit and implicit roles and responsibilities; capabilities and capacity for risk taking. There is also difference between a small farm and a producer group of small farmers.

---

[13] 125 million is still quoted by the Fairtrade Foundation with no reference.

How to cite this book chapter:
Vogt, M. 2019. *Variance in Approach Toward a 'Sustainable' Coffee Industry in Costa Rica: Perspectives from Within; Lessons and Insights.* Pp. 39–53. London: Ubiquity Press. DOI: https://doi.org/10.5334/bce.e. License: CC-BY 4.0

As coffee is often farmed for commercial purposes, the international industry has a significant influence on farming practices and, therefore, on how humans interact with the landscape. As a historic legacy of the colonial bean, coffee has been farmed intensively as a cash crop across many countries to satisfy national government requirements for foreign currency through export (Chirwa et al. 2007; Kennedy & King 2014; Montero 2014; Lekane 2017). National agricultural policy and planning is expected to be geared towards, and continually influenced by international market and industry trends. The price of coffee is a central consideration and can be an indication of success for producing landscapes, linked to the global supply and demand of the commodity as it ebbs and flows (Lewin et al. 2004; Osorio 2004). Coffee farming is also however a source of insecurity, both financial and non-financial, in producing landscapes. The international market and trade activity can ultimately influence outcomes in coffee farming landscapes and vice versa through supply and demand and have flow-on effects that translate to other coffee farming landscapes.

Brief history of coffee

No one has managed to confirm where the word or name 'coffee' originated or where it was discovered (*Black Coffee*, 2005; Abattouy et al. 2014). The word 'coffee' is a derivation of an Arabic word '*qahwa*', which means 'wine' (Weinberg & Bealer 2001: xiv) and coffee itself was often referred to in Europe as the 'wine of Islam'. One origin story introduces 'kaldi' (Weinberg & Bealer 2001), an Ethiopian goat herder who recognised a change in the behaviour of his goats, they danced, after eating fruit from a wild bush in the sixth or seventh century. The story of dancing goats intersects with written records of the Sufi using coffee for meditation and concentration in the monasteries of southern Arabia. The Sufi are considered the first to have brewed the bean into a drink; however, there are many stories of its discovery (Weinberg & Bealer 2001). In search of *marqaha*[14], coffee was sought after through the Middle East before its charm extended and spread to Europe. Coffee has been a revolutionary bean with an exotic, long and beautiful history. Eaten green by goats in Ethiopia, taken green and ground by the whirling Sufis and roasted by the Persians, coffee populated the ports of Yemen's Mocha and then Mecca, spreading cultivation from the Middle East and Africa to Asia and Sumatra since approximately the sixth century. Coffee arrived in the Americas in the seventeenth century, and then reached Hawaii. This only increased cultivation through much of the colonised world and consumption of the beverage in the colonising world. Pendergast (1999, 3–20) explains how consumption often stimulated social change by allowing uncommon public interactions between genders and often encouraged political discussion. It overpowered and endured legal bans throughout

---

[14] An Arabic term for the euphoria that coffee produces when consumed.

the Arab world in the 1500s as a response to political discussions emerging from coffee houses (Pendergast 1999, 6) and has been trafficked across the globe in imaginative ways. Coffee's arrival in Brazil depended on the exchange of a bouquet of flowers between a Governor's wife and a Portuguese Brazilian Official and mediator, hidden in the bouquet were coffee beans. A legacy of controversy and conflict through the history of coffee provides an interesting contrast to the social and unifying elements of the bean in cultivation and in consumption. A red herring amongst us.

Botanic background of coffee

The two species of coffee most grown in the world are, *Coffea Arabica* (*C. Arabica*) (arabica) and *Coffea Canephora (C. Canephora)* variety *Robusta* (robusta). On a smaller scale, *Coffea liberica (C. liberica*, 'liberica') is also grown for the market.

CLASSIFICATION OF COFFEE

Kingdom	Vegetable
Sub-kingdom	Angiospermæ
Class	*Dicotyledonaæ*
Sub-class	*Sympetalæ or Metachlamydeæ*
Order	*Rubiales*
Family	*Rubiaceæ*
Genus	*Coffea*
Sub-genus	*Eucoffea* **Progenitor**
Species	*C. canephora* (Guinea to Uganda)
	C. liberica (Ethiopia/Yemen) → *C. arabica*
	C. anthonyi (Congo & Cameroon)
	C. eugenoides (East Africa)
Commercial varieties	*C. arabica var typica.*
	C. arabica var. bourbon
	C. canephora var. robusta

Figure 1: Classification of coffee: species and varieties.

There is no one origin of coffee; instead there are multiple origins, divided by species and varieties, natural mutations and natural intra- and interspecific hybrids. The arabica plant was first classified in 1753 by Carl von Linné, a Swedish botanist (Charrier & Berthaud 1985). The varieties listed in Figure 1 are the most significant as commercial progenies and the most genetically and culturally significant, *Coffea arabica var. typica* (typica) and the natural mutation, *Coffea arabica var. bourbon* (bourbon). Bourbon is also considered a natural mutation of typica by some. Robusta is the most commercially grown and traded of the canephora species. *C. canephora var. nganda* (nganda), is not often grown or traded. There are approximately 60–120 species within the *Coffea* genus and over 25 varieties within the arabica family. Wild arabica and robusta varieties are often only found in their native environments, and different species and varieties are introduced to countries and regions of countries variably and for different reasons, normally influenced by an interest in the economic opportunity provided by the cash crop.

The commercial varieties listed in figure 1 represent sources of natural and laboratory-based inter- and intra-specific hybrids, natural mutations, with liberica, *C. anthonyi and C. eugenoides* as progenitors or gene donors for arabica. The majority of arabica mutations or hybrids will ascend from typica or the natural mutation of typica, bourbon. From here, numerous sub-varieties and hybrids have developed naturally or been purposely bred for their productive and resistant qualities. Within the *Arabica* species there are 25 varieties. Thus, the resulting varieties that are grown around the world vary for numerous historic and commercial reasons, they require different conditions for farming and there are physical and climatic characteristics that are more suitable for specific contexts.

Arabica requires different conditions dependent on elevation and climate, and typically grows across a narrower altitude range than robusta, requiring higher altitudes and it is known for high cup quality. While autogamous or self-pollinating, benefits from pollinators are noted as significant for tree health, fruit set and, occasionally, yield (Raw & Free 1977; Vergara & Badano 2009). The tree can reach up to five metres in height but is normally kept to two to three metres for harvest. It is an evergreen bush with dark green leaves that are shiny on top and matt green underneath. The grupes, the botanical name for the coffee berries, are slightly larger than robusta grupes and more oblong in shape. Arabica also varies by stages of flowering and berry ripening on the tree dependent on location. In lowlands experiencing constant rainfall every year, the order of the ripening of grupes and blooming of flowers is consecutive, whereas in semi-dry higher areas, the fruit and the grupe will be found on the tree at the same time (Mazzafera et al. 2010). Such characteristics provide arguments for and against shade-grown coffee particularly related to pest and disease management (Karungi et al. 2015; Pumarino et al. 2015; Jaramillo et al. 2013; Wrigley 1988; Gliessman 2007). Arabica is vulnerable to changes in climate and apart from some wild and natural hybrid varieties, geisha and hybrid of Timor, is highly susceptible to the international coffee leaf rust disease[15], one of various diseases[16] that have a significant effect on coffee farming internationally (Avelino et al. 2004, 2015).

In contrast, Robusta holds a different botanical profile to arabica. It is a more durable plant; it demonstrates resistance to coffee leaf rust and is suitable for an efficient and guaranteed coffee harvest and has a higher caffeine content. It grows taller, to seven metres, has an umbrella shape attributed to the top-weighted long branches and is allogamous, meaning that it requires cross-pollination. Robusta has slender branches, leaves that are dark green and narrower, flowers tinged red and berries that are purple when unripe and oblong when ripe (Nesbitt 2005).

It is amenable to growing at higher altitudes but is typically considered suitable for low-altitude cultivation below 800 metres and more suitable for withstanding temperatures up to 36 degrees higher than arabica. The caffeine content of the arabica beans, approximately 1% (Mazzafera et al. 2010) is estimated 1.2% lower than that of robusta, which is approximately 2.7% (Nesbitt 2005). Robusta generally sells at a lower price than arabica, which holds a higher market value and as such, is more commonly farmed representing 60% of all coffee traded internationally (ICO 2014). Robusta, while not unequal to the taste attributes of arabica, has therefore achieved a significant economic position due to distinct rapid growth, early and fruitful yield and disease resistance making it a valued species within the genera.

The Bean Belt: who wears the pants?

The geographic divide in the coffee industry bridges another parallel between coffee and oil and is representative of a dependent dynamic within the coffee industry. Most coffee grown in the world is located between the Tropics of Cancer and Capricorn, in the coffee belt. Shown in Figure 2.

The psychological, biological, financial and cultural dependence in consumer countries versus the financial, cultural and livelihood reliance on coffee within the coffee belt indicates a reciprocal dependence within the coffee trade. Dependency is a classification of poverty (World Bank 2000/2001, 28), yet interdependence is considered an aspect of sustainable development (Adams & Ghaly 2006). By dependence it seems the producers in *the belt* are more reliant on the periphery, *the pants (or skirt)*, as farmers are almost entirely reliant on

---

[15] CLR attacks the leaves of the coffee plant, causing the coffee cherries to fall earlier, which then affects harvest and yield.

[16] Pests and diseases that affect coffee cultivation internationally and within the two countries are discussed in later chapters.

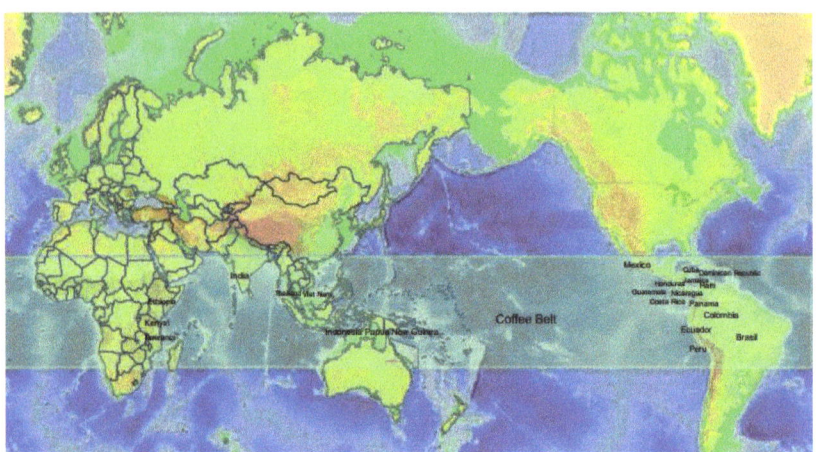

Figure 2: The bean belt.
Data source: Adapted from National Geographic Coffee 1999.

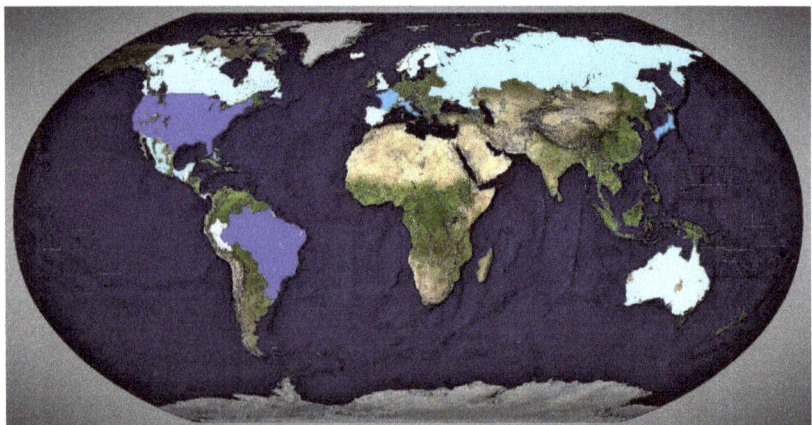

Figure 3: Periphery of coffee belt: Coffee consumption by country[17] (60kg bags/year).
Data source: ICO 2018.

---

[17] This is distinct to consumption per capita, which provides information about quantity consumed per person. This difference is significant, with many Scandinavian countries consuming the most per capita: Finland, 12.2 kg/capita; Sweden, 10.1 kg/capita; Norway, 6.68kg/capita; Iceland 8.43 kg/capita and Switzerland, 7.65 kg/capita (ICO 2018). In comparison, the USA, which imports the most at a global level, consumes 4.5 kg/capita. Consumption per country is provided here as a more general overview to compare where coffee is produced to where the majority is imported.

purchase by international companies. It is therefore in the relationship between farmers and consumers or roasters that efforts toward sustainable development and poverty reduction could be effectively aimed to transition from dependence to recognised interdependence. Data extracted from the International Coffee Organisation (ICO) illustrates the *periphery* of the coffee belt, the consumers, or importers of coffee. See Figure 3.

When these two diagrams are compared, it becomes apparent that for coffee to fulfill its destiny and be consumed, in turn providing income for producers in *the belt,* it must travel. Transport, infrastructure and oil are all necessary belt straps. This relationship as dependent or interdependent seems to be an appropriate area of focus to improve imbalance. The price paid for coffee increases and decreases frequently and constantly in producing countries. In consuming countries, the price maintains (Hallam 2003, 8) with occasional increases reflected in the cost of a coffee bought at a café. Seventy per cent of the world's coffee is grown on farms of fewer than 25 acres with most of these ranging between 2.5 and 12.5 acres. Small coffee farmers are amongst the poorest people in the world and the relationship between poverty and coffee becomes more contrary when considering the value of the international coffee industry, $125.1 billion in 2009 (Pendergast 2009). In an industry that represents such significant revenue at an international level, the suppliers and labourers of the industry are still considered poor and vulnerable. The distance that the coffee green and ready for roasting, *el café de oro* must travel is significant in terms of oil costs and logistics. With 25 million farmers reliant on coffee harvest for income, trends in the market and in farming techniques have a significantly global and interconnected reach. Berry (2004) in Garcia supplies the following diagram of the coffee sourcing chain which demonstrates the various and alternative channels. See Figure 4.

The additional line (orange) directly connects roasters with farmers, commonly referred to as Direct Trade. Various approaches to trade channels can influence the income of coffee farmers and processors. Figure 5 provides an idea of how the sourcing chain can differ based on country and industry context.

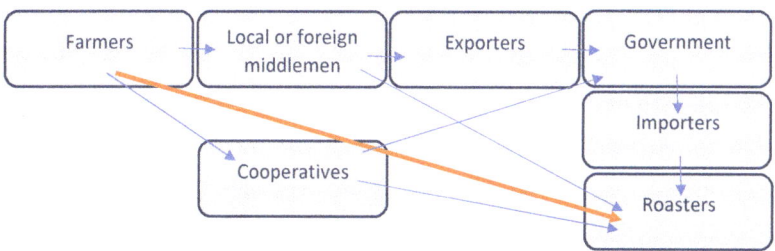

Figure 4: Basic In-country coffee sourcing chain.

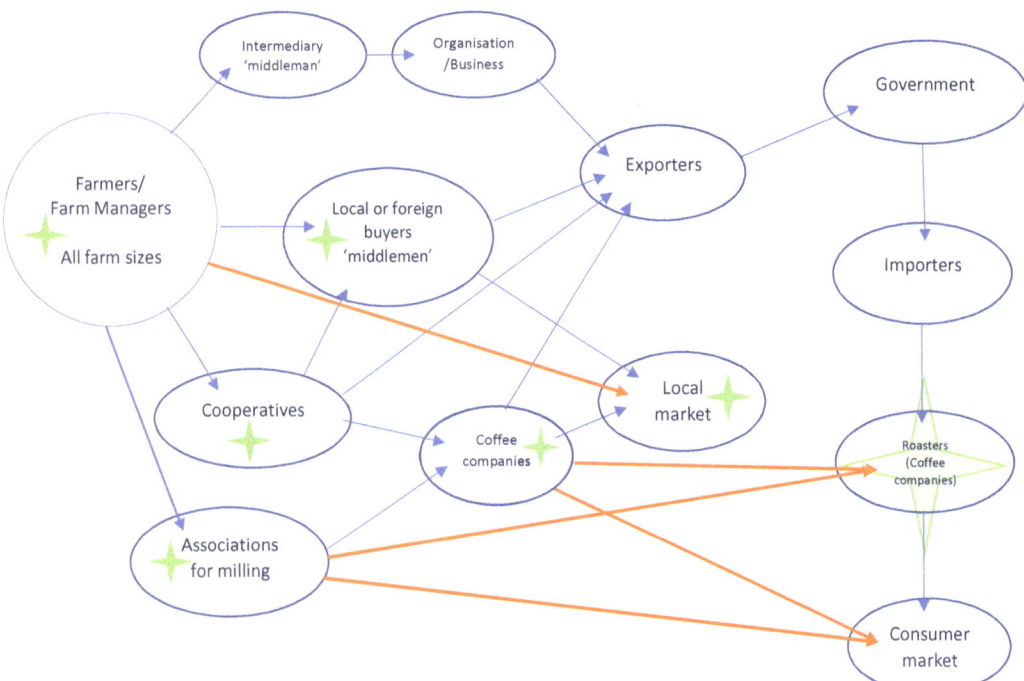

Figure 5: Example of variance in country specific sourcing chains.

The divide in profits through the supply chain particularly between roasters, retailers, processors and farmers is alarming where farmers bear the highest cost and risk in the coffee supply chain (Garcia & Lemos 2006, 15). From all profits of the coffee supply chain, growers are estimated to receive 10%, exporters 10%, shippers and roasters 55% and retailers 25% (Ransom 1997, 41) with possibility for variance dependent on the sourcing chain.

The power of demand remains with very few in the international coffee industry., see table 1. In 1998 Neumann and Volcafe dominated the international

Table 1. Major traders in coffee industry.

Leading coffee trader company 2010: subject to constant change	Million 60kg bags	Offtaker Trading Companies 2012	Location of HQ	% of world exports	Total bags purchased (million 60kg bags)
Neumann	13.5	Kraft Foods Inc	USA	11.8	13.5
Ecom	10	Nestle SA	Switzerland	11.2	12.8
Olam	8	Sara Lee	USA/ Netherlands	7.4	8.5
Volcafe	7	JM Smucker	USA	4.8	5.5
LouisDreyfus	6.5	Elite	UK	3.1	3.5
Noble	5	Tchibo	UK	2.4	2.8
Sucafina	4	Starbucks	USA	2.4	2.7
Amajaro[18]	3.5	Lavazza	Italy	2.1	2.4
Mercon	2.5	Melitta	Germany	1.7	2
		Segafredo	Italy	1.7	1.9
		Aldi	Germany	1.6	1.8

Data source: ITC 2011.

market of green coffee trade by holding 29% (Ponte 2004). In 2012 Neumann, Ecom, Volcafe, and Louis Dreyfus were the lead traders of coffee (Terazono 2013). Lead traders with a secured supply of beans, off takers differs slightly; with Kraft and Nestle representing 11% each of world exports. Nestle and Kraft purchased 1/4 of the world's traded coffee; and the top five coffee traders, represented 40% of all traded coffee (ITC 2011).

International traders, of whom there are few (Ponte 2004; ITC 2011; Terazano 2013), and then buyers 'wear the pants' within trade dynamics. However, the belt, the farmers and in-country processes, keep them up. Interdependence between international traders and farmers is evident.

Collapse of the International Coffee Agreement

Making a stand against what was considered a 'coffee paradox' (Daviron & Ponte 2005), Uribe, the New York Representative of Colombia's National

---

[18] Amajaro has since been acquired by Ecom.

Federation of Coffee Growers and the Chairman of the Pan-American coffee bureau sought to enlighten the US people. Including major coffee stakeholders, importers, marketers, baristas and end consumers of the actual value of coffee for farmers. Encouraging thought past what consumers pay for a cup of coffee and realising that only 38% of the $2.78 billion spent on coffee by US consumers went back to Latin American producing countries. He stated:

> We in Latin America have a task before us which is staggering to the imagination illiteracy to be eliminated, disease to be wiped out, good health to be restored, a sound program of nutrition to be worked out for millions of people. The key to all of this is an equitable price for coffee. (Uribe 1949 cited in Pendergast 2001, 194)

Colombia, Brazil and mainly the USA organised the International Coffee Agreement (ICA) to create a new quota system and raise coffee prices, a part of which involved the Colombian National Federation of Coffee Growers (Bentley & Baker 2000, 3–4). From 1958–1989, the coffee industry was regulated through the ICA. The ICO was established in 1963 alongside the first ICA in 1962. The agreement sought to regulate the price of coffee with a quota system which would prevent any member country from supplying the international market over their assigned quota. The ICA also allowed funds to promote the coffee industry, then operating under successive agreements. The move toward trade liberalisation and a preference for a free market political economy approach of the 1980s resulted in a global movement away from multilateral regulatory agreements and regulation of MNC activities in developing countries. By 1989 the US had withdrawn support for the ICA and resigned from the ICO. As a result, the ICA collapsed (ICO 2016) and the ICO price for coffee slumped. Following and reinforcing a free market approach the World Trade Organisation (WTO) was established in 1995 with the General Agreement on Tariffs and Trade (GATT). The agenda of the WTO was and is to liberalise international trade in goods and services through the removal of tariffs and subsidies. This includes restricting government regulation and promoting TNC investment in essential services such as water, health, education and the reinforcement of intellectual property rights.

GATT paused the quota system of the ICA as it sought to promote a neoliberal model of development through deregulation of international markets. Such an approach would reduce the state's ability to intervene in market activities. The collapse of this regulatory system resulted in disagreements amongst exporting countries, a boom in supplies due to new production techniques and liquidation of public stocks of coffee maintained by producing countries. An astounding rise in production of *Robusta* coffee from Viet Nam which went from being an insignificant coffee grower to the second largest producer in the world, was a contributor to increased supply.

Market Saturation

The collapse of the ICA in 1989 and removal of quotas as part of a global deregulation of international markets resulted in market saturation of *Robusta* coffee from Viet Nam and Brazil and significant fluctuations in global prices (Akiyama & Varangis 1990; Osorio 2004). Eventually a slump in the price of coffee resulted (Figures 7, 8 & 10). For example, in 1983, Viet Nam exported 44,000 bags of coffee, by 1990, this amount had increased to 1 million bags and in 2001, had jumped to 14 million bags (Luong 2003). At the same time, Brazil had increased its production and export quantity and the resulting saturation of the market with robusta rather than arabica drove the international price of coffee down further, below 50 cents per pound (Figure 8), leading to the 'coffee crisis' in 2001 (Osorio 2002; Igami 2015). In the same year, the first collapse of the Doha 'Development' Round occurred (Baldwin 2007), the subsequent four collapses were an additional strong indication of resistance to the proposed method for deregulation of international agricultural markets.

Resistance came from some of the countries whose concerns the agenda claimed to be meeting; Brazil, China and India refused to agree to the conditions offered (Bailey & Ranald 2006) creating an unpredictable environment for international trade, particularly between developing and developed countries. Figures 6 and 7 present coffee prices across 1969–2015 and 2009–2018, respectively, with cross-over in representation between 2009 and 2015. While

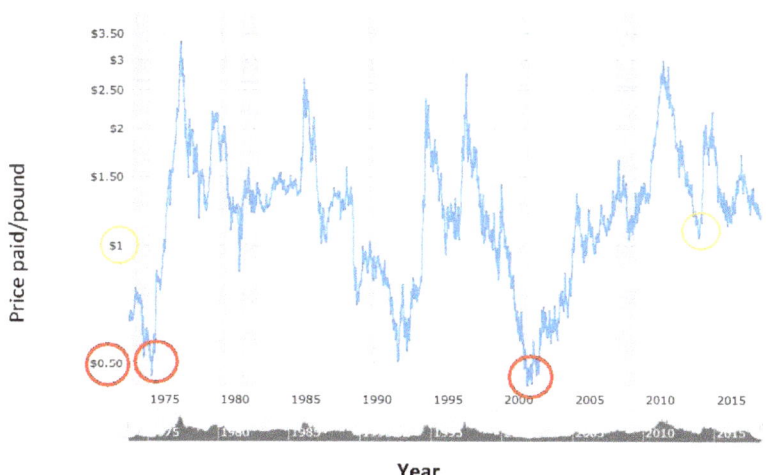

Figure 6: Coffee export price per pound (1969–2015).
Data source: Macrotrends 2018.

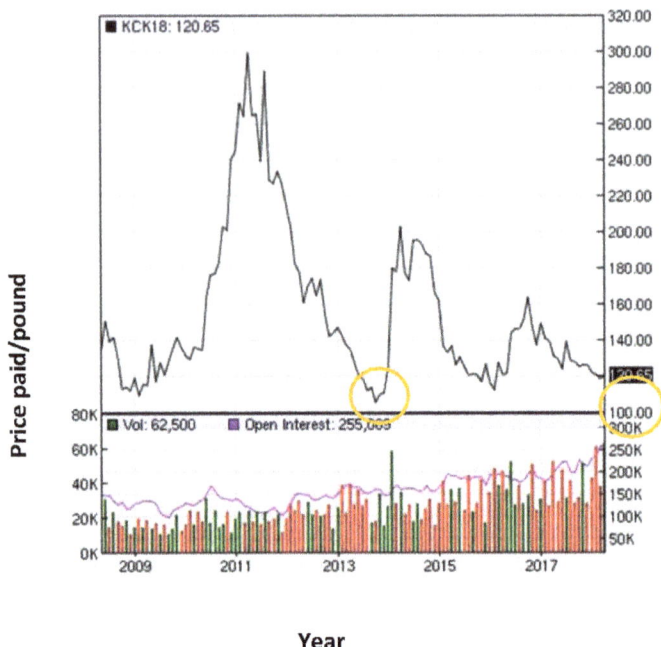

Figure 7: Coffee export price per pound (2009–2018).
Data source: NASDAQ 2018.

the price fluctuations appear similar across both figures, the price in Figure 6 does not drop below $1/pound. The low price highlighted in 2014 indicates this notable difference between the two figures.

The 2001 'coffee crisis' was one of the most significant occurrences in the coffee industry within 40 years. When considered alongside comparative maximum prices during the 1969–2009 period (nearly $3.50/pound)—and during the 2009–2018 period (nearly $3/pound)—the difference in minimum and maximum price is most significant between 1969 and 2009. In 2017 prices were just above 160 US cents/lb (IE Coffee futures 2019). How production and the price paid to the grower compared between Costa Rica, Brasil and Viet Nam are presented in figure 8 and 9.

The international price of coffee has again dropped in 2019, due to surplus supply, despite ongoing ideas that the supply of coffee is under threat due to climate change. The 2019 January price went from 101.56US cents/lb after a low of 99.16 US cents/lb (ICO 2019). It again decreased to 94 US cents/lb (ICE Coffee futures 2019). ICO (2019) state that 94 cents/lb (75 cents/lb for robusta) was the lowest since October 2006, on par with 2008 prices, figure 9.

The international coffee industry 51

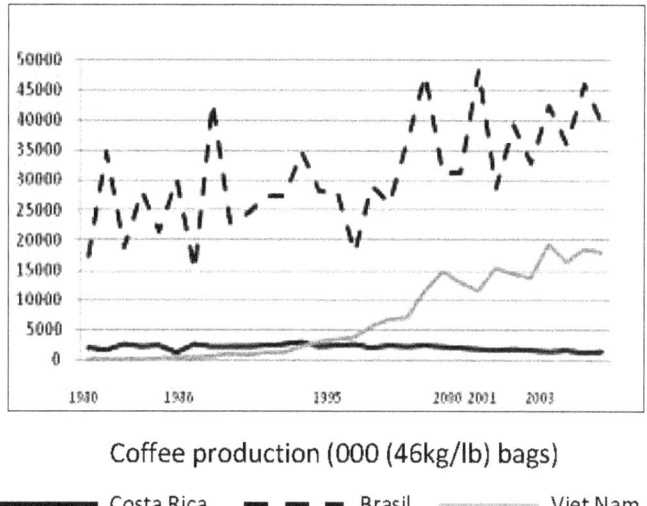

Figure 8: International coffee production during two coffee crises between (1990–2003).

Data source: ICO 2013.

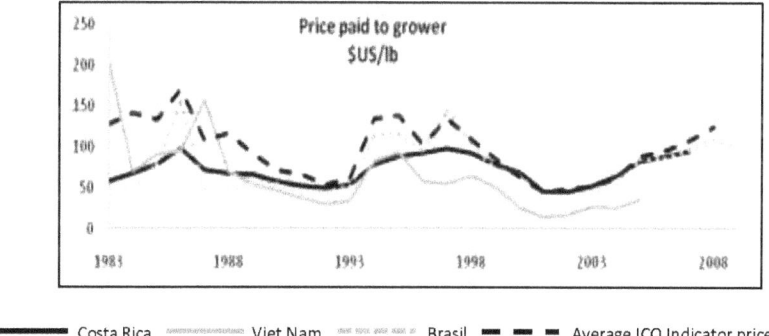

Figure 9: International coffee prices[19] during two coffee crises (1983-2008).
Data source: ICO statistics 2008.

---

[19] The above stated prices are composite indicators of the daily price of coffee exports.

The contrast of a coffee crisis

A low coffee price reveals the vulnerability of coffee farming landscapes' income to global supply trends. All quiet on the Western Front (Remarque 1929), while out of context, can encapsulate an international coffee crisis where the divide between the economically developed and emerging world creates an underlying dynamic for the coffee industry. The prices on the world market are only an indication of what a grower is paid for his or her coffee harvest per pound however fluctuations in this price determines incomes of Costa Rican farmers, a distinct cost of production by country is also influential. Figure 9 demonstrate how the price decrease differed by country. In Costa Rica it was less extreme compared to the standard price offered. The influence in Costa Rican coffee farming communities was however significant.

The retail price, what is paid at a café or for roasted coffee whole or ground, and retail sales are differentiated from sales of the café de oro (green bean). They are not an indication of the money flowing to coffee farmers or cooperatives. When the price of coffee dropped to 70 cents per pound in 2002, the lowest in real terms for 100 years (Osorio 2004, 1), it went unnoticed in the developed world where the prices for roasted and retailed coffee remained steady or *quiet* (Hallam 2003, 8).

> We believe that the soundest way of strengthening, from the outset, the economy of the Latin American countries, consists of paying a fair price for our products. During World War II the coffee market was fixed by the Office of Price Administration at a level that turned out to be one half of the market price when controls were released. This meant that coffee producing countries contributed to the war effort during the three or four years, fifty percent of the gross value of their main crop. We do not complain but we think that North American people should know about these things, especially since they are so frequently told of the inequities imposed upon them by the expense of their foreign aid programs. The healthiest source of income for any nation, as for any man, is the fair compensation for its own efforts. (Figueres cited in Martz 1959, 243–4)

It is important that consuming countries understand the significance of a fair remuneration for one's efforts in a producing country as it can facilitate an understanding of how their purchase preferences might influence the situation. For coffee farmers in the developing world, the slump in the global market price had serious implications such as forced migration through a necessary abandoning of farms and communities. Maintenance costs became higher than the sale price of green coffee. The perceived land value of coffee farms depreciated as perceived associated risk increased. Small and medium-sized traders could not compete with larger traders, the market at this level became more concentrated (Ponte 2001, 16).

Summary

An understanding of the international coffee industry clarifies trade's influence in development. The geographic and socio-economic divides conducive to negative influence have been identified by producing countries. While supply influence market prices, the international coffee industry can have significant influence on producing country landscapes. The international coffee industry is, like many commodity markets, volatile and risky for farmers. While this volatility exists within the belt, *the pants (or skirt)* – the consumers – remain up, supplied and *quiet*. How the sourcing chain[20] includes various stakeholders can influence distribution of economic benefit and may also influence poverty reduction and sustainability outcomes. The value of the industry and potential profit can influence prioritised farming and production approaches, and therefore, landscape outcomes.

---

[20] Sourcing rather than supply chain is used to better demonstrate the influence of a purchaser choice versus the quantity of coffee farmed. It is however recognised that where coffee supply reduces by uncontrollable circumstances this might better be described as a supply chain.

CHAPTER 4

Sustainability Certifications

Introduction

Sustainability certifications seek to encourage socially, and environmentally sustainable practices guided by exclusive standards and processes for implementation. They are uni or multi-stakeholder organisations, that work intra market and extra business to certify sourcing of natural resources that are major commodities, and more recently less conventionally traded. They can provide external advice and support for procurement and trade guidance for a business, through networks of certified businesses, or certify the business practice. While some certifications have been operating for nearly thirty years, they are still orientating themselves toward 'consistently positive' influence (Vogt 2019c, 2019e). Over the last decade they have been used more by multinational companies, originally only used by small businesses.

This chapter will provide a brief overview of sustainability certifications, and more detailed secondary information about two certifications, Rainforest Alliance (RA) and Fairtrade International (Fairtrade). Some quotes from fieldwork collected from an employee of RA are included in this section to provide direct information.

Sustainability certifications

As trade can influence development, certifications are considered capable of influencing the culture of a country (Watts 2005) by requiring compliance to a standard and therefore behaviour change. Each certification abides by a prerogative or ideological approach distinct from others, as such, the idea of what will result according to improved social and environmental outcomes is directed by the preference of each certification. The standards that form the foundation of voluntary certification are developed at an international level in most situations, and certainly at the beginning of the sustainability certification effort.

How to cite this book chapter:
Vogt, M. 2019. *Variance in Approach Toward a 'Sustainable' Coffee Industry in Costa Rica: Perspectives from Within; Lessons and Insights.* Pp. 55–66. London: Ubiquity Press. DOI: https://doi.org/10.5334/bce.f. License: CC-BY 4.0

Leclair (2002) questioned the longevity of sustainable alternative trade systems. Where relying on attitudes and behaviours of consumers he foresaw only a niche market stabilising. Since that time, the number of certifications globally has only increased, and what is required has also shifted influencing legitimacy and overall efforts of certifications amongst other legal, extra-market and internal to business efforts. Grainne de Burca (2005, 10–11) brings attention to the state like responsibility and role these certifications have and suggests that:

> An increasing number of transnational entities and networks are carrying out the kinds of governing functions which have normally or previously been carried out by states, [and as such] questions of authority and legitimacy – the source of any obligation to obey [arise].

The most common regulation approach for sustainability certifications is compulsory voluntary verification. Audits and other procedural techniques are used by certifications to more easily monitor and verify compliance. The order of being certified versus being compliant, and the standards required are areas of additional concern, with green washing (Dahl 2010) a common term for such situations, often observed. As the number of labels increases, with 464 eco-labels identified (Ecolabel Index 2018), and industry cross over within individual certification effort, and industries that can be certified by several different certifications. there is an increasing need to understand standard requirements and effective regulation.

Sustainability certifications and coffee

Coffee was one of the first commodities to be 'sustainably' certified. Alternative trade organisations for coffee emerged from the late 1980s to address ensuing poverty, environmental degradation and the increased demand for the lower grade coffee variety robusta. Fair trade, for example, originally aimed to allow small coffee farmers of arabica varieties direct access to markets with the intention of recognising and rewarding the use of organic practices. As more certifications for coffee emerged, it became clear that sustainable farming and trade approaches were guided by certification prerogatives or ideologies. For many consumers, sustainable coffee certifications represent an ethical purchase and a better choice compared to the standard products available. An understanding of what these certifications really mean is normally as detailed as information provided on the packaging for the consumer (Leclair 2002). The certifications allow the consumer to verify and identify products that are 'sustainable', and more are becoming available to verify ethical practices.

Of all sustainable green coffee sales as a proportion of global green coffee exports, 92% is conventional coffee; 6% sustainable coffee (multi stakeholder initiatives); and 2% sustainable coffee (private initiatives). UTZ certified, RA,

Organic, Fairtrade and 4C are included as multi-stakeholder initiatives. Private sustainable initiatives within these categories are clearly not defined but might be considered as corporate or internal to business codes of conduct (Pierrot et al. 2010; Fairtrade 2009; UTZ certified 2009). Average annual growth in sustainable coffee sales has been 153% for 4C association; 30% for Fairtrade[xix]; 19% for IFOAM (organic); 30% Utz Certified; 64% RA; 40% Total (excluding private sector initiatives). Five-year growth 278% for Fairtrade 142% for IFOAM; 187% for RA, and 433% in total (Giovanucci et al. 2010; Fairtrade Foundation 2019; RA/SAN 2019; UTZ certified 2009; 4C Association 2009).

Whether a niche or something more, there is an undeniable expansion of the coffee industry's demand for CSR programs including sustainability certifications. The growing popularity of sustainable coffee certifications in both consumer and producer countries could be a central reason.

History of Rainforest Alliance (RA) and Fairtrade coffee sustainability certifications

In 2007/8, sustainability certifications for coffee, and for other commodities were a new movement. In Australia, RA certified coffee was barely available, and Fairtrade had only been introduced to the market in 2006. Internationally, RA and Fairtrade certified products were more accessible and available. The number of labels and certifications was starting to increase, the major players for certifying coffee were Organic, Fairtrade and RA, with Utz Kapeh having some market presence outside Australia. 4Cs was a new sustainability program for coffee only just introduced to Costa Rica in 2009. Fair trade can be traced back to alternative trade organisations in America and Europe in the 1940s with the goal of relieving refugee and poor communities through direct trade of their handicrafts (WFTO 2019). The direct approach brought higher returns to producers and their handicrafts would be sold to higher socio-economic groups.

Coffee certifications date back to the late 1960s with organic coffee and in the early 1970s with Max Havelaar a fictional character from the book titled "Max Havelaar; the Coffee Auctions of a Dutch Trading Company" (Multatuli 1982) first published in 1860. The *anti-colonial* book's central character is a Dutch public servant, appointed assistant resident of an agency in West Java. An idealist, Havelaar attempted to work to prevent injustice and abuse of power in the Dutch East Indies. This book was successful in Holland, reaching multitude of readers and being effective in changing policy related to Dutch colonies. The label Max Havelaar was launched in 1988 and has developed to be known as the Fairtrade label. The initiative sought to improve payment to small farmers in disadvantaged regions. It started with a community of coffee farmers in Oaxaca, Mexico by arranging direct export to the international market where the coffee would be roasted and then sold, shortening the trade chain significantly.

Intentions were distinct to organic or sustainable farming factors as it focused more on trade and worker condition imbalances. In fact, this was one of the first intra-market sustainability mechanisms to counter the advantage taken by business of complicated trade routes (Meenu 2008; Vedel & Ellegard 2013). The label that is now known as Fairtrade was established in 1997 as Fairtrade Labelling International (Fairtrade International – Fairtrade) (WFTO 2019). The initial focus of RA in 1986 was prevention of rapid deforestation. The first RA office, a conservation media centre was set up in San José, Costa Rica in 1989. SmartWood, the first certification program, sought to improve forest management. Since that time, RA expanded standards through the Sustainable Agriculture Network (SAN) to cover numerous crops cultivated all over the world. There is now one set of SAN standards applicable for all agricultural crops.[21]

Costa Rica and sustainably certified coffee

Coinciding with the 1989 collapse of the International Coffee Agreement (ICA), Fair trade was introduced in Costa Rica. It was the second standard introduced to Costa Rica, the first was Organic certification in 1982. Coocafe R.L. ('Coocafe') (Consorcio de Cooperativas de Caficultores de Guanacaste y Montes de Oro) adopted the Fair-trading partners of both Coopecerroazul and Coope Santa Elena upon establishment in 1989. The strength of presence of certifications and the dominance of a few companies in the international coffee industry, where minimal effective consultation is carried out with producer groups, indicates a contribution to the *double loss* of farmers and processors where "whatever preferences might emerge out of their own experiences and worldviews are unlikely to be reflected in global messages indicating what goods, services, and practices are valuable" (Evans 2002, 58). The role of certifications internationally and nationally is multi-dimensional. To access a country's market, producer groups and farm managers must meet specific criteria which aim to benefit the farmer, the community and the environment. RA established first in Costa Rica and the standard for coffee developed in 1995, intended for plantation size farms.

Organisational structure of certifications

SAN standards set the foundation for RA certification.[22] They seek to promote the interest of workers, communities and the environment. As the secretary of

---

[21] Standards and Policy Technical Coordinator, 6 May, 2009.
[22] For more information, view http://www.rainforest-alliance.org/about.cfm

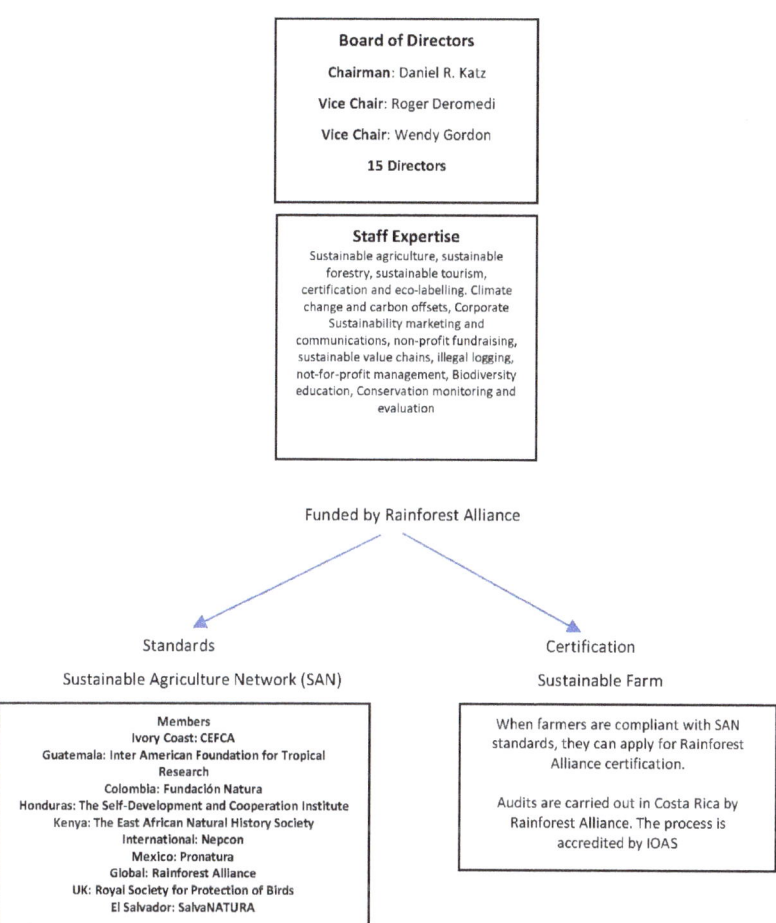

Figure 10: Rainforest Alliance organisational structure.

the network RA distributes the standards, coordinates the international technical committee, the directors and the strategic direction of the network. See figure 10. SAN did not therefore have much separation from RA (Ventura 2007).

Fairtrade[23] is the only certification scheme that sets out to tackle poverty and empower producers in developing countries. Through marketing slogans, it claims to be: "a partnership between the consumer and producer. A better deal for producers in the developing world"; and "Fairtrade helps producers take control of their lives." The Fairtrade standards and approach dictate interest

---

[23] For more information view www.fairtrade.net and www.flocert.net.

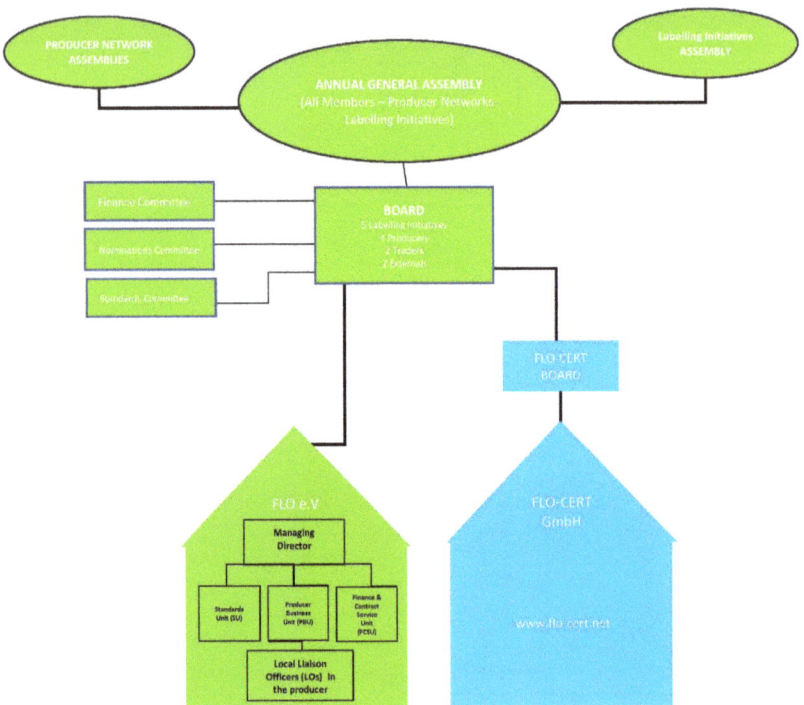

Figure 11: Fairtrade International organisational structure.
Data source: FLO[24] Annual Report 2005, available from Fairtrade Foundation 2019[25].

and approach to the lobbying message. Fairtrade alongside WFTO Network of European World Shops (NEWS) and European Fair Trade Association (EFTA) monitors European and International trade and development policies. It ensures a constant dialogue between the Fairtrade movement and political decision makers funded by the Fair-trade movement, see figure 11 for organisational structure.

Basic differences between Fairtrade and RA premise and standards

Interpretations of sustainability definitions also provide opportunity for misaligned and contradictory practices to purpose. The standards that guide

---

[24] Fairtrade Labelling Organisation – now Fairtrade International. – referred to in the text as Fairtrade.

[25] Please consult the Fairtrade International website for possible updates to the organisational structure, available in footnote 24.

international trade efforts toward a sustainable development are considered significantly influential. The level of detail required for such efforts may be skimmed over unless standards are well developed. High quality standards do not however directly translate to effective implementation or to certifications as the best approach (Vos et al. 2019; Vogelpohl & Verbandt 2019; Vogt & Englund 2019).

The core difference between RA and Fairtrade is the foundational and prioritised objectives which influence approach and preferred business structure. Fairtrade certification emerged from an economic justice platform seeking to reduce poverty for small farmers by offering a set of social standards and prioritising a minimum price and secured option of pre-harvest finance and long-term contracts. It also aims to provide socially orientated projects or organisational capacity building for cooperative structures through provision of a premium. Through involvement in the certification system it claims to facilitate international relationships between producer organisations and roasters or retailers of coffee. These measures aim to reduce risk to volatile international market prices, build capabilities of producers and provide opportunities for international networking within the industry (Raynolds 2003; Ronchi 2002). Fairtrade pays an additional premium for organic production.

RA originally prioritised forest conservation and now takes a holistic approach to developing standards with the goal of promoting sustainable processes on farms to contribute to the sustainable development of the coffee industry.[26] The approach emphasises strengthening the environmental and social pillars of development which will then allow economic viability, as a more sustainable approach. SAN standards used by RA to certify farms and producer groups are frequently revised. The first agricultural project of RA was with the largest banana exporter in Costa Rica, Chiquita. The standards were designed in a way that was not structurally compatible with cooperatives. The size of the farm certified is a key difference between Fairtrade and RA, and to poverty reduction efforts in 2009. Fairtrade only certifies cooperatives whose members were small farm holders. During 2009 a standard for farmer *groups* or cooperatives was developing and it is frequently revised. There were two RA certified cooperatives in Costa Rica in 2009, the rest were certified plantations.

The certifications support producers to meet the required criteria of standards and in gaining market access. Locally based liaison officers provide training and guidance on certification and facilitate relationships with buyers. Equally, they seek to provide a program which allows an independent business to engage in socially responsible behaviour to principled and/or prioritised criteria. See figure 12.

---

[26] For more information, view http://www.rainforest-alliance.org/about.cfm

Table 2: Comparing RA and Fairtrade standards 2017.

	Fair Trade	Rainforest Alliance
Standard Setting Body	Fairtrade International	Sustainable Agriculture Network (SAN)
Independence of Standards setting body	Membership based, not-for-profit Association. Membership open to Fairtrade labelling initiatives and producer networks	RA is secretariat of organisation. RA is arguably the most influential members of the secretariat
Standards		
Social Production Specifications	All farms must form cooperatives; collective use of social premium is decided within each producer group. Hired labour standard: Upholding ILO conventions Right to association Collective bargaining Freedom from discrimination and unequal pay No forced or child labour Minimum social and labour standards Right to safe and healthy working conditions	Less ILO conventions compared to Fairtrade Standard Principle 5: Fair treatment and good working conditions for workers (*not binding for audit purposes*) –Salary and benefits equal to legal minimum Workweek and work hours will not exceed legal maximums Worst forms of child labour prohibited Right to association: no discrimination Farms to offer employment opportunities and education to people in neighbouring communities; Adequate housing; Families living on farms have access to medical services and children have access to education Principle 6: Occupational Health and Safety Certified farms have an OHS program to reduce or prevent risk of accidents in the workplace; applicable to all workers.

Table 2: Continued

	Fair Trade	Rainforest Alliance
Ecological Production specifications	Standards for reduction in agrichemical use; reduction and composting of wastes; promotion of soil fertility; prevention of fires and avoidance of GMOs	Standards for ecosystem and wildlife conservation; integrated crop management and integrated waste management
Trade specifications	Minimum price; standard for trade relationship; long term contracts; credit advances	None
Production price premiums	Minimum price: $1.40/lb washed Arabica; $1.35/lb for unwashed Social premium: $0.28 Organic: $0.14	Variable Estimated in 2009 at $1.85/lb
Monitoring Body	FLOCert and independent monitoring body approved by organisation	Member organisation

Data source: Annual Reports from Trauben 2009; data sourced from Annual Reports from Fairtrade Foundation 2019; SAN 2019; RA 2019.

Before 2009 each respective certification developed its own standards autonomously; by 2009 the standards of both Fairtrade and RA were drawn up in consultation with ISEAL, the International Social and Environmental Accreditation and Labelling. In 2016, SAN introduced the 2017 SAN standard against which they measure their potential for performance with the SAI Platforms FSA tool. This indicates that the standard covers 100% of essential issues, 80% of basic issues and 50% of advanced issues (SAN 2019). ISEAL has strived to monitor and advise the standards that are required of developing country producers. Fairtrade was one of four members responsible for the inception of ISEAL, and RA and Fairtrade were among the eight founding members. In 2008 ISEAL membership doubled to sixteen and they have worked toward a code of good practice in measuring the impact of social and environmental standards, standard setting and verification. ISEAL aims to strengthen sustainability standards for the benefit of people and the environment. Twenty-two certifications and labelling organisations make up membership which is only a small proportion of the 464 eco-labels for sustainability certified products.

The three key differences between 2009 standards that figure 13 highlights are the independence of standard setting bodies to labelling bodies; the standards specific to trade included in each certification; and the detail of International

Labour Organisation (ILO) conventions in social standards. Across these differences Fairtrade is presented as having more independence in standard setting. Fairtrade involves itself in trade standards and includes ten ILO conventions in social standards where RA only "upholds a few" (Trauben 2009).

> Our mission is to find a balance of sustainable production that is good for the environment, respects workers while also ensuring that consumers are aware of this importance so that they recognise the value. It is consumer and market activism.[27]

RA does not offer a minimum price or price premium, they considered themselves to be more holistic with equal importance given to the three arms of sustainable development: the economic, environmental, and the social. Reforestation has been one of the key areas for focus within the SAN standards. RA was, in 2009, considering the benefits of participation in the carbon credit market through a program called carbon coffee.

Approaches to verifying compliance

Sustainable Farm Certification International monitors SAN standard compliance and determines if certification will be given based on the audit results. Audits are carried out by a country specific body and in Costa Rica, RA is that auditing body. The importance of having a third party to audit is recognised and a move toward this approach was indicated in 2009.[28, 29] A response to critiques from Oxfam DE in 2015 when compliance for workers was not met, replicated an explanation that a new upgraded standard and certification process would be launched in September 2016 (RA 2016a). There is now a 2017 SAN standard however verification of implementation through audit is not yet proven as consistent for all certified farms. FLOCert GmbH is an independently governed subsidiary of Fairtrade, employed and paid for by the certified organisation to audit and verify compliance with standards on behalf of Fairtrade. FLOCert auditing is intended at the trader, producer organisation, and producer level.

Compliance requirements for use of label

It is unethical and unacceptable to curtain socially irresponsible behaviour with a positive CSR message purely to maintain profit margins. Thus, it is

---

[27] RA Standards and Policy Technical Coordinator, 6 May, 2009.
[28] Standards and policy technical coordinator, 6 May, 2009.
[29] Recognition was also reported in 2007 when doubts were expressed about the legitimacy of the *third-party* auditing process (Ventura 2007).

important to distinguish *having* or purchasing a certification and label from being compliant with a standard. While 100% compliance with the SAN standard is not necessary to hold RA certification; a commitment to working toward full compliance is necessary. Standards for monitoring traders, roasters and retailers were under development in 2008 and any actor selling RA certified products must register on a public website. In 2009, to sell coffee with the RA label required a minimum of 30% of the coffee be RA certified. Presentation of the percentage of certified coffee was required but not then monitored. There is now information via a qualifying statement or disclaimer text that explains, 'with 30% certified coffee now, we're working towards buying all our coffee from RA certified™ farms by 2020!' (RA 2016b).

Fairtrade holds a standard for traders and importers consistent with all principles of Fairtrade, applicable to all Fairtrade payers. For a roaster and/or retailer to display the Fairtrade label specific to coffee they must use 100% certified coffee. A roaster or retailer is not liable to the certification body for breaches although in the case of Fairtrade, use of the certification is bound by standards specific to traders and if a valid contract is not honoured. "FLOCert will have grounds to sanction the operator" (FLOCert 2015). At the time of fieldwork, Fairtrade granted certification conditional to an ability to prove compliance through random audits. Where compliance was not evident a warning was issued. If the gap to compliance was large the cooperative would lose the certification.

Questions of jurisdiction, regulation and enforcement are prominent for CSR and certification approaches as all are an effort to improve social responsibility of corporations and companies directly and indirectly.

Summary

Certifications are a novel and distinct approach to internally developed and administered codes of conduct. They complement and can go beyond legislative attempts to encourage and regulate socially responsible corporate activity in source countries. The complexity of interests in a source country between foreign investment and economic value and respecting their citizens' rights and their environment can become a limiting factor. The intention of each certification differs, and this is reflected in organisational structure, approach, stated aims, the stakeholders involved and upon whom the certifications rely. Implementation of RA and location of operation demonstrates this difference; where Fairtrade developed from direct trade with small farmers and a social/economic approach, RA began with a plantation and environmental focus. The certifications follow categories of sustainable development, environment, social and economic. Standards of each certification do differ by detail, reflective of different approaches to sustainable development and the eventual objective of poverty reduction and sustainability. For certified traders, the difference in standards is evident for labelling. In 2009, RA appeared less strict with a minimum of 30% of all packaged coffee required as RA certified and sourced to allow use of the label. Fairtrade on the other hand requires 100% of packaged and sold coffee to be Fairtrade certified to allow use of the label. Each certification 'regulates' producers to ensure compliance, traders on the other hand are not well regulated.

CHAPTER 5

Overview of the contemporary Costa Rican coffee industry

Introduction

The detailed colonial history of Costa Rica, chapter 1, provides a contextual background for the study country, easing understanding of the contemporary coffee industry of the country. The contemporary experience of farming coffee in Costa Rica is significantly influenced by historic trends explained in chapter 1 for contextual background, including significance in economic development through independence, managing foreign relations, the green revolution, and coffee farmers capacity for organising and ensuring representation. Coffee was a vehicle of economic advancement for Costa Rica during independence as it successfully linked Costa Rica to the world market. Despite economic advances allowed through expansion of coffee farming and trade, the colonial relationship that tied it, albeit loosely, to Spain did not dissipate. Instead it changed form to a reliance on the world coffee, and to a lesser degree other commodity, markets (Seligson 1977, 216).

INEC (2010) indicates a similar structure today in the coffee industry as existed in the 1930s. Of all farms, 62 per cent are between one and five hectares and 86% have fewer than twenty hectares. In terms of land extension, 57% of all land occupied by coffee comprises farms of twenty to one hundred hectares. It is one of the few countries in the region to have small farms represent the largest proportion of all farms but not hectares. The reach of coffee cultivation through the Costa Rican population is therefore significant. The historic legacy of the coffee industry influenced this distinct land distribution pattern of ownership post- independence based on small farm holdings compared to neighbouring countries. The land distribution pattern also allowed allocation of income and experience with coffee to touch more Costa Ricans than other

---

How to cite this book chapter:
Vogt, M. 2019. *Variance in Approach Toward a 'Sustainable' Coffee Industry in Costa Rica: Perspectives from Within; Lessons and Insights.* Pp. 67–82. London: Ubiquity Press. DOI: https://doi.org/10.5334/bce.g. License: CC-BY 4.0

agricultural activities in the country at a political, economic, environmental and social or community level. The arabica only law and the harvest picked only by hand also distinguish Costa Rica from other countries and encouraged maintenance of small farms in the Central Valley. Robusta varieties could have more easily encouraged landholding conversion to plantations.

This chapter will provide more contemporary information about Costa Rica and the coffee industry of the country. Costa Rica is now a regional leader according to development indices, the country's approach to sustainability and poverty reduction has been influenced by intensive coffee farming trends and variable but well reputed conservation efforts during and after this intensive farming period. Common environmental and social challenges associated with farming coffee in Costa Rica are explained.

Costa Rica compared to regional indicators of development and happiness

Costa Rica is something of an exception within the Central American region. It is considered one of the most developed according to Human Development Index (HDI) ratings in the region and has been rated the happiest country in the world according to the Happy Planet Index (HPI). It has made conservation efforts and reached sustainability targets in a way that leave the country well regarded at an international level. Externally imposed situations and responses to various situations through the countries' history, some strategic, and some not, have created the current day situation. Costa Rica's government has a long-standing commitment to social welfare and has achieved prosperous economic development compared to neighbouring countries of the region, as demonstrated in table 3.

The HPI seeks to re-direct how governments think about development and economics and is dependent on three variables, one of which is ecological footprint. While Guatemala, Honduras and Nicaragua had smaller ecological footprints, Costa Rica ranked number one. They are living healthy and high-quality lives with a minimal ecological footprint. The regional success is a contrast to pre-independent Costa Rica when it was 'one of the poorest of Spain's American colonies' (Edelman 1979, 1; Hall 1985, 72), an *'ultimus inter pares'* (last among equals) (Molina & Palmer 2008, 28).[30]

---

[30] The Costa Rican economy pre-independence relied on the sporadic export of cacao, cattle migration, tobacco, leather and various other commodities, including the export of indigenous groups as labour from Nicoya and Nicaragua in the 16th Century (Molina & Palmer 2008, 20).

Table 3: Regional indicators.

Country	Rank by UN HDI (2007)	Rank by UN HDI (2017)	Rank by UN HPI (2007/2008)	Rank by HPI (2012)	Population in millions 2017	Life Expectancy (2007)	Life Expectancy
Costa Rica	**54**	**63 (0.794)**	**54 (3.7)**	**1 (44.7)**	**4,906**	**78**	**80 (2016)**
Nicaragua	124	124 (0.685)	68 (17)	7 (38.7)	6,218	72.7	75 (2012)
Panama	60	66 (0.789)	30 (6.7)	6 (39,5)	4,099	75.7	77 (2012)
El Salvador	106	107 (0.680)	63 (14.6)	17 (35.6)	6,378	71.3	72.1 (2012)
Honduras	112	133 (0.617)	61 (13.7)	65 (27.2)	9,265	72	73.5 (2012)
Guatemala	122	127 (0.650)	76 (19.7)	26 (34.2)	16,91	70.1	72 (2012)

Data source: HDR 2017; INEC 2010; WorldBank 2017; HPI 2017.

Land distribution nurturing cultural and social significance

The coffee industry is the largest agricultural industry dominated by small farmers and owned by Costa Ricans. Distributing the land into small lots for coffee fostered a sense of responsibility amongst the population and an understanding of and interaction with the land according to achieving a yield. Coffee allowed a commonality in the Costa Rican mentality and lifestyle and in daily habits and practices for many centuries, as the practice of farming coffee attributed to land distribution reached a significant proportion of the population. Oscar Arias Sanchez, elected as President in 1986 and re-elected in 2006 was closely linked to coffee through his parents and his business partner, the Peters family, the largest coffee processors in Costa Rica (Paige 1997, 3). As a cash crop it also provided shared exposure to the international market directly or indirectly.

While historically, socially, and culturally coffee is a strong industry, it is no longer what it used to be, having diminished in the last decade. The crisis of 2001 had a significant impact on coffee growing communities stimulating diversification of farming activities including subsistence farming, migration and a distrust of the coffee industry. Despite these issues, the cultivation of coffee remains an important cultural activity and, in true rural democratic fashion, the passion remains to maintain justice in the industry, and the voice of the rural community in politics and business.

Costa Rica: Coffee, sustainability and poverty reduction

Sustainability for the coffee industry refers not only to environmental influence but also to societal including income for farmers and the country. Coffee farmers work all year for the annual harvest and are paid once a year which provides a different context for income considerations. From 1950 to the 1970s land clearing and high-density planting to maximise yield and economic growth was encouraged. The coffee industry was perceived to be so important for the development of the Costa Rican economy that the lands of the Central Valley and the newly settled coffee growing areas of the country were gradually taken over by coffee (Samper 2000 146–8; Naranjo 1997, 94–104; Winson 1989, 107–110). Chapter 1 provides more detailed information. The Costa Rican coffee industry was most imbalanced during this time despite institutional conservation and sustainability effort prior to and during this time.

Conservation and sustainable development efforts during intensification

While conservation efforts occurred during the green revolution and prior to, they did not supersede or adequately compensate the extent of land clearing and intensive farming techniques. Steinberg (2001) referred to Costa Rican conservation policy as leading in the region. From 1926 to 1940 the National Agricultural College was the centre of environmental concern in Costa Rica. Agronomists and the Agriculture Secretariat was later to be known as the Ministry of Agriculture and Industry but the gap between the agronomists' principal ideas and platforms, and the politician deciding on law and policy remained. Costa Rican conservationists participated in the Inter-American on the conservation of renewable resources in 1945. This conference intended to promote collaboration between Latin American countries and recommended that, "International credit institutions, such as the Export-Import Bank, should obtain the approval of ecologist and conservationists on specific proposals for resource development" (Mejia et al. 1948, 162-4 in Steinberg 2001, 55), referred to as "a milestone in the history of conservation and conservation education" (RHE 1948, 433 in Steinberg 2001). In 1950, the Ministry of Agriculture and Industry sponsored the first Natural Resources Conservation Week. The goal was to inspire a sense of responsibility that every Costa Rican citizen must live in harmony with nature, promoting conservation (Steinberg 2001, 53). Up until this time the influence of technically proficient experts on conservation was non-existent and after this date it moved to inconsistent. Agronomist Alvaro Rojas elected to the Legislative Assembly introduced the Soil and Water Conservation Law of 1953.

In 1963, executive decree number 10 created the national reserve of Cabo Blanco, after that year and by means of a presidential decree, a series of reserves and national parks were created. An undertone to the economic focus of Costa Rican policy and programs was, and is, an active conservation and environmental movement which ultimately increased environmental security in Costa Rica. Costa Rica's conservation and sustainable development efforts in the last twenty years and prior have added to its international reputation as a successful and sustainable developing country. In 1968, a bauxite processing plant was proposed by the American company, Alcoa. There were student protests and beyond as the idea of an American company controlling Costa Rican resources with little evident benefit to Costa Ricans was considered unacceptable. This was an issue of nationalism and politics but also of the environment. These were the first protests of their kind in Costa Rica. While the processing plant went ahead the leaders for conservation policy for the processing plant were Costa Rican. Steinberg (2001) considers these protests as driving attention to conservation and environmental concerns, sensitizing a generation to foreign interference in domestic affairs.

The severe economic crisis that hit the country between 1978-1982, significantly contributed to deforestation and loss in biodiversity. By 1983; forest cover had reduced at an alarming rate of 17-26% (Sanchez-Azofeifa 1996; Fundación Neotropica 1988; Banco Central de Costa Rica 2016). In 1978, the Mesoamerican Federation of Non-Governmental Conservation Associations was formed, and the head office was in Costa Rica within the office of the Costa Rican Association for the Conservation of Nature (ASCONA). Deforestation was the key environmental issue because of the green revolution, the efforts made were protective and pre-emptive to restrict areas in which green revolution could occurred. An economic crisis was perceived as a threat to conservation efforts however this did not slow Costa Rica (Evans 1999). Initially denied by Vice President Carlos Manuel Castillo, the Ministry of Environment was established autonomous to the office of the Ministry of Agriculture and Livestock (MAG) to avoid conflict of interest. By 1982, law number 6794, ratified the decrees promulgated since 1963 for environmental protection and conservation.

The ecotourism boom of 1985 saw record numbers visiting national parks, adding financial and educational value to conservation efforts. Oscar Arias Sanchez became president in 1986 and established the Ministry of Environment, broadening focus from conservation to biodiversity. The office of biodiversity was established in 1987 funded by the MacArthur Foundation. The office established networks of foreign and national ecologists and meetings that resulted in an agreed need to start recording species diversity and bio- geographical patterns through the National species survey. INBio, the National Biodiversity Institute, was established in 1989. INBio aimed to reduce foreign dependence through identifying natural products that may be of interest to the private sector. INBio also took a participatory approach to the survey, employing unskilled workers from rural areas and providing training for specimen identification. Many other advances were made in conservation area and environmental NGOs worked consistently to ensure enforcement of laws. The bank of knowledge that exists in Costa Rica regarding conservation, biology and agronomy is a result of both national and foreign influences. According to Luis Faurnier, a Costa Rican biologist: "Costa Rican ecological thought developed from the numerous observations about the country's natural history in the past century and early decades of this century by foreign and national naturalists" (Evans 1999, 16).

In the 1980s and 1990s, following a severe economic crisis that hit the country (1978–1982), efforts were also made to change Costa Rica's export profile without abandoning coffee production. As an exporter of non-traditional products, (Vargas 2003, 40) the agriculture of change favoured the production of pineapple, cardamom, flowers, squash, among other products (Honey 1994, 71). In addition, tourism began to shape as a lucrative economic activity, going hand in hand with the protectionist measures of the various governments to protect part of the country's natural resources. In 1990, law number 7152, gave rise to the National Parks Service of the Ministry of Environment and Energy and with this institutionalized the network of Costa Rican national parks that had been operating since 1970. In 1994, José María Figueres became President and worked to increase awareness that Costa Rica is a sustainably developing country in the international political arena. Before the work of Broza and Ugalde, two Costa Rican biologists who transformed the national park program to ensure the establishment of parks, the previous technique of establishing National parks tended to involve planning and registration, the parks on paper approach. An active environmental non-government organisation movement (NGO), that is, as active as resources would allow, also assisted to hold Figueres accountable for international and domestic promises.

The gap between law and implementation that existed in the 1940s still exists as political issues with established environmental institutions like INBio and with the Figueres administration emerged (Steinberg 2005). The year 1996 saw a move past conservation efforts toward reforestation with the Forestry Law – N7575, which provides compensation through the Environmental Services Payment (PSA) for privately owned lands or forest plantation owners (WRI 2010). There are other private efforts toward reforestation with examples in Monteverde and San Gerardo de Rivas. To date, Costa Rica has 28 national parks and several biological and forest reserves.

The coffee industry in Costa Rica is private but the presence of state supervision and control through ICAFE regulates the industry (Ronchi 2002). Environmental and social laws regulate as they do for any other industry of the country. The cooperative movement strengthened the position of small farmers in Costa Rica through these times however insecurity and dependency existing since the early days of the coffee industry and manifesting from colonial times maintained. There are segmented efforts to improve biodiversity and encourage conservation within the Costa Rican coffee industry. Coocafe administers Café Forestal, MAG integrates such considerations into workshops for coffee farmers, and education institutes are accessible for extended advice. In 2012, a Nationally Appropriate Mitigation Actions (NAMAs) Steering Committee was established under the umbrella of the Agriculture and Livestock Ministry of Costa Rica. The NAMA seeks to deliver combinations of public and market incentives for adoption of measures aimed at increasing carbon dioxide sinks and reducing emissions of nitrous oxide and methane for the entire Costa Rican coffee sector. This seeks to address the coffee farm and the coffee mill (ICAFE 2013).

Physical suitability of coffee farming locations

The Central Valley was the original location of most coffee farms due to suitability of the land and climate. It was maintained as such due to the 1982 Arabica law. The green revolution through economic priority above environmental, and due to hybrid varieties, which were more tolerant to varying climatic conditions, resulted in coffee being grown in regions where it is not geographically nor climatically suitable. These factors can influence eventual long-term success of coffee farming in a region and make any effort to improve sustainability outcomes via coffee farming, difficult.

Coffee farming in Costa Rica (from the 2000s)

The coffee census[31] seeks to gain a detailed understanding of Costa Rican coffee growing regions. In 2007 it reported 76, 853 coffee farmers in Costa Rica. The measure is by household, and counts all members living in the house at the time of interview and those who live in said house for more than 6 months of the year. Seasonal migrant workers, the major constituents of labour during harvest, would not be included in the 24, 541 labourers on coffee farms (extracted from INEC 2006). There are 193, 205 hectares (1932 km² or 3% of Costa Rica) dedicated to farms that also hold coffee, and 98, 678 hectares (986 km² or 2% of Costa Rica) is dedicated to coffee trees (ICafe 2019; INEC 2006). In 2014, the agricultural census of Cosa Rica found there were 26, 527 farms covering 84, 133 ha. ICAFE estimated 93, 744 ha in 2012, 88% of these farms were less than 10ha. The coffee crisis of 2001 demonstrated the vulnerability of small coffee farmers particularly in the face of a volatile international market. See Figure 12. While quantity by export maintained, the price for exported coffee during 2001 dips dramatically.

The unit value of coffee was second highest of all exports (FAOstat 2019) and the importance of coffee farmer numbers across the country for the environment and future of Costa Rica is relevant. A culture of families helping each other and the farmers' affinity with the land they work because of ownership has contributed to a non-violent development of the Costa Rican coffee market, compared to neighbouring countries. This may have been influenced by, the *yeoman* theory, seeding a 'rural democracy' (Alfaro 1980).

By comparison, commercial agricultural farming on plantation size farms dominates agricultural exports by value (INEC 2011). The most productive agricultural crop was pineapple following a boom in the industry coinciding with World Bank Structural Adjustments Programs (SAP) of the mid-1980s. At this time, Del Monte planted and trialed the MD2 variety of pineapple, and from 1996 onwards this variety dominated the international market (Del Monte 2006). By 2015, bananas were the most significant agricultural industry by export. Medical (16%); Integrated circuits (6.7%); Orthopaedic appliances (4.4%) followed (MIT 2017; OEC 2015). The value and quantity of bananas and pineapples remain close to equal in the years leading to 2015. With pineapples demonstrating slightly higher value by quantity. See Figure 13.

In 2018, optical, technical and medical apparatus represented 24.57% of exports. Fruits and nuts represented 23%, miscellaneous food preparations represented 3.4%, coffee, tea and spices represented 3.3% (Workman 2019).

---

[31] The Coffee Census *Censo Cafetalero* is conducted by the National Institute of Statistics and Censuses in Costa Rica, *El Instituto Nacional de Estadísticas y Censos* (INEC) at the request of the Institute of Coffee in Costa Rica, *El Instituto de Cafe* (ICAFE).

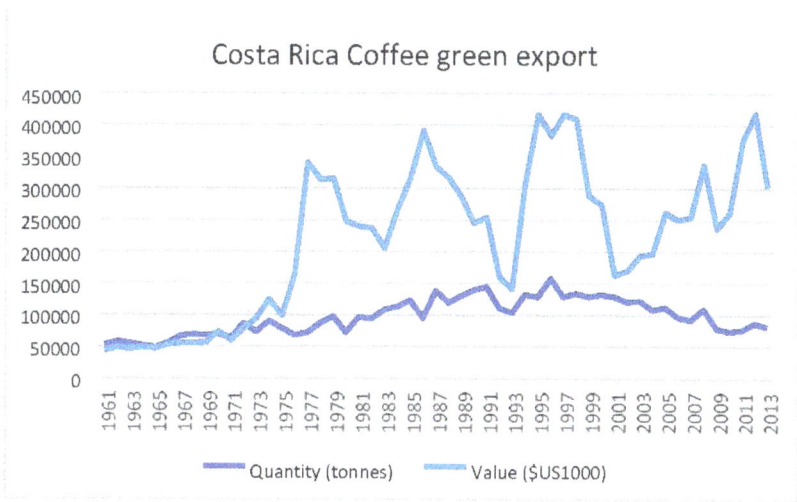

Figure 12: Costa Rican export of green coffee by quantity and value.
Data source: FAOStat 2019.

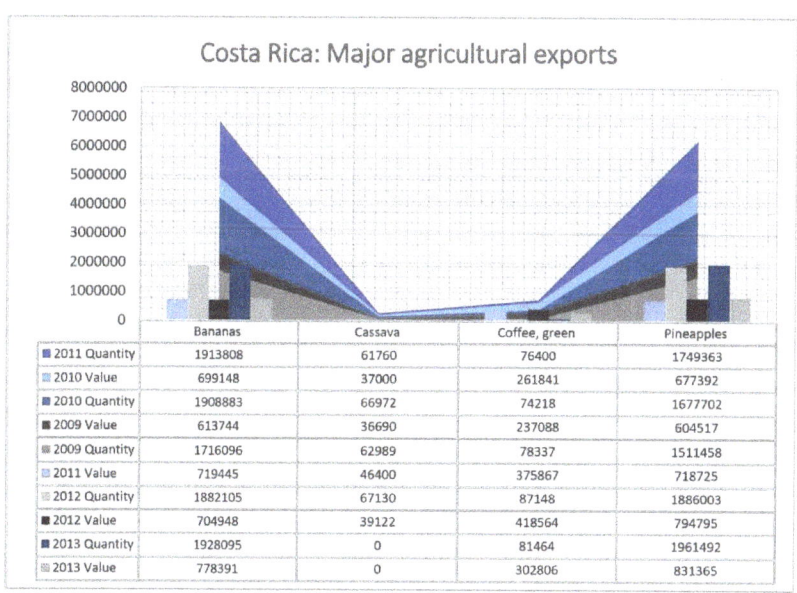

Figure 13: Costa Rica: major agricultural exports.
Data source: FAOStat 2019.

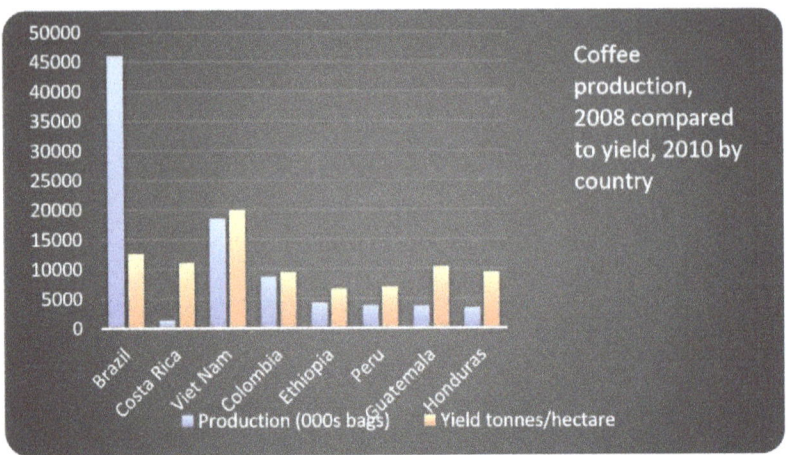

Figure 14: International coffee production yield per hectare.
Data source: FAOStat 2019; ICO 2019.

Table 4: Export trade matrix, coffee, green.
USDA Foreign Agriculture Service 2016.

Costa Rica Coffee, Green 60kgs bags	
Time Period	2014.2015
Exports for:	
U.S.	589,536
Others	
Belgium	165,904
Germany	57,841
Australia	51,060
South Korea	41,306
Italy	40,209
Netherlands	33,065
Total for Others	389,385
Others not Listed	182,762
Grand total	1,161,683

In 2008 Costa Rica was the fifteenth largest producer of coffee globally. The first was Brazil, the second was Viet Nam (ICO 2010b). In yield per hectare terms Costa Rica has been one of the most productive countries in the world (FAOStat 2019), see figure 14.

The largest purchaser of Costa Rican coffee by quantity is the United States, representing approximately 50% of all exported coffee purchased. See table 4.

Coffee Industry structure

When discussing the coffee industry in Costa Rica the structure can be recognised as a horizontally and vertically tiered, figure 15.

It is important to recognise the difference between a small coffee farm and a larger centrally owned and managed plantation. The difference is not only by number of people involved in managing the farm but also by the explicit and implicit roles and responsibilities; capabilities and capacity for risk taking. There is also difference between a small farm and a producer group of small farmers.

A farmer might live on or off-farm, and labour might be carried out by family or externally sourced. Small farm holders are not usually involved in processing or exporting coffee in Costa Rica. There are then plantations and small farm holdings where the manager or farmer lives off-farm and the land is only for farming, not processing. Plantations tend to include a mill, *beneficio* on-site; will use labourers managed by the farm manager and in some cases will export directly. The small farmer cooperative does the processing and exporting. They will occasionally include farms managed directly by the cooperative and farmers, in terms of a standard cooperative structure of members.

The resulting industry structures have encouraged types of dependency past those created through international trade dynamics. Centralised processing

Figure 15: Four horizontal and vertical tiers of coffee industry structure.

operations are an example. In Costa Rica large plantations and processors are separated from small farmers. While relinquishing the farmer of responsibility, it simultaneously creates a dependence on processors to buy their beans. In theory, and in the context of existing international trading systems, organising into cooperatives allows an increase in bargaining power for small farmers who bring their yield to the cooperatives' *beneficio* to combine with all members' yield. The National Council for Cooperatives (CONACOOP) were created in 1973. INFOCOOP works to promote new cooperatives and capacitate existing cooperatives through technical assistance, finance and investigation. CONACOOP works between government and the public to represent Costa Rican Cooperatives (INFOCOOP 2010). The predominance of small coffee farm holdings and a sense of solidarity and collectivism have in the past allowed a strong cooperative culture, *cooperativismo*. In 2009, there were fifteen coffee cooperatives in Costa Rica. Coopecerrozaul was one of the first to unite small coffee farmers to improve sales of their coffee harvest in 1961. Coocafe is an umbrella Consortium for nine of the coffee cooperatives in the country. This one consortium represented 2,200 producers of coffee, 4800 hectares and through associated member cooperatives accumulated indirect experience with Fairtrade for twenty years. Since 2009, studies approximate 22 coffee cooperatives are operating across the country (Snider et al. 2017), with an increased presence of private mills for individual farmers (Hofensitz 2017). Coocafe in 2019 is formed of seven cooperatives which have 2000 small farmer members. More than 30% of small farmer members are female (Coocafe 2019).

Lowering popularity of *cooperativismo*

Between 2008 and 2015 *cooperativismo* within communities of Costa Rica was becoming less of a popular culture or identity. Dissatisfaction with administrative approaches, management and suggestions of corruption have left some members inclined to remain independent as a simpler and more peaceful option. Within one community the local cooperative, the members of which were in the majority coffee farmers, had closed.[32] Within a different coffee farming community of Costa Rica, more coffee farmers were found with doubts about their local cooperative, stating dissatisfaction with organisational approach and corruption:

> Era un miembro de la cooperativa, mis padres también, pero en los últimos años me parecía más fácil cultivar y vender mi café para mí misma. Es más sencillo y menos estresante. No hay tanta confianza en la cooperative.

---

[32] Community member, personal communication, August 2014.

[I was a member of the cooperative and my parents were as well but in the last years it seemed easier to me to grow and sell my coffee for myself. It is simpler and less stressful. There is not so much trust in the cooperative anymore].[33]

The number of micro-mills on farm or in individual communities, increased since 2010 (Gunnerod & Hasse 2016; OECD 2017; Gyllensten 2017) which influences industry structure. Micro-mills as associations fit within the small farmer cooperative category without the administrative and democratic processes typically involved in cooperatives.

Farming coffee: complications and implications

Disease and pest epidemics

Insect infestations and pathogenic infections affect both robusta and arabica. It is estimated that 850 insects attack the plant (Le Pelley 1968, 1973). The most prevalent are coffee leaf miner, the coffee berry borer and coffee stem borers at an international level (Vega et al. 2006). Prevalence within each country differs slightly and species and varieties present distinctly. For example, coffee leaf rust rather than leaf miner is most prevalent in Costa Rica, and coffee berry borer and coffee stem borers are found in Costa Rica. Coffee berry borer causes three economic losses: reduced yield and quality of final product (Moore & Prior 1988); physical damage allows mature berries to become vulnerable to infection and further pest attack (Leefmans 1926); premature falling of the green berries. The consequences of most pest and disease outbreaks are similar in economic and environmental terms. Further information about pest and disease epidemics in coffee farms of Costa Rica is available from; Avelino et al. 2007; Waller et al. 2007; Avelino et al. 2011; Cerda et al. 2017.

Environmental impact

The impact of coffee production on biodiversity is disproportional to the area dedicated to farming (Donald 2004). Intensification is a common approach for maximising yield and therefore income for farmers with little regard for the influence on biodiversity that naturally exists in these landscapes and that contribute to global biodiversity. Full sun plantations have been found to leach nearly three times the amount of nitrates into surrounding environments than shade coffee systems (Babbar & Zak 1995). In addition to biodiversity outcomes, water management particularly at the stage of processing coffee berries,

---

[33] Farm owner, personal communication, August 2019.

often occurring in the farming landscapes or close by, will influence potential for water contamination (Arce et al. 2009; Beyene et al. 2011, Vogt 2019c). This is in large part due to the berries that are washed off to reveal the bean for consumption. The berries are highly acidic due to intensity of fermentation which then carry significant pollutant loads to water ways with toxic implications for water.

Environmental and health (in)security

Environmental insecurity, including deforestation, soil erosion and water contamination from the processing of coffee and the prioritisation of coffee cultivation over other crops, as strongly associated with the development of the coffee industry has affected the health of the population (see chapter 12). Food shortages were the result of the 1978–1982 crisis for many Costa Rican coffee farmers and for the nation. Cardoso comments that the "subsistence crisis became frequent and foodstuffs which had been very cheap at the time of independence became very costly" (Cardoso 1986, 209).

South-South Labour Migration: Destination Costa Rican coffee farms

A desirable destination for migrants of surrounding countries looking for work, there is also an increasing reliance on migrant labour in several Costa Rican industries and "the construction industry, coffee and sugar to mention a few would very probably enter into crisis if they had to count only upon national personnel" (NotiCen 2006). The Costa Rican coffee industry is distinctive in the region for the fact that coffee is only picked by hand, not by machines. Nicaraguans and Indigenous Panamanians, the *Ngöbe- Buglé* (ITUC 2008, 2; INEC 2000; OECD 2009, 229) are most found working seasonally in the coffee industry. Mazza and Sohnen (2010) claim that social scientists have found 100,000 Nicaraguans working in agriculture at peak harvest. This highlights a gap in Census Data collected by INEC and presented in the Coffee Census of Costa Rica, which claimed that 24 541 people were working in the coffee industry and confirms that seasonal migrant workers are not well documented or included in Census data. The seasonal labour population is the most vulnerable group involved in the Costa Rican coffee industry and the mobile nature of these workers has made documentation difficult. According to the IOM, 12,000 migrate to Costa Rica to pick coffee cherries (2008). Despite efforts to document and regulate them through IOM programs supported by various Costa Rican government departments, these labourers are in the majority undocumented and under recorded in Costa Rica. This has implications for their access to culturally appropriate health care, education for their children and social security services, as well as access to real protection of workers' and human rights. The

Ngöbe-Buglé fall in the category of highly mobile populations who travel and live between Panama and Costa Rica. The *Ngöbe-Buglé* population focus cultural appropriateness of international standards and norms. Schooling, housing and healthcare are all culturally specific and this population have their own ways, education is a challenge for the children of this population. Finca Sana was a new multi-stakeholder initiative of the IOM to work toward access to health care for the *Ngöbe-Buglé* population.

The movement of Nicaraguan seasonal workers into Costa Rica is considered more regulated now as a result of a project of the International Organisation for Migration (IOM) (State of a Nation Project 2001; IOM 2010; Martin 2011). Running from 2006 to 2009, the project was funded by the Spanish International Cooperation Agency for Development, *Agencia Española de Cooperación Internacional para el Desarrollo*, (AECID) and the Inter-American Development Bank component on remittances and Partners included the Ministry of Labour in Nicaragua, Ministry of Labour and Social Security, Costa Rica, Ministry of Foreign Affairs, Nicaragua, Ministry of Foreign Affairs, Costa Rica, Migration Offices in both countries, NGOs in both countries dealing with migrant population issues. The project sought to incorporate temporary migrants to the health care system (Lopez 2012).

Costa Rica had not ratified the Convention on the Protection of the Rights of all Migrant workers and Members of Their Families in 2009. It provides binding fundamental standards to address the treatment, welfare and human rights of documented and undocumented migrants, influencing a receiving country's security. In 2010, the new general law for migration; *ley general de migración y extranjería*, was introduced as a new immigration act. Previously Costa Rica acceded the 1951 convention for the status of refugees, ratified 1954 convention for the status of stateless persons, and acceded 1961 convention on the reduction of statelessness (UNHCR 2014). In 2011, Costa Rica adopted the Refugee Regulations to the Immigration Act, and in 2013, enacted the law against smuggling of migrants and the trafficking in persons by amending the Immigration Act. There are additional recommendations from the UNHCR to further improve the legal framework of the country (UNHCR 2014). Challenges presented by informal labour in the coffee sector of Costa Rica maintain.

Summary

This more contemporary history of Costa Rica and of the coffee industry of the country provides an overview of more timely information to consider as the following findings chapters are read.

Organised through considering fieldwork perspectives and opinions based on firsthand experiences of participants and the most relevant, commonly observed or controversial comments, the following chapters consider subtler advantages of sustainability certifications, the cost of sustainability certifications, the standards introduced, and how an increasing number of certifications influenced perspectives and experiences. Following on from these chapters, whether certifications are (1) intending to develop a reputation beyond their intentions, or intentionally developing a reputation beyond actual influence; and/or (2) reinforcing international trade power dynamics is considered. To summarise these findings, an overview of observed advantages and disadvantages is provided based on perspectives from within Costa Rica.

Perspectives from within Costa Rica

Determining effectiveness of any sustainability effort often relies on second or third hand information due to the distance between coffee farmers, the international market and consumers. Even today, ten years after original research for this study was carried out, reliable evaluations of certifications and associated consequences are sparse and not comprehensive (Vogt 2019e; Vogt & Englund 2019; Trolliet et al. 2019). To begin to address this fact, recognising that base research for this book was carried out in 2009, and planned for in 2008, the methodology and methods selected intended to provide primary information collected through interviews and focus groups.

An opportunity for direct understanding of what sustainability certifications mean in producing communities and countries is facilitated through an exploration of these perceptions and opinions. Some of the more complicated aspects of the certification effort can then be considered from in-country experience and perception.

CHAPTER 6

Methodology and Methods

Introduction

To achieve a type of exploration of 'in-country' opinions and perspectives, fieldwork was conducted in coffee farming landscapes and with coffee farmers and cooperative representatives in Costa Rica. Poverty, as a theme within sustainability, was selected to guide interview questions given the expansive potential influence of sustainability certification efforts which address trade, agricultural practices and community level activities in different ways. It allows consideration of several topics and where fieldwork was extended, further research could have selected common topics identified as areas for more specific research. The information and findings presented, resulting from the methods and methodologies selected, are not easily quantified. They remain focused on interview findings and identification of common observations and comments as a basis for further assessment. The method selected is therefore more an activity of starting a conversation to determine how outcomes associated with certifications are perceived within a producer country rather than presenting definitive findings on whether certifications are positive or negative. As such all quotes and findings are qualified by the Costa Rica context, and are limited to the farmers, cooperatives and in some cases communities where the interviews were conducted. It is considered a strength of the research that ten communities were visited which represented approximately 75% of all coffee farming communities in Costa Rica at that time. The quotes presented are not intended for direct extrapolation or to ponder what they 'actually mean' for this study. They are instead presented as a direct and unfiltered representation of how sustainability certifications are understood.

How to cite this book chapter:
Vogt, M. 2019. *Variance in Approach Toward a 'Sustainable' Coffee Industry in Costa Rica: Perspectives from Within; Lessons and Insights.* Pp. 85–98. London: Ubiquity Press. DOI: https://doi.org/10.5334/bce.h. License: CC-BY 4.0

Rainforest Alliance (RA) and Fairtrade

Sustainability certifications are often understood most in consuming countries as a logo or label representing sustainable trade for improved environmental and social justice outcomes. Available information was limited to slogans and marketing information. Upon meeting and discussing the details of Fairtrade with farmers from certified cooperatives in 2006 and seeing scholarly arguments against the minimum price approach of fairtrade, the actual detail involved appeared more complicated than a simple positive influence. Rather than engaging with the scholarly discourse straight away, exploring in-country experiences and perspectives appeared to me an interesting angle to consider how sustainability certifications were having influence and then if it was in fact positive.

The purpose of the study was therefore to provide an understanding of how certifications differ to address the geographic distance between consumers and producers which often results in reliance on marketing claims to determine sustainability.

At the time of developing this study, sustainability certifications for coffee, and for other commodities were a new movement. In Australia, organic certified products had been available for some years, and Fairtrade was introduced to the market in 2006. By 2008, RA certified products were beginning to enter the Australian market via larger corporate product lines. Internationally, RA and Fairtrade certified products were more accessible and available. The number of labels and certifications was starting to increase however the major players for certifying coffee were Organic, Fairtrade and RA, with Utz Kapeh having some influence. During fieldwork, information about 4C was provided to me as a new code of conduct which was expected to become popular, it was not however at that time used. Recognising that my understanding of the topic was coming from a consumer market perspective to develop to a producing country perspective understanding linked to the original perspective, the most prominent sustainability certification labels were of interest for a comparative study. RA and Fairtrade were receiving the most attention at that time and the difference between them other than the name and market entry approach were difficult to determine. One appeared more environmental, the other more about social justice, further differences were not obvious.

Starbucks C.A.F.E. Practices code of conduct was also operative and particularly in Costa Rica. It was however a company code of conduct rather than a sustainability certification which was starting to combine fairtrade certified coffee within its sourcing practice. Quotes that mention their code of conduct and approach to trade are however included for discursive comparisons related to the study, rather than as a focus for the discussion. Organic certifications were an omission in this study. While it is used in Costa Rica and encouraged through Fairtrade certified sourcing, the societal aspects covered by Fairtrade and RA led to their becoming the focal point for fieldwork discussions. Where organic certifications were brought up by participants, they are included as related comments rather than leading topics. The choice to consider two certifications only was an attempt to restrict possible topics for consideration, understanding that even one certification could provide adequate discussion points for such a study. The resulting discussion and quotes presented represent only a small proportion of all information collected.

Poverty as a guiding theme within sustainability for fieldwork considerations

Multi-dimensional poverty is a serious problem in agricultural areas, particularly for small farm holders (IFAD 2010). Sustainable development and poverty reduction seek to improve outcomes internationally for the environment and society. This is considered particularly in need while trade interests are prioritised over the two above mentioned elements. CSR has emerged as a means of correcting the imbalance and negative influence that international trade has had on the environment and society including in rural areas. There are guidelines and concepts under which business should act toward improvements for society and environment. One of the key values of CSR for the corporation is positive brand association and a strengthened reputation. As CSR is determined by the Code of Conduct to which the corporation must adhere and effective implementation of the standards within, its reputation should only be as strong as the principles that lay the foundation for these claims, approach to, and effective implementation. An increase in certification types differentiated by standards and certification processes appears to positively associate with outcomes for environment and society in producing countries. How such certifications influence practice depends on comprehensive standards and effective implementation. In most cases certifications claim to be working toward sustainability and poverty reduction outcomes to differing degrees. How they differ and what influence they have on coffee farms and farmers in Costa Rica were the key questions driving research.

Sen proposes that we evaluate development in terms of "the expansion of the capabilities of people to lead the kinds of lives they value – and have reason to value" (Evans 2002, 55). Ideas of freedom, development and wellbeing are connected. Achieved well-being is dependent on the capability to function. A reciprocal relationship between income and a person's capability is described as a "connection going from capability improvement to greater earning power and not only the other way around" (Sen 1990, 90). The capabilities approach broadens definitions of poverty to allow not only "opulence, utilities, primary goods or rights but functionings (doings and beings) – [as] a measure that encompasses these other units of evaluation" (Comin 2001, 4). A person's capability to achieve the functionings they choose will determine that "person's freedom – the real opportunities – to have well-being" (Sen 1992, 40). The more theoretical considerations of Sen (1992), Sen and Dreze (1999, 152), Evans (2002, 55) and Comin (2001, 4) complemented by the World Banks' report on the poor (Kanbur et al. 2000, 7) informed questions for fieldwork and writing of this monograph.

Ethics

Prior to commencing fieldwork, I received approval from the Human Research Ethics Committee (HREC) through my university, Flinders University of South Australia. All intended procedures, interview questions, communication methods were reported on in this document. I did find in country that there was a constant need to ensure participants did not feel a sense that their time had been or was being wasted. It was often mentioned that some post-graduate students had come past their communities, conducted interviews as part of their 'holiday' and then left with no mention or communication of their findings. While I was not conducting interviews to stimulate change in Costa Rica, instead improve understanding, I made sure to send a copy of my thesis to all participants via email once it was complete.

Methods

Interviews "are an excellent method of gaining access to information about ... opinions, and experiences" (Dunn 2010, 102). A question in an interview allows for an open response as opposed to a closed set of response options and "each informant can describe events or offer opinions in their own worlds" (Dunn 2010, 103). Underpinning this research approach is the consideration of conscientisation (Freire 1972) or a critical consciousness. Participating in the interviews not only assists the interviewer to collect an understanding of perspectives, opinions, stories and narratives that exist in Costa Rica within the coffee industry, it can provide the opportunity for participants to reflect. Sen (1990, 1992, 1999a) emphasises that informed and unregimented formation of our values requires openness of communication and arguments. The approach to research as face-to-face interviews and ethnographic methods is centred in Sen's fourth and fifth concept; that is voice and critical voice. In seeking to understand what coffee certifications 'mean' and how they influence coffee farmers and business owners in Costa Rica it is viewed as important that their voice be heard. This has set the foundation for this volume. The subjectivity of this approach is recognised, and common perspectives identified from interviews across the ten communities drive the critical points discussed.

Fieldwork

Original fieldwork was carried out in 2009, when ten coffee communities were visited across Costa Rica. The cooperatives were selected based on association with Coocafe, see the interview and fieldwork schedule and information about each cooperative according to the 2009 situation in table 5 and 6, and original communication was developed through a manager and member of Cooperative

Table 5: Interview schedule 2009.

Date	Category of participation	Interviewee	Organisation/ Cooperative	District, Canton
12/01/2009	Interview	Previous cooperative manager, coffee farmer and cooperative member	Coope Santa Elena	Santa Elena, Puntarenas
4/02/2009	Interview	Manager	Coope Pilangosta	Hojancha, Guanacaste
9/02/2009	Interview	Technical engineer and administrative manager for certification programs	Coopeldos	El Dos, Tilaran
12/02/2009	Interview	Manager	Coopeatenas	Atenas, Alajuela
13/02/009	Interview	Financial manager and assistant director	Coopetarrazu	San Marcos de Tarrazu, Tarrazu
17/02/2009	Interview	Farm Administrator	Finca Santa Anita, RA certified	Naranjo, Alajuela
20/02/2009	Interview	Manager	Coopepueblos	Agua Buena, Coto Brus
25/02/2009	Interview	Administrator of certification programs	Doka Estate	Alajuela
28/02/2009	Attendance of annual general meeting		Coopeldos	El dos, Tilaran
6/03/2009	Farm visits and interviews	Farmers 'Jose'; 'Esteban'; 'Ronny'	Coopepilangosta	Hojancha, Guanacaste

Continued

Table 5: Continued

Date	Category of participation	Interviewee	Organisation/ Cooperative	District, Canton
11/03/2009	Interview	Manager	Coope Santa Elena	Santa Elena, Puntarenas
11/03/2009	Informal discussion	Coffee farmer 'Ernesto'	Coope Santa Elena	San Luis, Puntarenas
14/03/2009	Attendance to Annual General Meeting		Coopepilangosta	Hojancha, Guanacaste
18/03/2009	Attendance to meeting and workshop of ministry of agriculture and livestock with coffee farmers, training to diversify farm activities		Coopepilangosta	Hojancha, Guanacaste
20/02/2009	Interview	Manager	Coope Llano Bonito	Santa Rosa de Santo Domingo, Heredia
20/02/2009	Interview	Director	Hijos de Campo & Café Forestal	Santa Rosa de Santo Domingo, Heredia
23/02/2009	Attendance to government conference		CONAPE	San Jose, Alajuela
23/02/2009	Interview	Committee Members	Hijos del Campo	San Jose, Alajuela
27/03/2009	Interview	Farmers: 'William'; 'Roman'; 'Walter';	Coopepueblos	Agua Buena, Coto Brus

Table 5: Continued

Date	Category of participation	Interviewee	Organisation/ Cooperative	District, Canton
31/03/2009	Interview and Cooperative visit	Manager	Coope Sarapiquí	San Miguel de Sarapiquí, Alajuela
13/04/2009	Interview and group discussions	Manager; employee of cooperative 'Javier'	Coope Cerro Azul	Nandayure, Guanacaste
6/05/2009	Interview	Standards and Policy Technical Advisor	Rainforest Alliance	San Jose, Alajuela
7/05/2009	Informal discussion	'Rosa'	CIDEHUM	San Jose
11/05/2009	Interview	International Marketing Manager	CoopeAgri	Perez Zeledon
11/05/2009	Informal discussion	Regional Director of Perez Zeledon	ICAFE	Perez Zeledon
12/05/2009	Coffee farming community discussion	Group discussion with coffee farmers	CoopeAngeles – some also members of CoopeAgri, all are previously members of CoopeAgri	Los Angeles de Paramo, Perez Zeledon
12/05/2009	Informal discussion	Peace Corps volunteer working and living in community	Peace Corps	Los Angeles de Paramo, Perez Zeledon
16/05/2009	Informal discussion with coffee farmer	'Juan'	Coopertarrazu	Cortes, Osa

Table 6: Information about cooperatives visited in 2009.

Cooperative	District, Canton	Established	Members	Certifications and CSR Programs
Coope Cerro Azul, COOCAFE	Nandayure, Guanacaste	1961	100	– FLO
Coope Santa Elena, COOCAFE	Santa Elena, Monteverde, San Luis, Puntarenas	1971	75	– FLO
Coope El Dos, COOCAFE	El dos, Tilaran, Abangares and Monteverde	1971		– C.A.F.E. Practices – Eco-logica – FLO – Utz Certified – ISO 14001
Coope Llano Bonito, COOCAFE	Llano bonito, Leon, Cortes	1972	600	– FLO – Rainforest Alliance – UTZ certified – C.A.F.E. Practices
Coope Pilangosta, COOCAFE	Hojancha, Guanacaste	1962	200	– ISO 9000, 14000 – FLO
Coope Sarapiquí	Sarapiquí, Heredia	1969	137	– FLO
Coopepueblos, COOCAFE	Agua Buena, Coto Brus	2005	80	– FLO – CAN
Coopetarrazu	San Marcos de Tarrazu, Tarrazu	1960	2600	– ISO 9001–2000 – FLO – Rainforest Alliance
CoopeAgri	Perez Zeledon	1962	10000	– FLO – Sustainable product of Costa Rica Certification – ISO 9001: 2000
CoopeAtenas At time of interview not a member of COOCAFE	Atenas, Alajuela	1969		– FLO – UTZ certified – Starbucks Coffee-C.A.F.E. Practices – Specialty Coffee Association of Costa Rica – ISO 14001

Santa Elena. Additional communities were selected based on my own research and networks while in country, the cooperatives are listed in table 6 according to association with Coocafe to make this difference clear. Themes for interview questions are provided in appendix A.

Cooperatives included in fieldwork visits in 2009

Coocafe, a consortium of cooperatives which has a two-tier structure and *Coope Ag*ri work with very small farm holders in Costa Rica. In 2009, Fairtrade certification was held by Coocafe member cooperatives and administered in part via Coocafe, and by *Coope Ag*ri. Since inception Coocafe was an umbrella consortium, in 2009 for nine coffee cooperatives in Costa Rica, with two arms for the development of education and funding for environmental and socio-economic programs *Hijos de Campo* and *Café Forestal*. In 2019 seven coffee cooperatives are now members of the consortium, many are different to the original nine, and certifications have increased by number including Organic USDA, Organic Eco-Logica, Certificación Europea, Fairtrade and local standards including Indicación geográfica and Esencial Costa Rica. Amongst the nine cooperatives in 2009, Coopecerroazul was the first coffee cooperative established in Costa Rica and it was from this cooperative and the cooperative Santa Elena that Fairtrade certification was adopted. *Coope Ag*ri was founded in 1962 by 391 small farmers located in the Central Valley around Perez Zeledon. In 2019 it has over 8000 coffee farming members, through which over 700 temporary and permanent workers are employed.

A follow-up fieldtrip in 2014 allowed observation of changes since the original fieldwork in two communities, Santa Elena and Agua Buena. Figure 16 and 17 provide a visual representation of the location of the communities visited in 2009 and 2014.

Triangulation of fieldwork information

The process of considering and organising all fieldwork interviews, observations and discussions involved continual reference to the original perspective that I came to the study with – how the consumer country perspective aligned with actual outcomes in producing communities. Sustainability and poverty reduction were anchors for this process. In addition, the premise or intention of each sustainability certification was maintained for consideration. The frustration, variable positive associations, the other sustainability efforts in country, the business or commercial context compared to environmental context, and the marketing versus actual implementation of standards were commonly communicated and included as prominent findings. My own personal

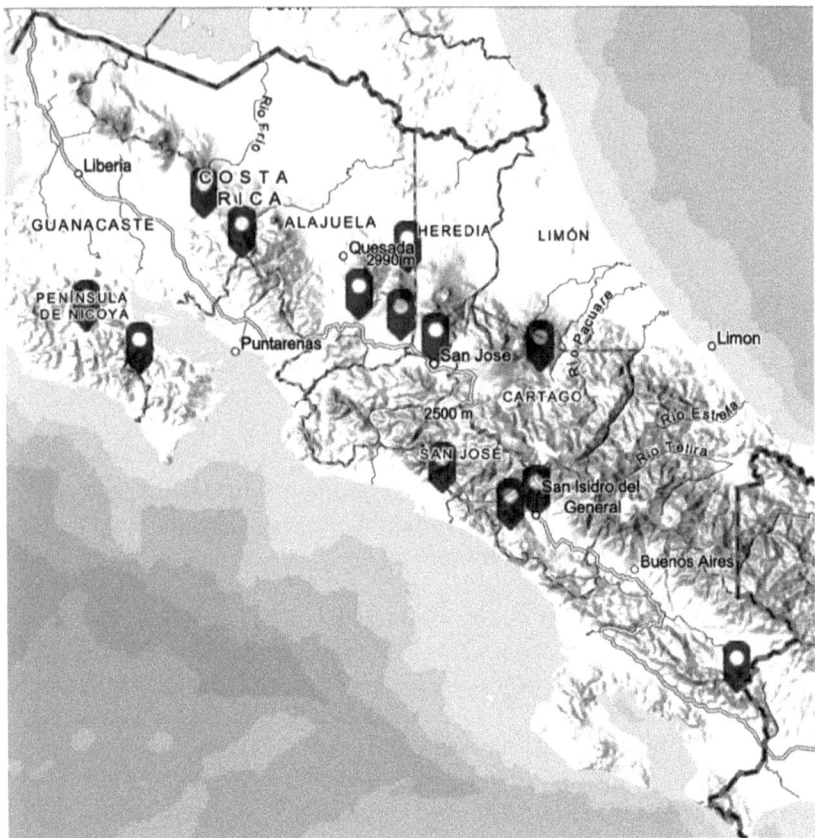

Figure 16: Ten coffee farming communities and three cooperative, certification or foundation bases visited in 2009.

Data source: Vogt 2019d.

reflections would often consider how sustainability between large land holding and small farms could be considered the same, or prioritised, and how several oversights in the process could allow products to be sold with a logo that represented contrary outcomes. During and after fieldwork it became clear that the study would not be about discussing a range of definite advantages, and instead about understanding the sustainability certification process in a balanced way and ensuring the in-country perspective was represented. While opportunity for serious critique was certainly available, the benefits were also obvious. I found it important to bring the fieldwork findings and considerations back to the intricate context within which they work, as intra market and extra business autonomous mechanisms for sustainability. The triangulation process involved: reviewing interviews, observation notes and discussion notes with the anchors

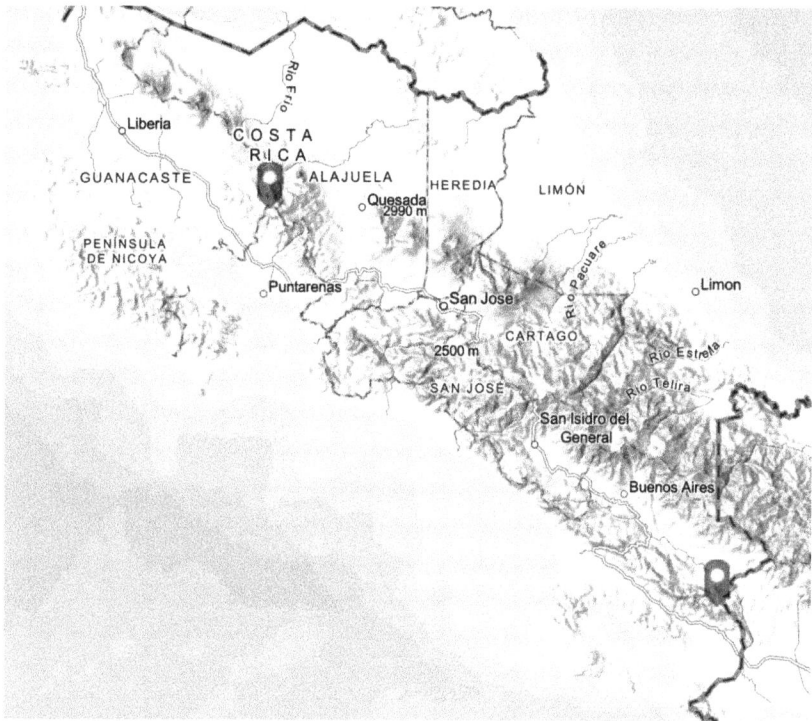

Figure 17: Two coffee farming communities visited in 2014.
Data source: Vogt 2019d.[34]

I mention above in mind, to consider and explain the influence, by opinion or in fact, sustainability certifications were having.

Presenting common opinions, quotes and results

Key topics emerging through the triangulation process have determined chapter titles and subheadings presented in the findings chapters, chapter 6–13. They are an opportunity to constructively critique for improvement. Beginning with the subtler advantages allows a reader to know that there are definite benefits, the following chapters and key topics within proceed to explore the more intricate opinions, perspectives and experiences and demonstrate where these efforts could improve. Identifying a problem, or advantages and disadvantages versus understanding and finding effective solutions are recognised

---

[34] Information from follow-up fieldwork available from Vogt 2019d.

as distinct. The rationale behind fieldwork explains why such opinions and experiences with sustainability certifications are important to present without an exhaustive assessment or critique from an external person. Discussion and communication of identified issues and benefits preludes a broader discussion about alternatives and potential for improvement. In some cases, in-field quotes are complemented with secondary literature and information to support in-country critiques and opinions with peer reviewed literature. Presenting the opinion and experience from stakeholders within Costa Rica is however the intention of the methodology selected and is considered important with or without supporting peer reviewed literature.

Addressing subjectivity and representation of fieldwork presented in results

The benefit of interviewing cooperative representatives was the opportunity to obtain opinions based on organisations that represented a significant proportion of all coffee farmers in each region. The downside to this approach was an inability to obtain individual opinions from all farmers in each community. As many interviews were seeking to understand how certifications were understood, speaking with cooperative managers, certification technical advisors and marketing managers was considered appropriate and valuable. Certainly, their opinion could be considered biased or subjective however the intention of the research was to shine a light on their opinion. At the time of fieldwork and even today most information available about what sustainability certifications are achieving in producing communities is limited, and somewhat reliant on marketing and trade-based forms of communication and information. All quotes and associated comments should therefore be understood in this way. There was not an intention to interrogate but there was an ability to further explore opinions. The stronger opinions presented are considered evidence of levels of dissatisfaction that could probably be better explored by the certifications themselves or understood as part of a greater legacy of international trade. Some fieldwork quotes taken from interviews with the RA office in Costa Rica are presented in the background section of the book, they are not considered opinions or perspective based, instead, they are voiced expressions of operational procedures by a representative of the RA certification

Quantified summary and assessment according to poverty reduction indicators

To conclude the presentation of extensive fieldwork observations, opinions and findings presented in chapters 6 to 13, a quantitative summary is presented according to poverty reduction indicators. Poverty reduction according to the definition used by Sen (1992) as outcomes of development, well-being and opportunity for well-being, and freedom were considered as indicators. See table 7 for these definitions presented as indicators.

Identified issues from fieldwork were organised by theme and discussed as elements of accepted definitions of poverty reduction within sustainable development to facilitate understanding of alignment with the key intentions of certification efforts. To ensure a simple approach, orientation for each indicator is allowed as positive or negative, and the fact that each might be inter-related and influential to another is accepted. The quantitative summary is presented in the conclusion.

Not all points of discussion about how certifications work towards sustainability and poverty reduction easily intertwine or align with this approach to assessment. They therefore remain discursive. The discursive presentation of findings and results provides the necessary detail to understand how intricate these considerations can be, and how many perspectives there are to consider. The quantified aggregated summary of findings from quotes and discussion points provides an additional layer for understanding rather than being a focal point for findings.

Table 7: Poverty reduction indicators to summarise fieldwork.

Outcomes	Indicators	Orientation*	
Development	Capability to achieve the functionings they choose	Positive	Negative
	Social and Community Relations		
Well-being/ Opportunity for wellbeing	Health		
	Social Security		
	Assets		
	Infrastructure: water, roads etc.		
Freedom	Participation in decision making		
	Empowerment		
	Earning power		

* *May depend on corresponding indicators and outcomes associated with an identified influence*

Qualifying how findings should be used and understood

All discussion and findings are specific to the Costa Rican context, and not necessarily reflective of how certifications operate in the context of other countries. The discussion provides an understanding of in-country understanding perspectives, opinions and situations resulting from certification efforts within accepted definitions of sustainability and poverty reduction. The understanding is expected to be useful for background study and could perhaps provide guidance for researchers of this topic in the future. They are considered likely to become more prevalent and perhaps relevant to other countries.

Findings

To develop fieldwork findings into presentable results a form of triangulation was used. The triangulation sought to identify common observations, opinions and perspectives across the coffee farming communities visited leading to chapter headings for this section. Information available in the background section complement and provide context for the following chapters.

In some cases, perspectives and opinions are supported by secondary literature and in other cases they are simply presented as a series of direct quotes which address a similar topic. To avoid misrepresentation or too much of an external assessment, all quotes are presented as they were given with limited ponderings of what each means. In some cases, they are used to contribute to existing discussions related to the influence of, and role taken by sustainability certifications and contextualised for Costa Rica. There was no intention to quantify information or force topics that might be considered more important from a scholarly perspective, or retrospectively relevant.

To quantify relevant topics against poverty reduction indicators a table is presented at the beginning of this section and in the conclusion section. It serves as an additional layer for understanding and should not distract from discursively presented opinions which are more difficult to quantify. Where an identified topic is relevant to poverty reduction indicators a note is included below the subheading explaining which indicator it is related to. To determine whether the association is positive or negative table 8 can be consulted.

CHAPTER 7

The subtler advantages of 'sustainability' certifications

Introduction

The idea of certifications as 'foreign' efforts in Costa Rica often encourages, or is combined with, negative and intrusive connotations. There are however advantages from certifications in the Costa Rican coffee industry. The advantages do not necessarily outweigh the disadvantages discussed. They are subtle yet valued by producer groups in Costa Rica and contribute innovatively to intentions for improved sustainability and poverty reduction through trade. The advantages include orientation in the international market, with a redistribution of national power dynamics; influence of standards on law; facilitating access to credit.

Orientation in the international market and redistributing national power dynamics

(Included in quantified summary, table 8)

Access to international markets and facilitating successful operation within them is a commonly identified need. Fairtrade certified markets expand international networking and increase information available for coffee producer organisations. This in turn facilitated a redistribution of power through the Costa Rican coffee industry:

> Antes de que fuera un exportador domestica que dominaba el Mercado y poca información llegaba a los productores, en general la comercialización de café en Costa Rica dependía de dos personas – y en FEDECOOP.

How to cite this book chapter:
Vogt, M. 2019. *Variance in Approach Toward a 'Sustainable' Coffee Industry in Costa Rica: Perspectives from Within; Lessons and Insights.* Pp. 101–106. London: Ubiquity Press. DOI: https://doi.org/10.5334/bce.i. License: CC-BY 4.0

Eran como dioses y no había información para los productores. Ahora cualquiera puede vender café. Saben cómo funciona el mercado; Pueden vender por Internet. Puedo saber lo que está sucediendo en el mercado cada día, hora. Acceso a la información proporciona acceso al mercado.

[Before it was a domestic exporter who dominated the market and little information reached the producers, generally the commercialisation of coffee in Costa Rica depended on two people – and on FEDECOOP. They were like gods and there was no information for the producers. Now anyone can sell coffee. They know how the market functions; they can sell by internet. I can know what is happening on the market every day, hour. Access to information gives access to market].[35]

Members of Coocafe have had similar and varying experiences and responses to changes in the coffee industry and in the Fairtrade system. What was consistent is the fact that certifications represent access to the market of various countries. RA 'opened the door' to Japan, North America, and Australia[36], and Fairtrade is international.[37] The previous Deputy Minister of Agriculture in Costa Rica, co-founder and president of *Fundación Hijos del Campo,* Children of the Field Foundation and *Fundación Café Forestal,* Café Forestal Foundation explained that the organisational structure required by Fairtrade improved direct relationships, secured contracts, facilitated political activism and allowed access to information about international markets that were previously difficult to access:

Fairtrade ofrece una visión, formamos parte de un grupo nacional e internacional; Mejora nuestra visión de lo que está pasando, lo que nos permite dialogar con el gobierno sobre lo que necesitan los productores de café de Coocafe. Para hacer cambios en la ley y la política es difícil como es identificar lo que necesita ser cambiado, el análisis es absolutamente necesario.

[Fairtrade provides a vision; we are part of a national and international group; it improves our vision of what is happening which allows us to dialogue with government about what coffee producers of Coocafe need. To make changes in law and politics is difficult as is identifying that which needs to be changed, analysis is absolutely necessary].[38]

In addition to the international network provided through Fairtrade, CoopeAgri identified Fairtrade principals that complement a cooperative structure:

---

[35] Cooperative manager, 12 February, 2009.
[36] Administrator of certification program, 25 February, 2009.
[37] International marketing manager, 11 April, 2009.
[38] Director *Hijos del Campo* and *Café Forestal,* 20 February, 2009.

Para mi Fairtrade llama mi atención porque tienen una red grande a través del mundo, y puedo hablar con la gente en el Reino Unido, los EE. UU., Australia y Alemania así que al menos con esta calidad de miembro puedo participar. Yo, como productor en Costa Rica por lo menos puedo hablar con el mercado.

[For me Fairtrade calls my attention because they have a large network throughout the world, and I can talk to people in the UK, US, Australia and Germany so at least with this membership I can participate. I, as a producer in Costa Rica can at least speak with the market].[39]

Law and certification standards: correlation, causality and influence

Various mechanisms encourage and assure sustainable practice (Vogt 2019a), including law, or intra-market voluntary mechanisms. In Costa Rica how different mechanisms successfully assured more sustainable practices was of interest. In the opinion of some participants, Costa Rican law "tiene más peso que cualquier certificación" [holds more weight than any certification][40] as the repercussions for noncompliance are more serious involving jail time, and payments of civil compensation (Mauri 2002). When Fairtrade and SAN standards used by RA overlap with national law, they default to the law. Some certifications' standards and criteria were identified as more thorough than state law.[41] There are differences between environmental and industrial relations legislation and requirements of certification standards for example.

Costa Rica has ratified all ILO conventions but has not ratified the UN Migrant Workers Convention[42] designed to protect the rights of documented and undocumented migrants. This is relevant to the coffee industry in Costa Rica considering much of the labour force is classified as undocumented mobile migrant workers. The mobile nature of seasonal workers, particularly the *Ngöbe-Buglé* makes schooling for children an additional issue to be addressed. RA considers the SAN standard as complementary to industrial relations law

---

[39] International Marketing Manager, 11 May, 2009.
[40] Financial manager and assistant director of cooperative, 13 February, 2009.
[41] Administrator of certification programs, 25 February 2009.
[42] The UN Migrant worker convention is the first universal codification of the rights of migrant workers and members of their families, formally known as the International Convention on the Protection of the Rights of All Migrant Workers and Members of their Families. The convention was adopted by the UN General Assembly on the 18 December 1990. It took 13 years to obtain the support of twenty countries for it to become an international legal instrument, and therefore entered into force 13 years later, July 1, 2003.

and is applicable to all certified producers, "hay cosas que la ley no se puede hacer, no tenemos un enfoque tan blanco y negro que la ley tiene, estamos construyendo la capacidad de la gente" [there are things that the law cannot do, we do not have such a black and white approach that the law has, we are building the capacity of people].[43] The manager of Doka Estate, a RA certified plantation explained that national industrial relations law pertaining to seasonal workers is not suitable for the actual patterns and circumstances of these workers:

> El 95% de nuestros trabajadores estacionales son indocumentados de Nicaragua, no tienen documentos por lo que tenemos que registrar cuantos hay por casa, cuando llegan, cuando salen, si tienen un accidente. El problema es que están aquí un día y no el siguiente, por lo que el seguimiento de ellos es difícil y no hay contrato. El Ministerio de Trabajo exige que se integren en la seguridad social, pero para la seguridad social es necesario un plan mensual y, en realidad un plan diario es todo lo que podemos trabajar considerando sus patrones de movimiento. Para evitar esto, hemos desarrollado un plan, si se lesionan a sí mismos pueden ir al hospital y decir que trabajan en nuestra granja y no tienen ningún problema.
>
> [95% of our seasonal workers are undocumented from Nicaragua, they do not have documents, so we must register how many there are per house[44], when they arrive, when they leave, if they have an accident. The problem is that they are here one day and not the next, so keeping track of them is difficult and there is no contract. The Ministerio de Trabajo (Department of Industrial Relations), require that they be integrated into social security, but for social security a monthly plan is necessary and, a daily plan is all we can work with considering their patterns of movement. To work around this, we have developed a plan, if they injure themselves, they can go to the hospital and say that they work on our farm and they have no problem].[45]

SAN standards were identified as making a significant difference as they were more detailed than national environmental and labour legislation. The construction of warehouses to store agri-chemicals separately is required by SAN

---

[43] Standards and policy technical coordinator, 6 April, 2009.
[44] Seasonal workers are provided with housing ($5m^2$ minimum per person), potable water (and analysis to prove that it is), treatment of grey water for cleaning clothes, if there is no kitchen, wood for cooking, waste removal systems. They do not pay rent and are paid $US1.67 per basket of coffee cherries or *cajuela*. They are also provided with childcare which is a requirement of Rainforest Alliance and is not a part of state law.
[45] Administrator of certification program, 25 February, 2009.

and Fairtrade standards but were not required by law.[46] The use of uniforms when handling chemicals, childcare provision to prevent child labour, standards for housing and facilities provided for workers were all required in SAN standards but not in state law. A comparison between farms certified by RA and those not, confirmed this[47] where SAN standard requirements were expected to and did improve conditions for labourers. Compliance to SAN labour standards was however identified as an issue by Oxfam DE in 2015. The Fairtrade standard for hired labour (hired labour standard) is separate to the generic Fairtrade standard and was only approved in 2008. It had not yet been implemented in Costa Rica. The required standards were however more advanced than the SAN standard, see figure 13. Chapter 9 explains the hired labour standard in detail with advances past legal requirements, but also how the standard allows the possibility for excluding labourers.

Where chronologically the certification is ahead of the law there are examples of the law 'catching up'. For example, a RA certified coffee plantation was already recycling as required by SAN standards before waste management legislation of 2010 was passed. In May 2009, a RA employee confirmed that, "la ley no cubre el reciclado aun en Costa Rica" [the law does not cover recycling yet in Costa Rica].[48] It was not until May 2010, that the Integrated Waste Management Bill (GIR) became law in a unanimous vote (Ben-Haddej et al. 2010–2011). The possibility that standards might influence, and progress national law is therefore considered a subtler advantage of certifications.

Eventual improvement in required environmental and hired labour practices for Costa Rican coffee farms rely on a legitimate and reliable auditing process, and effective standard development that allows for the difference in hiring approach between plantations and small farms. Further information about possible improvements are provided in chapter 9 and would only encourage opportunity for the law to 'catch up' improving how adequately sustainable legal requirements are.

Access to credit

(Included in quantified summary, table 8)

As an activity that includes an annual harvest and therefore income, access to credit is a relevant consideration for all coffee farmers in Costa Rica. Across every coffee farming community, it was observed that Fairtrade certified cooperatives more easily secured access to credit from local banks.

---

[46] Administrator of certification program, 25 February 2009; Cooperative manager, 11 March, 2009.
[47] Administrator of certification programs, 25 February 2009.
[48] Standards and policy technical coordinator, 5 May, 2009.

Summary

(Orientation in international market and redistributing national power dynamics; access to credit included in quantified summary).

There are subtler advantages of Fairtrade and RA which assist producer groups to overcome self-identified challenges within the international coffee industry. The categories identified through fieldwork associate certifications with global efforts for improved sustainability and poverty reduction through trade, and occasionally as more advanced or progressive compared to legal requirements. While there is no direct correlation or contributing association between a certification standard and changes in state law; the identified distinction between requirements can allow certification standards to address local situations more appropriately than national law. While not yet a perfect process, the standards introduced by Fairtrade and RA can be considered complementary to sustainability principles, particularly where work toward the overall objective is appreciated as a staged or progressive approach. How different standards progress international and national legal requirements and complement implementation of existing legal requirements is suggested as a valuable consideration for future research. These subtler advantages of certifications run in parallel with misaligned intentions and outcomes.

Misalignments between intentions and outcomes vary by certification. Improving an understanding of how misaligned intentions to outcomes eventuate provides an opportunity for improvement. The following chapters explain these misalignments as existing or possible according to investment versus benefit; standard criteria; the number of certifications being demanded; over representing reputation compared to actual outcomes; and reinforcing international trade dynamics.

CHAPTER 8

The cost of 'sustainability' certifications: intention versus outcome

Introduction

The intra market location of certifications can remove focus from the intended aim due to a dominant business focus. The standards and codes of conduct to which the business complies must be highly principled and developed in consultation and consideration of local contexts to achieve intended benefit. Effective implementation and independent monitoring can assist to align intentions with outcomes where standards and codes of conduct are appropriately geared. Access to the market is fundamental for business success and survival[49] but it comes at a price. Organisational development and international networks resulting from involvement with sustainability certifications and certified markets have been highly valued. The payment ahead of harvest, essentially pre-finance for farming activities, is commonly identified as a benefit of the Fairtrade system as discussed in the previous chapter. The Fairtrade minimum price and secure trading partners "cushioned" the impact of the 2001 coffee crisis. However, the Fairtrade minimum price and prices gained through RA certified markets for small producers, the Fairtrade price premium, and the cost of audit raise questions around how sustainability and poverty reduction intentions are and can be achieved.

A minimum price

The minimum price offered by Fairtrade intends to provide stability within a volatile international market situation. Within poverty reduction terms this is

---

[49] Cooperative manager, 12 February, 2009.

How to cite this book chapter:
Vogt, M. 2019. *Variance in Approach Toward a 'Sustainable' Coffee Industry in Costa Rica: Perspectives from Within; Lessons and Insights.* Pp. 107–113. London: Ubiquity Press. DOI: https://doi.org/10.5334/bce.j. License: CC-BY 4.0

a positive offering. It was suggested by interviewed cooperative representatives that the secure price offered by Fairtrade ensured survival through the coffee crisis of 2001.[50][51] Member numbers decreased dramatically, as did coffee farming as entire farms were abandoned[52] during this time. In 2009 while security through long term trading contracts and relationships, organisational capacity building and participation of producers in the Fairtrade system was variably observed, cooperative representatives claimed to be losing money through Fairtrade certified market channels. The Fairtrade minimum price did not cover the cost of production in Costa Rica despite the poverty reduction objective. While a FLAANZ and Oxfam report (2010) affirms the benefit of this approach from the perspective of a coffee producer from the Kilimanjaro Native Cooperative Union, "Pay us a fair price for our coffee, and we will make poverty history for ourselves," Costa Rican interviewees clarify, "Este ano Fairtrade hizo que el productor perdiera el dinero a través del mercado Fairtrade. El mercado convencional este ano es $2.57 y Fairtrade $1.87, causo una perdida" [this year Fairtrade made the producer lose money through the Fairtrade market. The conventional market this year is $2.57 and Fairtrade $1.87, it caused a loss][53], and this was confirmed by other interviewees:

> Los clientes que tenemos hacen tener la certificación Fairtrade vale la pena, pero el premio y el precio no vale la pena. Si vendemos café a $1.87 no es atractivo para mí, no cubre los costos. Costa Rica es diferente a otros países, el costo de producción es más alto, el transporte y la mano de obra es casi el doble que el de otros países.
> [The clients that we have make having the Fairtrade certification worth it but the premium and price is not worth it. If I sell coffee at $1.87 it is not attractive for me, it does not cover the costs. Costa Rica is different to other countries, the cost of production is higher, transport and labour is nearly double that of other countries].[319]
>
> Para tener estas certificaciones es un poco caro para nosotros, hemos estimado que, para cumplir con todos estos criterios de las certificaciones, la inversión es de aproximadamente 27 centavos por quintal 60 de café, es una inversión, por lo que cubre muchas cosechas, pero si es una producción de 100 quintales por 3 hectáreas, hay que hacer mucho para hacerse confirme. Tienen que reconocer el trabajo que tenemos que hacer para lograr estos cambios. Cualquier certificación porque incluso si es una responsabilidad de hacer las cosas bien, si vendemos

---

[50] Cooperative manager, 13 February, 2009.
[51] Cooperative manager, 4 February, 2009.
[52] Cooperative manager, 13 April, 2009.
[53] Cooperative manager, 13 April, 2009.

café al precio Fairtrade, no es sostenible. Hay personas que pueden vivir con estos precios, pero en qué condiciones, pueden comer, pero no pueden pagar la escuela. Fairtrade garantiza un tipo de vida, pero no vendemos un 40% a través de Fairtrade. Cuando del precio del café es bajo vendiendo 25% comercio justo y 75% al mercado por $1.11 es insuficiente. Fairtrade exige que invirtamos en salud, medio ambiente, etc. pero cuanto café estamos vendiendo a través de su mercado?

[To have these certifications is a bit expensive for us, we have estimated that to comply with all these criteria of the certifications, the investment is approximately 27 cents a quintal 60 of coffee, it is an investment, so that covers many harvests, but if it is a production of 100 quintales[54] for 3 hectares, you have to do a lot to become compliant. They must recognise the work that we must do to make these changes, any certification, because even if it is a responsibility to do things well, if we sell coffee at the Fairtrade price, it is not sustainable.

There are people who can live with these prices, but under what conditions, they can eat but they cannot afford school–Fairtrade guarantees a type of life, but we do not sell all our coffee, we sell 40% through Fairtrade but when the conventional coffee price is low, 25% Fairtrade, market $1.11 at 75% and this is insufficient. Fairtrade demands that we invest in health, environment etc., but how much coffee are we selling through their market].[55]

Ese es el problema que tenemos estoy hacienda un estudio comparativo de costos en Centroamérica, para demonstrar el problema que tenemos con los altos costos que el precio mínimo no cubre. Tenemos costos de producción más bajos en Costa Rica y tal vez en Centroamérica debido a la eficiencia, pero en la producción en la agricultura, no podemos manejar, trabajamos a mano, tenemos que pagar la seguridad social, etc. no podemos manejar esto.

[That is the problem that we have, I am doing a comparative study of costs in Central America, to demonstrate the problem we have with high costs that the minimum price does not cover. We have lower production costs in Costa Rica and maybe in Central America because of efficiency, but in production in farming, we cannot manage, we work by hand, we must pay social security etc…. we cannot manage this].[56]

---

[54] 60 Quintal = fanega = 46kg =1lb = 10 cajuelas.
[55] Financial manager and assistant director of Cooperative, 13 February, 2009; Cooperative manager, 11 March, 2009.
[56] International marketing manager, 11 May, 2009.

Selling a minimum percentage through Fairtrade certified markets caused Costa Rican farmers to lose money in 2009. Contracts with a fixed but superior price were signed in years when the conventional market price was on average lower. In the following years the cost of production maintained or increased, and the conventional market price increased. After carrying out research on sustainable production costs globally in coffee, Fairtrade increased the minimum price for certified coffee by an average of five cents per pound to $US1.24 per pound for unwashed arabica, and $US1.28 per pound for arabica coffee (FLO 2009a). This new minimum price intends to cover sustainable production costs for coffee producing organisations. It was again increased in 2011 to $US1.35 per pound for unwashed arabica and $US1.40 for washed arabica. It might not however consistently or effectively cover the cost of production in Costa Rica. The RA price, in comparison, depends on the buyer and is not fixed. RA certified farms received a superior price in RA certified markets while working holistically toward the three pillars of sustainability. The economic benefits of RA were clear for large plantations, the work involved to become certified was demanding but realistic. The superior price of 41–48 cents per pound above the standard market price balanced out the effort.[57] Certification was financially beneficial, superior to the conventional market price for plantations but not for cooperatives, "RA desde el fondo no protege a usted y los tostadores que comprar RA comprar 83 a través de los precios del gobierno a la tasa de Mercado abierto de $1.73 y recibimos 97 centavos" [RA from the bottom it does not protect you and the roasters that buy RA buy 83 through government prices at the open market rate [of] $1.73 and we receive 97 cents].[58]

The Fairtrade premium

(Included in quantified summary, see table 8)

The price paid for coffee in Costa Rica is regulated by ICAFE, "para un contrato abierto el precio pagado será el precio de Nueva York y un adicional de 36 centavos, el precio ICAFE" [for an open contract the price paid will be the NY price and an additional 36 cents, the ICAFE price][lix]. Fairtrade provides a 28-cent premium for organic production and a 14-cent premium additional to the price paid for a pound of coffee. This premium is intended for the social and economic development of the cooperative or the community:

> A lo largo de este ano la prima total recibida de Fairtrade por Coocafe fue de $5560, en términos de becas, representa básicamente nada más que para otros programas, aunque es una pequeña cantidad que ayuda a los pequeños costos operativos de las cooperativas y contribuye a otras

---

[57] Administrator of certification programs, 25 February, 2009.
[58] Cooperative manager, 20 February, 2009.

actividades, pero la cantidad varia y desde hace dos años las ventas a través de Canals de comercio justo cayeron, ahora está empezando a aumentar.

[Over this year the total premium received from Fairtrade by Coocafe was $5560 this, in terms of scholarships, it represents basically nothing but for other programs, although it is a very small amount it helps for small operational costs of cooperatives, and it contributes to other activities, but the amount varies and since two years ago the sales through Fairtrade channels fell, now it is starting to increase].[59]

El premio generalmente permitió algunas mejoras en la comunidad para un campo de futbol, salón comunitario, carreteras o reparaciones de carreteras en EL Dos, donde yo era el gerente. Aquí (en Atenas) el premio, como votado por nuestros miembros en 2008 es incorporado al precio final pagado al productor, por lo que la gente lo recibe directamente.

[The premium generally allowed some improvements in the community, for a football field, community hall, roads or road repairs in El Dos, where I used to be the manager. Here (in Atenas) the premium, as voted by our members in 2008 is incorporated into the final price paid to the producer, so the people receive it directly].[60]

The social premium intended for community projects is sometimes used as an additional payment to farmers almost as a coping mechanism against the insufficient price paid. However, even with the premium payment, costs were not covered. The premium was again increased in 2011 to 20cents.

Auditing

Certified producer groups and plantations spend time and money on the audit process. It was not always absolutely third party in 2009, and an extensive audit process was not identified for either of the certifications. One Fairtrade certified cooperative stated that only 5 of 50 farms were visited, 10%, and that they were selected randomly. The producer group paid to fly an auditor to the communities to complete the task and the cost of audit was a common cause for complaint, particularly where alternative systems operating in the country did not include this cost. The Community Agroecology Network (CAN) is an example:

En Fairtrade tenemos que invertir en un auditor, con CAN que nos dan asesoramiento técnico de forma gratuita. Con Fairtrade, los precios no

---

[59] Committee member *Hijos del Campo*, 23 February 2009.
[60] Cooperative manager, 12 February 2009.

son tan justos, por el momento Fairtrade no cubra el costo de producción para la cooperativa o las granjas. Tenemos un mercado fuera de Fairtrade que es $2.08, esto es más que Fairtrade. Vendemos 75% al mercado Fairtrade.

[In Fairtrade we must invest in an auditor, with CAN they give us technical advice for free. With Fairtrade, the prices are not so fair, at the moment Fairtrade is not covering the cost of production for the cooperative or the farms. We have a market outside of Fairtrade which is $2.08, this is more than Fairtrade. We sell 75% to the Fairtrade market].[61]

Tenemos que pagar dinero por la inspección, por la membresía, y por cada exportación que hacemos. Lo mismo sucede con Rainforest, con todas las certificaciones. Por ejemplo, con productos orgánicos, si usted tiene Maya-cert para venir e inspeccionar, usted paga por el transporte desde Guatemala.

[We must pay money for the inspection, for membership, and for every export that we do, the same thing happens with Rainforest, with all certifications. For example, with organic, if you have Maya-cert to come and inspect, you pay for transport from Guatemala].[62]

RA recognised in 2009 that the cost of monitoring, and of studies to confirm the existence and growth of specific trees required, was a barrier to more farmers benefiting and being part of their certified market. RA's idea to combine auditing that verifies stringent compliance with measuring carbon sequestered by trees planted, to earn carbon credits, was developing at this time. The monitoring costs would decrease and "credibility of the results would be high".[63] One RA certified farm manager mentioned involvement in the program as a positive development.[64]

Summary

RA and Fairtrade certifications require investment and resources for implementation toward compliance which represents an additional cost to standard operations. The auditing process for each certification body is an associated cost for the certified producer group or plantation farm. The cost included transport costs for the auditor visit, preparation of paperwork and potential visits involved in an audit process.

---

[61] Cooperative manager, 25 February 2009.
[62] International marketing manager, 11 May, 2009.
[63] Standards and policy technical coordinator, 6 May 2009.
[64] Administrator of certification programs, 25 February 2009.

The benefit of the Fairtrade price was variable since the early 2000s, and despite an increase in the minimum price offered in 2011 the conventional market price for arabica coffee on average remained above the Fairtrade minimum price. It was therefore problematic when contractual agreements settled on a price equal to or just above the Fairtrade minimum price rather than ensuring that it is above the conventional market price and that it covered cost of production. Due to contractual arrangements with limited price flexibility, many cooperatives were feeling locked into making a loss through Fairtrade certified trade channels, and similarly for limited experiences with RA certified market. The subtler advantage of improved access to credit was almost, in this situation and circumstance, irrelevant or compensatory to the situation being imposed but remained valued. The Fairtrade premium provided an opportunity to compensate these loses when used to compensate farmer payments. By comparison, RA does not guarantee a minimum price but successfully obtained consistently higher prices than conventional market prices for plantations and covered the cost of certification. This was not the case for certified cooperatives.

On a purely financial basis, benefit versus the cost of Fairtrade was not balancing or benefiting all or most certified farmers or cooperatives in Costa Rica in 2009. Increases in the minimum price since 2009 did not indicate an improved ability to cover costs in 2019. Individual trade contracts confirm this more thoroughly. The superior price achieved through RA certified channels were exclusive to plantations and were not assured for cooperatives. For plantations, it covered expenses associated with becoming certified and this was not expected to change.

CHAPTER 9

Standards for producers: variance in objective and approach

Introduction

RA and Fairtrade clearly communicate distinct intentions and approaches to improving environmental, economic and social outcomes, and how they prioritise each pillar of sustainability. RA has historically certified plantations rather than producer groups and cooperatives, while Fairtrade maintains attention to coffee cooperatives only. Where they are similar is their approach to standard development, external to a farming community. Their standard criteria do reflect the difference between RA and Fairtrade, and the ISEAL Alliance provide foundational guidance as a standards monitoring body. Procedures for RA and Fairtrade standard setting are in line with the ISEAL Code of Good Practice on Standard Setting. Representatives of the certifications are also involved in ISEAL standard setting discussions.

Standard development: politics of change and a top down approach

A top down versus consultative approach in standard setting is addressed by Giovannucci and Ponte (2005) who discuss the importance of including farmers in key decision-making processes in sustainability initiatives:

> If developed country actors decide alone what is included in standards and how they are measured, the impact of sustainability initiatives is likely to remain limited. Although some sustainability certifications may yield substantial benefits for producers, power relations may remain essentially unaltered if producers are still on the receiving end

---

How to cite this book chapter:
Vogt, M. 2019. *Variance in Approach Toward a 'Sustainable' Coffee Industry in Costa Rica: Perspectives from Within; Lessons and Insights.* Pp. 115–124. London: Ubiquity Press. DOI: https://doi.org/10.5334/bce.k. License: CC-BY 4.0

of key decision- making processes. In order for standards to work for developing country producers, the following four factors must be assured: (1) transparency and clarity of the standards and their requirements; (2) effective participation by developing country producers in key decisions over standard setting and monitoring procedures; (3) reasonable access; (4) just compensation for the efforts required of producers to meet and monitor elevated standards.

There are then specific differences to how Fairtrade and RA approach standard development beyond ISEAL guidance, and to reflect the philosophical difference between each certification approach.

Standard development according to certification

Standard detail can reflect intentions for or changes in practices in a more detailed way. They determine required and encouraged improvements and can be influenced by additional programs operating in the same area. For example, tree varieties planted for shade that are not specified by a standard, instead distributed by the local government. Fairtrade and RA operate separate departments for standard development and compliance monitoring for certification.

Fairtrade operates two independent branches FLOCERT GmbH and FLO eV and works on standard development through the Standards Unit and decision making through the Fairtrade standards committee level, a multi-stakeholder committee. Within the Fairtrade standard there are generic trade standards (Fairtrade International 2019a); product specific standards for small producer organisations (FLO 2009; Fairtrade International 2019b) and hired labour standards (Fairtrade International 2019c). The standards apply to all producers and traders. The Fairtrade standard has minimum and progressive criteria over a three-year period[65] allowing scope for organisations that are not 100% compliant to work toward this goal. Fairtrade has prioritised small holding farms and farmers organised into groups, and an economic and social standard via a minimum price and price premium. Fairtrade also provides opportunity for producer groups alongside a range of other stakeholders to be involved in organisational processes and provides a discretionary advantage to producer compared to buyers in trade agreements.

RA on the other hand uses the SAN standard and are committee and board members. The premise of RA compared to Fairtrade is an intended *holistic* approach with environmental and social sustainability leading to economic sustainability as explained in chapter 8, they began by certifying plantation size farms only. They have a standard for small producer groups, revised in 2009 however they still deal mainly with coffee plantations instead of small

---

[65] Cooperative Manager 11 March 2009.

producer groups. The politics of the minimum price is not relevant for RA like it is Fairtrade.

RA credits ISEAL as a major influence on SAN standards for their certification together with national research institutes such as CATIE[66] and technical groups:

> The number of crops that we were certifying began to grow and we could not compile a guide for each crop, so in 2008 all these additional criteria for each item, they brought together. This is not only the decision of the network, there are groups of technicians in the background and what the market demands. Influencing our standards are lots of technical groups, what the market asks, ISEAL asks. So really it is influenced by what the whole world is doing, these are the rules... influence comes from ISEAL, which is influenced by what the market asks.[67]

The difference in approach of the two certifications influence how standards can be changed on a contextual case by case basis, and then as an official standard. The SAN committee, the standard setting body for RA certification, meet twice a year to discuss changes to standards or strategy. There are local interpretation guidelines for specific crops and countries updated in 2015. For coffee, these guidelines exist for Honduras, Brazil and El Salvador.

Producer involvement in standard setting

Giovannucci and Ponte (2005) argue that producer participation is key to poverty reduction and sustainable livelihoods. A RA representative explains that, "no estamos 'en medio' de grandes corporaciones y productores "[we are not 'in the middle' of large corporations and producers].[68] In comparison, the Fairtrade approach while not explicitly seeking to be in the middle does provide an opportunity for such situations indicating a detailed difference in philosophical understanding of sustainability and intentions between each certification. For Fairtrade certified farmers, financial negotiations and secure contracts present some of the greatest challenges. While discretionary preference is given to farmers instead of buyers, in some instances having Fairtrade support in these situations was mentioned as necessary.

Fairtrade works to empower producer groups through involvement in the Fairtrade system and must consult with these groups as well as with ISEAL. RA consults with SAN and ISEAL, but not directly with planation managers, or small producer groups. Involvement of farmers is only possible through the

---

[66] For more information, view http://www.catie.ac.cr/magazin.asp
[67] Standards and Policy Technical Coordinator, 6 May, 2009.
[68] Standards and policy technical coordinator, 6 May, 2009.

SAN committee. With the idea that farmers will equally participate in Fairtrade debates and discussions, Fairtrade consistently seeks to include and consult. There is the opportunity for ISEAL to include farmers, or for Fairtrade to either represent their interests or include them in ISEAL discussions. However, from the farmers' perspective, interaction between producer groups and certifications does follow a "enfoque de arriba hacia abajo" [top down approach][69] and this idea was supported:

> En cuanto al feedback entre el productor y el consumidor, veo más y esto en Fairtrade que Rainforest Alliance porque siento que en realidad con Rainforest hay tres criterios básicos ambientales, sociales y económicos, por lo que estos son los fundamentos para el productor. Para mí, el problema que veo con Rainforest es que es una Multinacional que está operando en los EE. UU. y que tiene un enorme valor en los EE. UU., Canadá y el Reino Unido, etc. Así que tienen una alianza y de esa manera tienen participación pero que esta distanciado.
>
> [In terms of feedback between producer and consumer, I see more of this in Fairtrade than Rainforest Alliance because I feel that with Rainforest there are three basic criteria environmental, social and economic, so these are basics for the producer. To me, the problem I see with Rainforest is that it is a Multinational that is operating in the US and it has huge value in the US, Canada and the UK etc. So, they have an alliance, and, in that way, they have participation, but it is distanced].[70]

Examples of contextually inappropriate and ineffective standards from findings include water management standards; the fairtrade minimum price; labour standards; land title requirements; and independent monitoring.

Inappropriate Standards

Water management and RA

(Included in quantified summary, see table 8)

SAN standards applied to small producer groups for RA certification were identified as out of context for small farmers in one region of Costa Rica, specifically related to *el ojo de agua*, the source of water.

> Cuando los inspectores de la RA vinieron a auditor nuestras fincas sentimos que sus preguntas estaban un poco fuera del contexto histórico, cultural y social para el granjero, por ejemplo, en una pequeña comu-

---

[69] International Marketing Manager, 11 May 2009.
[70] Ibid.

nidad en San Luis, el inspector fue a finca y le pregunto, '¿proviene de un sistema público, de la comunidad? Si no, es una falta del estándar.' El campesino dice, 'Bueno primero tengo que dar la gracia por tener agua, si no tengo un sistema público el sistema no ha existido o en los últimos anos en esta área no ha sido necesario'. Aquí en esta área hasta ahora, hay una fuente de agua en cada finca, por lo que este requisito que determinaría el cumplimiento de las normas RA y por tanto la certificación no parece relevante para nuestra comunidad.

[When the RA inspectors came to audit our farms, we felt that their questions were a little out of historic, cultural and social context for the farmer, for example, in a small community in San Luis, the inspector went to a farm and asked 'The water that you consume, does it come from a public system, from the community? If not, it is a breach of our standard.' The farmer says, 'well I first have to give thanks that I have water, if I do not have a public system it is not because I do not want to, it is because the system has not existed or in the last years in this area it has not been necessary.' Here in this area until now, there is a source of water in every farm, so this requirement which would determine complying with RA standards and therefore achieving certification does not seem relevant to our community].[71]

Fairtrade minimum price

(Included in quantified summary, see table 8)

The minimum price may also be considered an inappropriate standard for the Costa Rican context. Costa Rica by law will only farm the arabica species, it achieves the highest international market prices compared to the other popular coffee species, robusta. The distinction between price influences how the Fairtrade minimum price compares to conventional market prices. The average international market price for coffee, which averages prices of arabica and robusta are closer to the price set by Fairtrade however they can remain above the minimum $1.35. Where prices of arabica separately are compared, the difference is significant, and the Fairtrade minimum price does not appear reasonable. Within ICO pricing, Costa Rica sells within the 'other mild' category of arabica. The average price of this coffee in 2017 was $1.44 (ICO 2017a); in Costa Rica, the average price paid to growers since 2011 has been above $1.70 (ICO 2017b). The Fairtrade minimum price is a valuable standard when the conventional market price is below the standard rate. Where the minimum price is used in trade contracts and fixed for the length of the contract, the disadvantages become more obvious particularly when taking the information

---

[71] Previous cooperative manager, coffee farmers and cooperative manager, 12 January, 2009.

regarding conventional market prices and cost of production into consideration. Ensuring the minimum price covers the cost of production according to each countries' requirements, alongside allowing stability and security in trade terms, would more adequately cover all aspects of poverty reduction. Ensuring a stability in income that allows costs to be covered is essential. One without the other is not considered a sufficient poverty reduction measure or achievement.

Labour standards

(Included in quantified summary, see table 8)

Labour standards are about more than wages as outlined by International Labour Organisation (ILO) conventions. The conventions include, minimum age (convention 1920); right of association (convention 1921); equality of treatment (convention1925); and various other standards (ILOLEX 2010; Lyutov 2010). The detail of each standard is important in terms of setting clear objectives for best practice. The comparative table demonstrates the difference between labour standards of the two certifications (Table 2).

Certifying larger plantations with a specific group of workers or employees is possibly a simpler process to understanding numbers of workers, as permanent across numerous small farm holdings.

The practice of and requirements for hiring labour for plantations is different from small farms with a definite formality for plantations. The common practice for Costa Rican producers of small farm holdings that *hire* seasonal workers, was informal. At times as simple as word of mouth or loyalty; some workers were considered family friends for small farmers. "Las mismas personas regresan cada ano, y les preguntamos si conocen a otras personas que podrían estar interesadas en venir a trabajar" [The same people come back every year, and we ask if they know other people who might be interested in coming to work].[72] The relationship that developed over this time was explained:

> Hemos tenido la misma familia y trabajamos en nuestra granja durante los últimos 5 o así anos, incluso estamos pensando en ir a Nicaragua para visitarlos ya que también son los granjeros de café que viajan aquí por algún dinero extra, similar a unas vacaciones de trabajo. También compartimos información sobre técnicas de cultivo de café.
>
> [We have had the same family come and work on our farm for the past 5 or so years, we are even thinking about going to Nicaragua to visit them as they are also coffee farmers who travel here for some extra money, similar to a working holiday. We share information about techniques in coffee farming as well].[73]

---

[72] Coffee farmers, Los Angeles de Páramo, 12 May, 2009.
[73] Previous cooperative manager, coffee farmer and member of cooperative, 12 January, 2009.

Such a positive situation cannot be assumed in all cases. The labour standards can assist to ensure consistency, however an increase in cost for the farmer could result. This would include training of staff, upgrading qualifications and new organisational policies and procedures including Occupational Health and Safety (OHS), and sexual harassment grievance procedures (FLO 2009c). Infrastructural adjustments may also be necessary for housing of labourers and the provision of childcare which requires more investment. The RA standard might not be as detailed as Fairtrade in labour standards (Labour Rights 2009, figure 13) however the standards for RA are applicable to all employees working on a plantation, a point of difference from Fairtrade. In 2008, the Fairtrade standard for hired labour (hired labour standard) was newly introduced as a separate standard to the generic Fairtrade standard. Fairtrade standards define small producers as "those that are structurally dependent on permanent hired labour and that are managing their farm mainly with their own and family labour" (Fairtrade 2009a, 4). The definition of *worker* referring to all waged employees of the producer organisation and of its members.

The definition of worker includes "migrant, temporary, seasonal, subcontracted and permanent workers" (FLOCert 2009, 24) and they must be *unionisable*. Those that were consequently included in the standard are conditionally based on a group that can be unionised and make up a *significant* number of workers founded on national law. Within the updated hired labour standard a minimum of 25 permanent workers must be employed to use the standard. The definition of permanent worker was not fully elaborated on and scope for variance in definition certainly existed within each community and country. Issues for temporary seasonal labour employed by small farmers could also continue to arise as Fairtrade's hired labour standard did not effectively apply to all small holding coffee farmers. If farmers themselves were hiring 'a significant number' of workers as defined by national law and the standard itself, they are required to seek certification under the hired labour standard. Without a *significant* number of workers, all Fairtrade labour standards for coffee default to generic Fairtrade standards. With a significant number of workers, small farmers become certified external to their cooperative, raising issues of expense and process for a small farmer, and therefore feasibility.

These definitions indicate that the responsibilities of small holding coffee farmers to their employed labour will be governed by the Generic Fairtrade standards and not the specific hired labour standard unless the producer independently seeks this certification as necessary. Necessity, determined by a *significant* number of workers, becomes an issue as members of a cooperative are, as a group, employing many seasonal migrant workers. Due to the size of the farms each farmer may only employ one or two people, an insignificant number by Fairtrade standards. The hired labour standard can therefore easily be excluded from requirements for producer groups, and farmers of small holdings. Where they are applicable, the required investment is relevant.

When the Fairtrade price is locking farmers into a price that does not cover costs, it seems contradictory to expect that they adequately take care of their labourers within the same agreement. There are also some cultural considerations related to any international hired labour standard that require additional consideration (Vogt 2019b).

Formalising land title

Property rights and land-titling have become a focus of conflict and debate in Costa Rica through reforestation efforts tied to Costa Rica's environmental policy. In 1996, the Forestry Law – N575 (WRI 2010) combining land-title with financially subsidised reforestation efforts was introduced, easing reforestation effort but only for owners with formal land title. Formalising land title was identified by a group of farmers in Costa Rica as an additional cost and issue[74] as there was resistance to the formal registration of land with the state. These issues are relevant to coffee farmers of small holdings and examples how a popular poverty reduction approach might not necessarily achieve the stated aims. This observation highlights the need to understand local culture and equity from a local perspective and distinguishes between identifying a problem and requiring conditions to resolve it, versus developing local understanding and finding effective solutions within a similar process. How sustainability certifications and cooperatives require formalised land title through standards is therefore an additional consideration related to appropriateness, particularly according to culture and local context.

Transparency and independent monitoring

(Included in quantified summary, see table 8)

The certification bodies aim to assist producers with implementation of the standard criteria and the producer organisation is not financially penalised if standards are not complied with. Instead they will receive a warning or lose the certification depending on the offence and their previous record of offences, and realistic ability to become compliant. Fairtrade revises administrative processes at the business and *beneficio* level and then visits member farms. RA and FLOcert auditing bodies select farms at random when monitoring. "Fairtrade selecciona tres cooperativas de Coocafe y da aviso con tres días de antelación" [Fairtrade select three cooperatives of Coocafe and give three days' notice before they visit].[75] "Visitan el 10% de las fincas miembro" [They visit 10% of

---

[74] Coffee farmers, Los Angeles de Páramo, 15 May 2009.
[75] Cooperative Manager, 11 March 2009.

member farms][76] . "Visitan las fincas por si mismos; No vamos con ellos" [they visit the farms by themselves; we do not go with them].[77] RA follows a similar pattern for visits. RA viene una vez al año y pasa tres días, un día en cada granja y un día con papeles [RA comes once a year and spends three days, one day on each farm and one day with papers].[78] Producers are also regulated by the Ministry of Agriculture and Livestock (MAG). "Regulan el certificador en Costa Rica y vienen una o dos veces al ano" [They regulate the certifier in Costa Rica, and they come once or twice a year].[79] Fairtrade inspectors visit before harvest[80], which would influence an ability to monitor conditions for seasonal labourers who come only for the harvest season.

Summary

(Approach by each certification; inappropriate standards for water management; Fairtrade minimum price; Labour standards; Transparency and independent monitoring included in quantified summary, see table 8)

Standards and effective implementation are considered central to the influence each certification will have in coffee farming practices and communities related to poverty reduction and sustainable development. Implementation of standards and ensuring adequate monitoring of implementation represent additional costs but are essential to ensure aligned outcomes. The influence of standards is determined by the sustainability philosophy used by each certification, criteria inclusion, how consultative standard development is, and effective implementation. RA and Fairtrade certifications maintain an international, centralised, and external to community standard development approach. While the intention to develop standards centrally but in consultation with stakeholders exists, in implementation this was not identified as consistent nor as an effective process. In addition, inappropriate standards required processes contrary to local physical geography contexts, leaving producers confused about the sustainability value of such certification processes.

Most hired labour for coffee farms in Costa Rica are migrant workers and the legitimacy of their visas and ability to work in country can vary. Fairtrade and RA developed hired labour standards to ensure that labourers, legal or illegal, are provided adequate conditions. The difference between hired labour for a small holding farm or a cooperative managing across all member farms, and a plantation is a significant difference. The Fairtrade standard for hired

---

[76] Cooperative Manager, 20 February, 2009.
[77] Cooperative Manager, 11 March 2009.
[78] Administrator of certification programs, 25 February 2009.
[79] Technical engineer and administrator of certification programs, 9 February 2009.
[80] Cooperative manager, 12 February, 2009.

labour was introduced after labour standards were included in SAN standards therefore implementation of RA labour standards was comparatively more advanced. While the Fairtrade standard for hired labour is detailed, it is separate to the Fairtrade generic standard and only deemed relevant for farms that employ a 'significant' number of workers according to the Fairtrade standard, and then where 25 permanent workers are employed within the hired labour standard itself.

While RA tries to remove itself from power dynamics between farmers and buyers, Fairtrade works between and alongside producer groups and buyers, most are small holding farmers, and is truly engaged in the *social concept* of Fairtrade. Fairtrade prioritises social and economic justice for coffee farmers however financial negotiations and secure contracts are perhaps the most challenging to achieve. When buyers of Fairtrade certified coffee are MNCs they might source certified products for market presence, positive brand association and increasing brand equity (Raynolds 2007; Vogt 2019a, 2019b) while negotiating contracts against the best interests of producers. With such a range of interest groups involved, changing a standard to benefit farmers could become complicated and make the process, possibly the certified product, more expensive.

As in-community standard development, implementation and audit emerge (Vogt 2019b), RA and Fairtrade maintain the external to producer community approach for standard development, introduction and certification of compliance. Fairtrade maintains its resolve and commitment to stated aims and objectives that benefit farmers while continuing to balance with interests of roasters and buyers of certified coffee. Despite these power relations, Fairtrade has managed to change its standards in accordance with ISEAL, but still struggles to balance the producer voice in the process of change. There is therefore some complication when critiquing and changing the Fairtrade standards. This could be considered a problem in terms of encouraging poverty reduction through building capabilities for effective participation. RA seeks to revise and update standards on a regular basis, and comparatively the process is more removed from stakeholder involvement than Fairtrade.

CHAPTER 10

Increasing the number of certifications and associated benefits or disadvantages

Introduction

While Fairtrade appeared the only sustainability certification, alongside organic in 2006–2009 in Australia, the number of certifications operating in the Costa Rican coffee industry with sustainability intentions were significant. They included RA; Fairtrade; Organic for different countries; UTZ Kapeh; 4Cs, Starbucks C.A.F.E. Practices, ISO for processing. Every business interviewed in Costa Rica was certified by at least two or three certifiers or socially responsible programs for coffee. How realistic implementing an increasing number of certifications was for producer groups became a point for discussion. As did how the number of labels evidences a market orientated effort, rather than a producer community orientated sustainability effort.

Top down demand

Given a perceived benefit, and the increase in popularity of certified coffee markets, many cooperatives commented that compliance to more than one certification was often at the demand of existing clients. A top down demand approach motivated by the improved reputation offered by certified coffee, or an opportunity to meet intentions to improve CSR efforts appeared evident. "Ahora tenemos clientes que vienen y demandan café basado en la certificación" [We now have clients who come, and demand coffee based on certification][81, 82]:

---

[81] International Marketing Manager, 11 May 2009.
[82] Ibid.

How to cite this book chapter:
Vogt, M. 2019. *Variance in Approach Toward a 'Sustainable' Coffee Industry in Costa Rica: Perspectives from Within; Lessons and Insights.* Pp. 125–132. London: Ubiquity Press. DOI: https://doi.org/10.5334/bce.l. License: CC-BY 4.0

> Nuestro cliente solicito que seamos certificados con RA. Fairtrade está en un proceso de cambio en el momento de ser más completo y detallado en la implementación sin embargo es el apoyo de los departamentos gubernamentales según los entrevistados que están ayudando a hacer cambios en el terreno para satisfacer las demandas de sus clientes.
>
> [Our client requested that we become certified with RA. Fairtrade is in a process of change at the moment to be more thorough and detailed in implementation however it is support from government departments according to interviewees that are assisting in making changes on the ground to satisfy demands of their clients].[83, 84]

The financial manager and assistant director of Coopetarrazu explained in more detail:

> Nos certificamos con Fairtrade porque en ese momento, el precio era bajo en café… y algunos compradores de café estaban buscando un café Tarrazu que fuera certificado Fairtrade y no existía así que decidimos certificarnos para ofrecer esta combinación al mercado. Entramos en C.A.F.E. Practices de Starbucks porque teníamos clientes demandando que cumpliéramos y luego teníamos otros clientes demandando café certificado RA, así que también trabajamos para ser certificados bajo el programa de RA.
>
> [We became certified with Fairtrade because at that time, the price was low in coffee and some buyers of coffee were looking for a Tarrazu coffee that was Fairtrade certified and it did not exist, so we decided to become certified to offer this combination to the market. We entered C.A.F.E Practices of Starbucks because we had clients demanding that we comply and then we had other clients demanding RA certified coffee, so we also worked to become certified under the RA program].[85]

The first RA certified small holding coffee farm in Costa Rica achieved certification in 2007.[86] There have been other RA certified cooperatives, and some are members of Coocafe. Despite complying with SAN standards none of these cooperatives were selling through RA certified markets in 2009[87][88], indicating a difference in focus and appropriateness of the two certifications dependent on the size of farm holding and the organisation type.

---

[83] Administrator of certification programs, 25 February 2009.
[84] Farm Administrator, 17 February 2009.
[85] Financial Manager and assistant director, 13 February 2009.
[86] Standards and policy technical coordinator, 6 May, 2009.
[87] Cooperative manager, 13 February, 2009.
[88] Cooperative manager, 20 March, 2009.

Symptom of a supply chain power imbalance?

An increasing number of certifications in the market seems to reinforce a power imbalance between producers, traders and consumers. Producers are obliged to be certified several times to access different markets. The subjectivity is evident as the choice is more with buyers than producers, and the power imbalance in this situation becomes obvious. Several managers and administrators mentioned that MNCs develop quotas or percentages for certifications and these quotas are based on the whim of consumers' preference and their own administrative interests.[89, 90] If a cooperative does not have the certification required in a market, they must either pay and work toward compliance to maintain the trade relationship or lose the sale. The implications of such supply chain dynamics and requirements contribute to considering the role such certifications play in producing countries, particularly as their intention is to improve sustainability. It appears that the resulting administration required by producer organisations and companies is creating something of a mess of efforts, requiring more with minimal overall benefit and possibly harm from becoming certified. This particularly seems the case where standard development and introduction may not adequately address 'sustainability' issues. As more time passes merges between certifications such as that between RA and UTZ in 2018, and a facilitated internal and independent amalgamation of standards could become more common.

Limited capability for market access

A consistent perception evident through interviews with Fairtrade certified cooperatives was the cost of Fairtrade and RA, and market access benefits. This is before any assistance or support for implementing farming and trade standards. In 2009, the benefits of Fairtrade were not so easily identified. Rather than changing farming processes it seemed the certifications were more useful for market access and stable buyers, for certified producer organisations, "las certificaciones son necesarias para acceder a los mercados especializados" [The certifications are necessary to access speciality markets].[91] This opinion was confirmed in other interviews. "Básicamente las certificaciones son para acceso al Mercado" [Basically the certifications are for market access].[92]

---

[89] Administrator of certification programs, 25 February, 2009; Farm administrator, 17 February, 2009.
[90] International marketing manager, 11 May, 2009.
[91] Regional Director of Pérez Zeledón, 11 May 2009.
[92] Technical engineer and administrator of certification programs, 2 February 2009.

At the same time barriers to increasing certified markets exist, this was also an issue for CAN. Certification efforts rely on funding from roasters and producer cooperatives, and producers are then reliant on these efforts to access markets; thus, they become certified as suits strategic ambitions or may not, because of strict financial constraints, a similar situation for every certification which must be paid for. The need to juggle certifications (Vogt 2019c) can be considered symptomatic of uncoordinated efforts. The financial and resource implications, for cooperatives particularly, may outweigh the benefit of market access. Ultimately the claimed or perceived benefit of increased market access, while evidenced and observed for long-certified cooperatives is still limited.

Certifications as a market movement

While the market value of certifications for producer organisations is recognised by most interviewees, more than 50% of coffee cooperatives in Costa Rica hold the idea that certifications are "simplemente un capricho del Mercado y del consumidor "[simply a whim of the market and consumer].[93, 94] Over 75% required support from government departments and international funding bodies for implementation of the required standards. Aside from certifications, quality is a major influencing factor in choosing green unroasted coffee in the specialty market; overall the prominence of certifications in Costa Rica indicates their importance.

The significant strength of influence through the supply chain of client demands on coffee producer businesses follows a demand for certifications in 'consumer' countries. The certifications allow the end buyer to verify and identify products that are *sustainable*. There is then a market *vote* for CSR and sustainable practices. In this context, sustainable certifications represent an ethical purchase and a better choice compared to the standard products available. The understanding of what these certifications really mean is as detailed as the information provided on the packaging and word of mouth (Vogt 2019a, 2019b) which could be considered a limitation (Shaw & Black 2010). When the influence of this choice is significant it is indicative of a certification system subject to the psychology of the market which can be alarming. As intra-market mechanisms, sustainability certifications are likely to experience such market demand reliance, and this could be considered a limitation (Shaw & Black 2010; Vogt 2019b).

---

[93] Ibid.
[94] Cooperative Manager, 20 February, 2009.

The producer perspective: observed and understood difference between certifications

The manager of Coope Tarrazu explained how their cooperative was managing three certifications:

> Hemos empezado a fusionar los diversos estándares en un estándar para la cooperativa. Si no hacemos esto los diferentes estándares son demasiado segregados para nuestros miembros y para nosotros y nos ahorramos tiempo.... Parece la forma más inteligente para gestionar toda esta información y el trabajo de papel.
> [We have started amalgamating the various standards into one standard for the cooperative. If we do not do this the different standards are too segregated for our members and for us and we save ourselves time. It seems the smartest way for managing all this information and paperwork].[95]

The amalgamation of standards within a cooperative would not allow farmers to know which specific standards pertain to each certification. Effective implementation of all-inclusive criteria would arguably be sufficient, particularly if use of financial and organisational resources reduces. The farmers' awareness of certifications compared to the importance of standards as opposed to labelling was highlighted by the regional director of ICAFE in the Pérez Zeledón region who explained. "Este es un miembro de Coope Agri y él no sabe que él es un 'campesino Fairtrade'" [This is a member of Coope Agri, and he does not know that he is a 'Fairtrade farmer'].[96] What appears most important for a farmer is in fact the change in practices required, and how it will influence their income, perhaps also their health and wellbeing rather than a preferred label. The importance of standards compared to a certification label and associated marketing claims about a certified farmer becomes more pertinent and relevant. The difference between market preference compared to actual outcomes in farming communities is emphasized.

While the standards and auditing methods of certifications were becoming similar[97] in 2009, the fact that some cooperatives were amalgamating standards to facilitate the juggle of several certifications indicates how different some standard requirements are. The premise of each certification remains distinct and this will continue to dictate the prioritised approach of each certification also. The difference is noticeable for certified organisations and from a cooperative level perspective were quite clearly communicated.

---

[95] Financial and assistant director, 13 February, 2009.
[96] Regional director of Perez Zeledon, 11 May, 2009.
[97] Cooperative manager, 12 February, 2009.

> Fairtrade realmente trata de unir a las comunidades a través de sus criterios tenemos una mejor visión de la producción, la industria y de la comercialización. La red de iniciativas, de países y organizaciones de Comercio Justo a través del mundo es más fuerte que Rainforest"
> [Fairtrade really tries to unite the communities and through their criteria we have a better vision of production, the industry and of commercialisation. The network of initiatives, of countries and organisations of Fairtrade through the world are stronger than Rainforest].[98]

Fairtrade is viewed as more community orientated compared with RA. This perception stems from the requirement that any organisation certified by Fairtrade must be a cooperative. "Fairtrade no solo certifica, sino que supervise, tiene premios y programas. Ayuda a tomar importantes decisiones económicas y políticas" [Fairtrade not only certifies but it supervises, it has premiums and programs. It assists in making important economic and political decisions].[99] The RA approach is identified as different to Fairtrade by a representative of RA, "Rainforest tiene un concepto que analizan, pero no organizan, aquí es donde veo la gran diferencia" [Rainforest has one concept that they analyse but they do not organise, this is where I see the big difference].[100] The RA representative explained their approach:

> Somos una de las certificaciones que integran los tres pilares de la sostenibilidad a través de la red. No buscamos un premio de precio fijo. Es más holístico, y no da prioridad a un pilar sobre otro.
>
> [We are one of the only certifications that integrate the three pillars of sustainability through the network. We do not look for a fixed price premium. It is more holistic, and it does not prioritise one pillar over another].[101]

Fairtrade prioritises social justice by intending to provide economic security and organisational capacity building. One cooperative manager explained, "las dos certificaciones tienen una diferencia, Fairtrade desde la base te protege un poco, desde lo alto son las mismas" [The two certifications have a difference, Fairtrade from the base it protects you a little, from the top they are the same][c]. Becoming evident through interviews was the fact that Fairtrade is changing in the way it sets standards and monitors implementation. "Me hace reír porque Fairtrade está estableciendo un nuevo modelo de auditoria y lo que parecen estar hacienda es copiar otras certificaciones." [It makes me laugh because

---

[98] International marketing manager, 11 May, 2009.
[99] Director of *Hijos del Campo* and *Café Forestal*, 20 February, 2009.
[100] International marketing manager, 11 May, 2009.
[101] Standards and policy technical coordinator, 6 May, 2009.

today Fairtrade is establishing a new model of audit and what they seem to be doing is copying other certifications].[102]

> Antes Fairtrade era como una asistencia social, oh usted es pobre, necesita ayuda, pero ahora Fairtrade es más como una certificación, mirando a la salud, el medio ambiente. Es más similar a otras certificaciones ahora y este año se centran mucho en los estándares ambientales.
> [Before Fairtrade was like a social assistance, oh you are poor, you need help, but now Fairtrade is more like a certification, looking at health, environment. It is more similar to other certifications now, and this year they are very much focused on environmental standards].[103]

The influence of ISEAL and their work towards unifying best practice through codes and verifying implementation could be reason for an increase in environmental Fairtrade standards. Despite an increasingly common or agreed approach, several core differences between the certifications remain.

The influences of a top down, market demand-based approach

(Included in quantified summary, see table 8)

Identified top down approaches are not only relevant to standard setting. The increase in demand for different certifications appears to result from buyer and market demands for certifications, and from country specific regulatory requirements for sustainable imports. Certifications provide producer groups or certified farms with new trade networks and demonstrate compliance to distinct import country requirements. The demand for multiple certifications does therefore appear something of a symptom of supply chain power dynamics and therefore a top down approach as market access is identified as a significant motivator for becoming certified. Further discussion on this point is provided in chapter 12.

For producer groups the difference in approach between certifications is identifiable if not obvious not only through standard requirements but also through philosophical approach to sustainability. While most farmers will not be aware of the name of each certification or that they are in fact a 'Fair trade' [or other] farmer, the required changes in practices are relevant for all producers.

The standards and compliance processes do therefore appear most relevant in the producing country, however, the need for market access and stable trading partners can significantly determine which certifications will be complied with. The demand for several certifications by corporations or buyers in producing countries is however generating an administrative juggle for producer

---

[102] Cooperative manager, 12 February, 2009.
[103] Cooperative manager, 11 March, 2009.

organisations. One method developed in Costa Rica to assist with the juggle of multiple certifications is to internally amalgamate all standards. Producers become compliant to multiple certifications without an internal distinction between certification specific standard requirements. Merges between certifications are more recently occurring and might also assist to reduce the producer organisation juggle which inevitably influences resource investment requirements toward compliance and the identified cost versus benefit issue.

CHAPTER 11

Reputation beyond intention and influence

Introduction

Intentions of different certifications are presented within a 'sustainability' frame without clarification of the definition of sustainability used, or of actual outcomes. The distance between farmers and consumers easily allows misalignment between a certifications' reputation, their intention and the actual outcome. The need for market demand often allows marketing communication and promotion that exaggerate or selectively present positive stories. In other cases, marketing approaches can remain so simple that opportunity for reputation to exceed intention or outcome are provided. Fairtrade and RA required improved standard criteria and approaches to ensure and verify implementation and compliance despite quite positive marketing communications. There is also a consideration of how and if certifications are in fact influencing change compared to other in-country sustainability programs, and whether the influence they have is adequate and appropriate.

Subsistence farming, and regulated and reduced chemical use

New coffee varieties introduced during the green revolution were detrimental to the livelihoods of farmers in Costa Rica:

> En la década de 1930, cuando el café era de buena calidad, solo tenía arábica de lo que sé, pero luego más café vino a mejorar la cosecha, pero no la calidad. Era un árbol que producía más. Después de 3 años llego la primera cosecha, pero la cosecha fue tanto que la técnica no era necesario. Este mató a la comida encima de ella.

How to cite this book chapter:
Vogt, M. 2019. *Variance in Approach Toward a 'Sustainable' Coffee Industry in Costa Rica: Perspectives from Within; Lessons and Insights*. Pp. 133–142. London: Ubiquity Press. DOI: https://doi.org/10.5334/bce.m. License: CC-BY 4.0

[In the 1930s when the coffee was good quality, we only had Arabica from what I know, but then more coffee came to improve the harvest but not the quality. It was a tree that produced more. After 3 years came the first harvest, but the harvest was so much that technique was not necessary. This killed the food on top of it].[104]

Conservation efforts juxtaposed intensified expansion of new coffee varieties, and deforestation required to accommodate the expansion. Reforestation, conservation, diversification of farm activity, and subsistence farming all contributed to significant changes in coffee farming techniques after the farming trends of the 1930s. The coffee crises of the 1990s and 2000s introduced additional difficulties to coffee farming communities. Costa Rica's export profile, without abandoning coffee production, shifted to non-traditional products (Vargas 2003), favouring the production of pineapple, cardamom, flowers, squash, among other products (Honey 1994). In addition, tourism became a lucrative economic activity working hand in hand with the protectionist measures of the various governments to protect part of the country's natural resources. "Desde la crisis de 2001 hemos aprendido que nuestros agricultores deben dedicar parte de su finca a la agricultura de subsistencia" [Since the 2001 crisis we have learnt that our farmers must dedicate some of their farm to subsistence agriculture].[268] Diversifying farming techniques was also identified as advantageous, "ahora incluso si el precio cae al menos siempre hay algo para comer" [Now even if the price falls at least there is always something to eat].[105]

The 2000/2001 coffee crisis reduced the use of agricultural chemicals and fertilisers, and diversified farming activities as a financial necessity. The chemicals and fertilisers necessary to maintain the introduced hybrid variety of coffee also depleted the soil of nutrients. Health impacts were, and still are, an issue for farmers and their families throughout Costa Rica with reports of infertility through the country.[106] Specific to the region of Coto Brus:

> Over ninety percent had heard of or knew someone that had suffered from agrochemical use-related health problems. Illnesses included minor intoxications, vision problems, cancer, birth defects, sterilization, gastrointestinal issues, and death. (Garcia 2006, 39)

Irrespective of being members of the local cooperative, farmers in the region of Agua Buena, Coto Brus and Hojancha, Guanacaste reduced agri-chemical use and diversified farm activities for the same reason, they could no longer afford the chemicals. "En la mayoría, no usamos productos químicos por dinero,

---

[104] "Esteban," coffee farmer, 6 March 2009.
[105] "Ronny", Coffee farmer, 6 March, 2009.
[106] Director *Hijos de Campo and Café Forestal*, 20 March, 2009.

no por una conciencia ambiental" [In the majority, we do not use chemicals because of money, not because of an environmental conscience].[107] "Tuvimos que dejar de usar productos químicos, Ya no nos lo podíamos permitir pagar" [We had to stop using chemicals; we could no longer afford it].[108] The benefits of reducing the use of chemicals particularly on health are well recognised by farmers throughout Costa Rica:

> La salud de la familia, esto es muy especial al menos para mí. He visto que solo necesito aplicar productos químicos una vez al año no 8–9 veces. El ambiente es completamente diferente porque el café estaba completamente al sol, ahora hay sombra.
> [The health of the family, this is very special at least for me. I have seen that I only need to apply chemicals once a year not 8–9 times. The environment is completely different because the coffee was entirely in the sun, now there is shade].[109]

Mi camisa y pantalones no huelen mal, la ropa se fue en la lavadora con ropa de la familia y creo que no era saludable. Ahora utilizamos menos agroquímicos, la cosecha ha disminuido pero la salud es mejor para los agricultores, el medio ambiente y para los consumidores. El cambio vale la pena es importante.
[My shirt and pants do not smell bad; the clothes went in the washing machine with the family's clothes and I think it was unhealthy. Now we use agro-chemicals less, the harvest has decreased but the health is better for the farmers, the environment and for the consumers. The change is worth it, it is important].[110]

Ahora mis hijos pueden correr a través de la granja y el bosque (secundaria) y no tengo que preocuparse por las consecuencias. No tengo que preocuparse por su salud de hecho sé que son más saludables para vivir en esta granja con el espacio para correr y aprender sobre los árboles en la granja y el bosque.
[Now my children can run through the farm and forest (secondary) and I do not have to worry about the consequences, I do not have to worry about their health in fact I know they are healthier for living on this farm with the space to run and learn about the trees on the farm and the forest].[111]

---

[107] "Walter" coffee farmer, 27 March 2009.
[108] Cooperative manager, 31 March, 2009.
[109] "Roman" coffee farmer, 27 March 2009.
[110] "Willian", coffee farmer, 27 March, 2009.
[111] "Ernesto" San Luis, 11 March 2009.

El agua, el suelo, la familia, el producto es más saludable. Nuestros padres aplicaban muchos productos químicos venenosos y nosotros y ellos vivíamos la intoxicación. Los niños recolectores de cerezas también fueron afectados.

[The water, the soil, the family, the produce is healthier. Our parents would apply lots of poisonous chemicals and we and they lived the intoxication. The children collecting cherries were also affected].[112]

The principal influence of reduced chemical use by small holding farmers was economic. Members of *Coope Sarapiquí* attributed organic practices to unaffordable agri-chemicals, implemented in consultation with MAG, ICAFE, INFOCOOP and other coffee cooperatives in the region, rather than by Fairtrade or RA. Fairtrade offers a price premium for organic practices. The manager of *Coope Santa Elena* explained that the work practices of a member group are 100 per cent organic, "pero esto no es debido a una certificación, es debido a la conciencia ambiental de los agricultores" [But this is not because of a certification, it is because of the farmers own environmental conscience].[113]

The producer perspective: the difficulty of assigning influence of change to certifications

In relation to the environment, several cooperative managers mentioned a continuing national effort toward sustainability:

Costa Rica siempre ha tenido el ambiente consciente. Desde los años 60/70 Costa Rica y Figueres, el presidente había comenzado la reforestación. Hemos tenido 50 años con este enfoque a través de la educación escolar. Es una estrategia nacional, una estrategia verde.

[Costa Rica has always had an environmental conscious. From the 1960/70s Costa Rica and Figueres, the president started reforestation. We have had 50 years with this focus through school education. It is a national strategy, a green strategy].[114, 115]

While not necessarily effective for the coffee industry during the green revolution, the quote indicates an ongoing effort from the government to create awareness and/or support conservation intentions. Changes in the Costa Rican coffee industry were however rarely identified as prompted or supported by a certification, and one representative of the Costa Rican coffee industry went

---

[112] "Esteban", coffee farmer, 26 March 2009.
[113] Cooperative manager, 11 March, 2009.
[114] For more information, visit http://www.rainforest-alliance.org/about.cfm
[115] Cooperative Manager, 16 March 2009.

as far as to say that, "la certificación Fairtrade no ha influido en la industria cafetalera en Costa Rica" [Fairtrade certification has not influenced the coffee industry in Costa Rica].[116] How influence is understood must then be considered, a change in mentality, in practice or encouraging and/or incentivizing after any change is made to ensure it continues. The manager of Coope Llano Bonito explained his understanding of the situation:

> Green Peace ha hecho más de un caso a conciencia que cualquier certificación. Los cambios en el uso de los productos químicos no son debido a una certificación es debido a nuestra propia conciencia. Costa Rica está muy informada por el gobierno y la ley – es obligatorio que productos químicos no se pueden usar… agua y desperdicio de agua, pero lo cierto es que no hay fondos para hacer estos cambios.
>
> [Green Peace has made more of a case to consciousness than any certification. The changes in use of chemicals are not because of a certification it is because of our own consciousness. Costa Rica is very informed by the government and the law – it is obligatory what chemicals you cannot use… water and waste of water but the thing is there are no funds to make these changes].[391]

While funds must also be sought out or used to implement standard criteria, this comment complements Steinberg's idea of the important role that environmental advocates play in influencing national environmental policy (Steinberg 2001, 51–76). Within these considerations and entry points for influence, the certifications could be interpreted as having a softer intra-market approach. That is, they reinforce a change that comes from within the business, within the market, rather than at a national policy and/or legal level, considered external to the business. How influencing change and consciousness is understood versus assisting standard implementation for changed practices could be further considered to complement the point made.

Frustration with Fairtrade

(Included in quantified summary, see table 8)

There were varying levels of frustration with the sustainability certification approach and one message is clear from all Fairtrade certified cooperatives. The praise that the certifications and specifically Fairtrade receive for their poverty reduction and sustainable development work is a cause for complaint when:

- It does not adequately or uniformly support the implementation of the standards;

---

[116] Director of *Café Forestal and Hijos del Campo*, 20 February, 2009.

- Is not considered to have influenced significant change and, is contrary to Fairtrade's stated objectives.
- Is locking farmers into a financial loss through a contractually fixed minimum price agreement.

Certifying existing practices?

The multi-entry point of influence for change in farming practices beyond international and certification activity was discussed by one cooperative manager. "No es solo Fairtrade que hace la diferencia en el parte social; es las otras actividades, las otras situaciones vividos por la cooperativa dentro del Mercado Nacional" [It is not just Fairtrade that makes the difference in the social part; it is the other activities, the other situations lived by the cooperative within the national market].[117] The standards introduced and intended for implementation on plantations or member farms are seen to reinforce the existing processes already used or required by law. "Están certificando lo que ya está allí, el Mercado pide café de sombra, así que obtenemos certificaciones RA, pero tengo que certificar lo que ya tengo" [They are certifying what already is there, the market asks for shade grown coffee, so we get RA certifications, but I have to certify what I already have].[118, 119] The Technical engineer and administrator of certifications for Coop El Dos explained and reinforced:

> Todas las normas son muy importantes, muy importantes. ¿Pero nuevas cosas? No, realmente no puedo decir que hay nuevas cosas que las certificaciones nos están ensenando porque las practicas que hemos estado llevando a cabo durante mucho tiempo, incluyendo la organización. Si nos organizamos, y aunque importante, también es algo que ya teníamos aquí.
>
> [All of the standards are very important, very important, but new things? No, really, I cannot say that there are new things that the certifications are teaching us because the practices we have been carrying out for a long time, including organisational. Yes, we organise ourselves, and although important, it is also something that we already had here].[395]

From these points of discussion, the function of certifications could be considered as additional or complementary to national policy and law, and existing practices.

---

[117] Cooperative manager, 12 February, 2009.
[118] Cooperative manager, 20 February 2009.
[119] Technical engineer and administrative manager for certification programs, 9 February, 2009.

Scope for improvement: more recent changes

While the recognition of change stimulated by certification is low, in the past few years Fairtrade has focused more on education for effective implementation of standards, related particularly to the environment.[120, 121] Although considered minimal, there were detailed standard criteria were identified as stimulating a change, in practice and in attitude. "Las granjas que no están certificadas por RA están atrasadas en uniformes, calidad de almacenamiento para productos químicos y educación, proveemos cuidado de niños para niños de obreros y cuidado de salud siempre por si acaso" [The farms that are not RA certified are behind in uniforms, quality of storage for chemicals and education, we provide childcare for labourers' children and health care always, just in case].[122]

> Este ano (Fairtrade) se ha vuelto muy estricto, ya que sus estándares están cambiando totalmente y lo sentimos mucho más y tenemos mucho que cambiar para cumplir con los nuevos estándares y todavía estamos trabajando en esto a nivel de Coocafe. Están trabajando de un sistema de control y revisión de la implementación de las normas.
>
> [This year (Fairtrade) became very strict, as their standards are totally changing and we felt it much more, and we have a lot to change to become compliant with the new standards and we are still working on this at the level of Coocafe. They are working on a system of control and revising the implementation of the standards].[123]

As with changes required by national law, changes in standards come at a cost. "Ahora estamos buscando fondos y explicando a nuestros miembros porque tienen que construir un espacio de almacenamiento personal para productos químicos" [We are now looking for funds and explaining to our members why they have to construct a personal storage space for chemicals].[124] Each certification has a plan for reducing the use of toxic chemicals on farm and this has assisted in educating and facilitating a reduction in incremental stages. Despite these recent organisational level changes, neither Fairtrade nor RA are considered to have had a major influence in stimulating change toward sustainable practices for small holding coffee farmers.

---

[120] Cooperative manager, 11 March 2009.
[121] Technical engineer and administrative manager for certification programs, 9 February, 2009.
[122] Administrator of certification programs, 25 February, 2009.
[123] Technical engineer and administrative manager for certification programs, 9 February, 2009.
[124] Cooperative manager, 11 March, 2009.

*Requirements for implementation:
Minimal support or building capacity?*

(Included in quantified summary, see table 8)

Ensuring that all farms are compliant to a standard is necessary to demonstrate implementation and ensure associated outcomes. It seems the FLOCert approach to monitoring is not effective in knowing if 100% compliance to the standard is occurring. The comparison that *Coopepueblos* was able to make between the implementation of a university study carried out on many members' farms and the implementation of Fairtrade standards indicated a gap between being certified and knowing the compliance *status* of each member farm:

> Tenemos un estudiante que esta hacienda un estudio de las granjas para desarrollar su propia certificación o estándar. Estará aquí por un ano. A partir de este estudio podemos ver exactamente lo que hay en la finca de cada miembro, van de finca a finca, ver cuantos arboles hay y podemos ver lo que podemos mejorar. Cuando Fairtrade viene no van a todas las fincas y las pagamos, mientras que este estudio que es gratis ha ido a todas las granjas. Así que ahora sabemos exactamente lo que hay en cada finca. Es un estudio real, más real que el comercio justo. Fairtrade visita 5 de las 50 finca, no siquiera es lo mismo.
>
> [We have a student who is doing a study of the farms to develop his own certification or standard. He will be here for a year. From this study we can see exactly what there is on every member's farm, they go farm by farm, seeing how many trees there are, and we can see what we can improve. When Fairtrade comes, they do not go to every farm and we pay them whereas this study, which is free, has gone to all the farms. So now we know exactly what there is in every farm. It is a real study, more real than Fairtrade. Fairtrade visits 5 out of 50 farms, it is not nearly the same].[125]

Assistance toward an educated change in social and environmental standards is supported by various government and non-governmental programs. Several Costa Rican institutions can provide support including MAG, ICAFE, CATIE, UNDP, foreign and local universities, and research institutes. As the manager of Coope Santa Elena explained. "No tengo ningún problema en ir y buscar apoyo y siempre encuentro algo, del gobierno o de un instituto de investigación, está ahí" [I have no problem going and looking for support and I always find some, from the government or a research institute, it is there].[126] While the option or

---

[125] Cooperative manager, 20 February, 2009.
[126] Cooperative manager, 11 March, 2009.

indeed the need to seek out this financial and technical support is positive, it also highlights a fine line between capability building through providing minimal support and expecting too much. Complementary to these considerations is the cost involved in implementation.

Summary

Certification efforts intend to improve economic, societal and environmental outcomes for certified producers and perhaps for the producer community. While initial intentions vary by certification premise and approach, both RA and Fairtrade have adjusted standards over the years to become more similar. Ensuring implementation is the easiest way to demonstrate improvement. Fairtrade is arguably operating in a more complex space, there are multiple farms to work with and to monitor for standard implementation and the minimum price and price premium are also distinct from other certifications. The space within which RA and Fairtrade certifications operate leaves scope for interpretation of intentions for producer countries alongside their necessary marketing efforts to maintain or increase market access. Marketing efforts and eventual reputation of certifications appeared almost grandiose and, in some cases, simply inaccurate where compared to the reality of operation and implementation in Costa Rica in 2009 and compared to actual outcomes. The marketing claims where accessible in producing countries do leave producer groups wondering how certifications can possibly claim or portray such outcomes as solely their doing. There was an ongoing frustration felt toward Fairtrade and all certifications for this reason amongst other factors.

Sustainability and conservation efforts in Costa Rica over decades sought to resolve the green revolution to tip or force a reduction in chemical use and diversification on farms. Certifying existing practices and requiring implementation of standards with no support offered are two commonly identified issues and sources of frustration with certifications.

RA appears to allow the business to regain financial ground with a superior price for certified coffee sold, their standards and approach did not however appear useful or appropriate for small farm holdings at that time. Fairtrade was also ensuring a financial loss while increasing standard requirements and associated investment for compliance. This contradiction becomes more obvious and frustration grows where an alternative and superior system operates in the same community as was observed in Agua Buena. There is therefore some work to be done to find a balance between certification requirements and the realities of the producer community and country. During 2009, any adjustments in certification requirements had not managed to iron out all observed kinks, and closer to 2014 some of the certified cooperatives visited had closed, possibly caused by how appropriate a landscape was for coffee farming, and dissatisfaction with cooperative structure and processes. An increasing preference for individual farmer operations and independent trade partners, and micromill associations was evident. Popularity of sustainability certifications in Costa Rica had declined which can be attributed to inconsistency in improvement, and to alternatives which provide superior price, but may or may not be adequately sustainable by standards encouraged (Vogt 2019c).

CHAPTER 12

Reinforcing international trade power dynamics?

(Included in quantified summary, see table 8)

Introduction

Fair trade originally represented direct trade between small farm holders and small coffee roasters and retailers. While small roasters have developed a strong and growing presence in the international coffee market, increasing the market share of specialty coffee, their representation and strength across the entire international coffee market is small. As larger corporations and plantations maintain greater power (Ponte 2004; Terazono 2013; ITC 2011) through provision of and access to market opportunities and by selecting which farms are sourced from and which practices are therefore encouraged, a centralisation of power remains. A "centralisation of power over the cultural flows that shape preferences are a subtler form of *unfreedom* than those that Sen highlights but no less powerful" (Evans 2002, 59). How and whether the certification standards and processes re-balance existing trade dynamics requires consideration. The need to increase market demand for certified coffee is an issue identified for Fairtrade (Murray et al. 2003, 23; ITC 2017) and relies on dealing with larger corporations and market players unless small roasters can significantly increase their market share. RA has entered the certified market of many countries through these larger market players with limited contrary ideas due to their certifying plantations more than producer groups.

Increasing certified markets and resulting compromises

Demand and awareness are starting points for expanding certified markets but distribution to allow purchase is also necessary for such a formula to succeed.

How to cite this book chapter:
Vogt, M. 2019. *Variance in Approach Toward a 'Sustainable' Coffee Industry in Costa Rica: Perspectives from Within; Lessons and Insights.* Pp. 143–148. London: Ubiquity Press. DOI: https://doi.org/10.5334/bce.n. License: CC-BY 4.0

To increase certified markets, Fairtrade has been seeking to develop relationships and secure contracts with larger market players. These MNCs represent an opportunity for the Fairtrade label to increase brand salience, distribution and sale of certified products. An increase in sales of certified coffee is a benefit for certified producers. MNCs have established distribution channels that Fairtrade can piggyback on for increased market presence while the MNC benefits from positive brand association. Despite criticism that MNCs are not 100% certified, Fairtrade defends these relationships seeing the benefit of MNCs' involvement as financial risk mitigation and only those products bought under the standards and conditions of Fairtrade hold and display the label.[127] Permitting MNCs to trade Fairtrade products could be considered a conflict of interest, or a marketing ploy however a need to increase certified markets must be considered. The certified products they source, and sell are also 100% Fairtrade certified.

Voluntary regulation and vulnerability to power dynamics
Interdependence between corporation and certification

Complementary to considerations of standards and approaches of each certification regarding inclusion and participation of producers, how international trade dynamics are managed through certified market channels is a relevant consideration. Despite being a regulatory mechanism, contracts drawn up between the producer and buyer/*consumer* governed and limited by certification standards are vulnerable to power relations. The inter-dependence of the corporation and certification organisation is an evaluation topic for consideration alongside the producer, buyer dynamic. For the certifying organisation, financial viability depends on demand for their label and purchasing power. RA primarily negotiates and engages with larger firms and causes less controversy for certified plantation instead of producer groups. There is limited explicit marketing and standards related to social justice also as RA does not seek to negotiate for producers nor be 'in the middle' of these two stakeholders. In 2003, RA signed memoranda of understanding with Volcafe Group and Neumann Kaffee Gruppe (Alvarez et al. 2015). In 2018 Nespresso was sourcing 40% RA certified coffee (RA 2019).

Fairtrade standards by comparison are specific to producer groups/cooperatives of small holding coffee farmers. The space and conditions for negotiation within contracts are covered by Fairtrade standards and are, therefore, theoretically regulated by FLOCert. While maintaining the Fairtrade floor price, the agreed upon and fixed price should be at the discretion of the producer group not the buyer according to Fairtrade standards. The allowance of MNCs

---

[127] Only a percentage of Nestlé's product line is Fairtrade certified as it is not a Fairtrade certified company.

to trade through these channels raises issues of monitoring the negotiation process which is difficult and ultimately left to the two parties involved. If the balance of negotiating power leans toward the buyer, the price negotiated despite the context of a voluntary standard will depend on the negotiating ability of a producer organisation rather than regulation of a standard. Fairtrade has not demonstrated effective at ensuring contractual agreements are in the best interest of the producer. Starbucks's tendency to negotiate a low price was mentioned in 2009 interviews. Some cooperatives successfully negotiated an above minimum price; other cooperatives prefer to avoid dealing with the consistent pressure to lower the price:

> Starbucks aseguraran que paguen el precio mínimo pero este ano tuvimos un problema porque el precio mínimo del comercio justo es $1.87 por quintal. Vendimos a Starbucks con contratos abiertos. El contrato abierto es el precio de mercado de Nueva York y un adicional de 36 centavos este contrato no tenía un precio fijo. Todavía dependía del precio de mercado de Nueva York. Hubo un tiempo cuando el precio cayo a $1.51 que es de $1.87 y Starbucks era bastante exigente que fijamos el precio en ese punto. Hubo una gran discusión y debate que dijimos que no estamos de acuerdo, no estamos fijando el precio ahora. Finalmente llegaron a un acuerdo.
>
> [Starbucks ensure they pay the minimum price but this year we had a problem because the minimum Fairtrade price is $1.87 per quintal. We sold to Starbucks with open contracts. The open contract is the NY market price and an additional 36 cents, this contract did not have a fixed price; it was still reliant on the NY market price. There was a time when the price fell to $1.51 which is $1.87, and Starbucks was pretty much demanding that we fix the price at that point. There was a big discussion and debate we said that we are not agreeing, we are not fixing the price now. They eventually agreed].[128]

Issues with Starbucks are relevant as they planned in 2009 to source all coffee through Fairtrade and C.A.F.E. Practices channels. Yet according to an international marketing manager of a Fairtrade certified cooperative, "decidimos no vender más a Starbucks. Negociaciones con Starbucks, ¿querían negociar el precio? Si siempre" [We decided to not sell to Starbucks anymore. Negotiations with Starbucks-did they want to negotiate the price? Yes, always].[129] Negotiations through Fairtrade certified market channels can strengthen the leverage of producers and the negotiations are not exclusive to price:

---

[128] Cooperative Manager, 12 February 2009.
[129] International Marketing Manager 11 May 2009.

Había un comerciante en los Países Bajos que se quejó de que el precio se basa en mediciones de libra, que quería en kilogramos o en toneladas. Enviamos una carta a Fairtrade que estábamos cumpliendo con los criterios, no lo fueron. El problema es que muchos de los países centroamericanos se quedan callados. Tenemos un poco más de experiencia y tenemos 55 compradores en el mercado así que podemos decir que si no lo vendemos a otra persona y eso es todo. Esto no es realmente el case para otros países.

[There was a trader in the Netherlands who complained that the price is based on pound measurements, he wanted it in kilograms or in tons. We sent a letter to Fairtrade that we were compliant with the criteria, they were not. The problem is that a lot of the Central American countries stay quiet. We have a little more experience and we have 55 buyers in the market so we can say if we do not sell it to you, we will sell it to someone else and that is it. This is not really the case for other countries].[130]

The above examples demonstrate the capability of cooperative managers to negotiate effectively with clients *through* the Fairtrade system. It seems that context and negotiating power can influence whether:

- A fixed price is negotiated at the discretion of the producer not the buyer.
- Monitoring of a negotiation process is ultimately left to the two parties involved. This is distinct from negotiation *with* Fairtrade where the voice of producers is not always heard.[131, 132]

Power dynamics between producers and certifications

A meeting between Coocafe and Fairtrade representatives was scheduled in 2008 to negotiate an increase in Fairtrade's minimum price. The development of functioning capabilities relies on the real participation of farmers in the Fairtrade system which is an intention of Fairtrade. Fairtrade intends to provide the opportunity for producer groups to participate and have their critical voice heard, however, for Costa Rican coffee producers this is yet to happen. "El productor que escuchan mínimamente. Escuchan más a los tostadores y minoristas" [the producer they listen to minimally. They listen more to the roasters and retailer].[133] "Coocafe es el que se involucre en este… No sentimos que tenemos

---

[130] Ibid.
[131] International marketing manager, 11 May, 2009.
[132] Cooperative manager, 13 April, 2009.
[133] Cooperative Manager, 13 April 2009.

la fuerza para cambiar el precio" [Coocafe is the one that gets involved in this.... we do not feel that we have the strength to change the price].[134] It seems that for the Costa Rican context, farmer involvement and consultation with Fairtrade happens at levels quite distanced from the farming community. Effective representation of 'farmer' opinions would therefore rely on strong internal consultation processes of each cooperative.

Monitoring producers more than traders and roasters

Another criticism of RA and Fairtrade certification programs is the fact that only the producer organisation is audited for compliance to the certification standards, not the trader or roaster.

> Estas certificaciones nos están cobrando mucho y Fairtrade 'aquí arriba' revisan todo, la transparencia económica, etc., pero la gente, la gente en el centro, no. Nos quejamos a Fairtrade directamente.
> [These certifications are charging us a lot and Fairtrade 'up here' they review everything, economic transparency etc. but the people, the people in the centre, no. We complained to Fairtrade directly].[135]

SAN is looking at developing standards for roasters and retailers involved in the supply chain. In 2009, audits were carried out most consistently at the producer level and variably at the trader and roaster level.

Summary

There are twenty-five million farmers working to supply the world with coffee and a handful of companies hold purchasing power in the industry. To increase sale of certified products and market share, certifications must engage with MNCs. This growth can only be positive if they are able to maintain their objectives while doing business with such powerful stakeholders. The voluntary regulatory approach alongside such power dynamics suggest two scenarios. The first that implementation and correct process may more easily move to the MNC's orientation and interest particularly where the certifications require the MNC's for market access, despite standards requiring the opposite. The second is that the MNCs prefer such scope and therefore uptake of certifications will increase which is considered as positive; apart from an increase in scenario one.

In these situations, producers' voice within the Fairtrade process might not result in improved conditions, as fairtrade and other certifications find a need

---

[134] Ibid.
[135] International Marketing Manager, 11 May 2009.

to satisfy what is necessary to achieve an increase in certified products available in the market and sales. Maintaining the producer voice and involvement does however allow a level of understanding of their point of view and within specific situations and contexts ensuring the standard is followed and having Fairtrade take on the role to mediate such situation at the very least provides a level of security and support not always available through other certifications.

CHAPTER 13

Summative discussion

Introduction

Sustainability certifications generate outcomes and influence through philosophical understanding of sustainability. Standards, and approach to encouraging implementation and monitoring of compliance are subsequently influenced. For the coffee industry there are aspects of sustainability to consider and perhaps favour, including the size of the farm certified and how that ultimately contributes to improved sustainability including poverty reduction. Certifying plantations compared to producer groups, or small farm holdings is an important consideration when determining how each certification contributes to sustainability outcomes in Costa Rica. The existing structure of international coffee industry leaves producer groups "relatively poor in a rich community" (Sen 1999, 71). The difficulty of maintaining a family, the crop and labourers on a small coffee farm was commonly identified and communicated in interviews, reinforcing the importance of supporting small farmers (IFAD 2010), and building collective capabilities (Sen 2002). The environmental implications of plantations versus small farm holdings is another relevant consideration, as are hired labour situations.

A social and environmental approach for small farm holdings would therefore be necessarily different to plantations, as requirements are distinct. In contrast, a RA certified plantation manager did not consider the coffee industry a challenge,[136, 137] one administrator clearly states, "no es difícil vender el café"

---

[136] Farm administrator, 17 February 2009.
[137] Administrator of certifications, 25 February 2009.

How to cite this book chapter:
Vogt, M. 2019. *Variance in Approach Toward a 'Sustainable' Coffee Industry in Costa Rica: Perspectives from Within; Lessons and Insights.* Pp. 149–166. London: Ubiquity Press. DOI: https://doi.org/10.5334/bce.o. License: CC-BY 4.0

[it is not difficult to sell coffee].[239] The situation between coffee farmers does therefore differ, and while sharing similar experiences, routines and cultures they should not be assumed as a homogenous group within the coffee industry. Land holding size is only one differentiating factor.

Certifications as intra-market voluntary systems operate amongst a range of efforts that are intra and extra-market. Policy, law, company codes of conduct, non-governmental organisation efforts, and educational organisations are examples. While RA entered the market with an idea of being an NGO and not for profit, Fairtrade entered the market as a direct trade model of business which adapted to become an external to business certification process. Instead of being a strictly in-producer community NGO they intertwined with international and national supply chain dynamics, and more so as they seek to increase market reach and uptake from the larger corporations and businesses of the coffee industry. Certifications are not necessarily in the middle of these dynamics, but they do need to interact with them. How and whether they are in the middle of these dynamics depends on the certification and their sustainability intention and philosophy.

All certifications regulate implementation voluntarily with compulsory monitoring, beneficial for uptake as repercussions for non-compliance are light. This lighter approach taken by certifications compared to legal requirements can also reinforce existing power dynamics through negotiation of implementing processes, an ability to avoid regulation, and little repercussion for non-compliance. In addition to regulating compliance, the intentions and outcomes of Fairtrade and RA can misalign, as already discussed, and imbalance between numerous stakeholders involved can also occur. As certifications adjust standards, organisational structure and process, and, where applicable, stakeholder involvement, alignment of outcomes with intentions varied over time dependent on standard quality and effective implementation. Changes in any of these aspects was not therefore synonymous with changes in outcomes.

Considerations and concerns identified

From the in-country perspectives and observations presented in chapter 6 to 12, some common considerations and concerns were identified:

- Stately marketing claims;
- Expense and resources required for effective implementation;
- Inadequate resource support for implementation, particularly where comparative systems operate alongside and demonstrate better outcomes for producer communities;
- Forced financial loss for producer groups; and
- Limited effective producer participation in Fairtrade certification processes.

all contributed to an idea from Costa Rican producers that certifications were in 2009 a whim of the market.

Outcomes associated with RA and Fairtrade

The philosophical difference between the RA and Fairtrade approach to sustainability and then how it is intended through certification is highlighted here. RA demonstrated most effective for larger plantations which is where their attention originated, while Fairtrade only certifies small farmers and small producer groups. As more small farmer groups were interviewed compared to larger plantation, the findings in this monograph reveal more about Fairtrade compared to RA. Whether certifying larger plantations compared to small producer groups improves sustainability outcomes or vice versa is not addressed at length or in detail in this monograph but could be in the future. RA and Fairtrade have created significant opportunity and benefit for producers and their communities within sustainability areas. RA was not however successful in certifying small producer groups and their small producer group standard required improvement for local community appropriateness. Fairtrade by comparison was locking Costa Rican coffee farmers into a loss. This was happening in two ways.

The first is economic in that the minimum price and contract detail did often lock in a percentage of harvest dedicated to the Fairtrade market at an immediate financial loss due to cost of production. Compounding this foundational issue is the cost of introducing and implementing new and existing standards and the cost of auditing compliance. The 'lock' of a minimum low price not only limits effective implementation of the standards as implementation represents an increase in time and cost for producers and their organisations. Contract negotiation was subject to producer discretion according to the Fairtrade standard however FLOcert variably regulated this aspect.

The second is involvement and influence within the Fairtrade and RA system, directly related to centralised power dynamics. Capacity building in terms of international networking and political activism for the coffee industry were identified as benefits of the Fairtrade system. Producer groups are allowed and invited to sit at the table, listen and speak but do not seem to have the necessary bargaining power to affect decision-making within the Fairtrade system. The power in the Fairtrade network is perceived to sit with the roasters and retailers rather than with the producers, which can also influence how and whether Fairtrade will effectively intervene in contract negotiations that do not respect reasonable producer discretion or preference. Centralised decision-making structures and limited functioning collective capabilities (World Bank 2000/2001; Sen 2002) in a system that is aiming to reduce poverty is a contradiction.¹³⁸ The lack of effective participation of small producer groups in the Fairtrade system can therefore be considered an indicator of poverty.

An economic loss

The certification role aligns with a first attempt socially conscious, not for profit business which operates external to the sourcing and trading company. The learning curve and mishaps that occurred while they experimented with this organisational model, by location amongst business, NGO, and law, and amongst existing sustainability efforts were occasionally at the expense of the producer. At the time of interviews, the price offered by Fairtrade to certified cooperatives was not considered attractive. The Fairtrade minimum price was often locking cooperatives into the contracted stable minimum price compared to conventional market prices for a percentage of their harvest over time. This consequently left the cooperative and producers with the choice of either mitigating risk with a stable price which might not cover an increasing cost of production nor the cost of being certified but would if the international coffee price reduced as it did in 2001. Or, earning significantly more per pound through uncertified markets when conventional coffee prices exceed the Fairtrade minimum price with no secured minimum price. For RA certified plantations the cost of becoming certified made financial sense with RA certified markets paying well above the high conventional market rate in 2009. RA certified small producer groups did not however report the same level of financial benefit.

The issue with the Fairtrade minimum price and the standard price paid through RA markets relates to the cost and the identified financial risk of becoming certified for small producer groups. "Es difícil justificar el pago de una certificación cuando no hay garantía o certeza de que se pagara un mejor precio" [It is difficult to justify paying for a certification when there is no assurance or certainty that a better price will be paid].¹³⁹ Strict requirements for existing certification schemes therefore make it difficult for resource poor producers to risk changing production methods for the supposedly more lucrative alternative of certification through access to markets (Garcia, 2006; 5). Deciding whether to adopt an additional certification standard is therefore a significant decision for a cooperative. When deciding if becoming certified by RA was a rational decision for a cooperative:

---

¹³⁸ The issue of participation in standard development is extremely important in relation to consultation with seasonal worker populations; however, that is not explored in this thesis which focuses on the producer groups' effective participation within the FLO system.

¹³⁹ Previous cooperative manager, coffee farmer and cooperative member, 12 January, 2009.

La primera pregunta de los agricultores es, '¿Cuánto más nos van a pagar para ser certificados?' Entonces,' ¿Cuál es la diferencia entre esta certificación y otra certificación?' Otros preguntan, '¿por qué no combinamos lo que ya tenemos dentro de Fairtrade y fortalecemos los estándares ambientales?'

[The first question from farmers is, 'How much more are they going to pay us to become certified?' Then, 'What is the difference between this certification and another certification?' Others ask, 'Why do not we combine what we already have within Fairtrade and strengthen the environmental standards?'].[140]

In the eyes of the cooperative managers and employees interacting with the Fairtrade or RA systems, both are an arm of the market and their financial expense tends to outweigh their financial benefit. The cost of auditing is commonly identified with complaint. Issues with the cost of auditing increased when alternative systems developed in the same community:

En fairtrade tenemos que invertir en un auditor, con CAN que nos dan asesoramiento técnico de forma gratuita. Con Fairtrade, los precios no son tan justos, por el momento Fairtrade no cubra el costo de producción para la cooperativa o las granjas. Tenemos un mercado fuera de Fairtrade que es $2.08, esto es más que Fairtrade. Vendemos 75% al mercado Fairtrade.

[In Fairtrade we must invest in an auditor, with CAN they give us technical advice for free. With Fairtrade, the prices are not so fair, at the moment Fairtrade is not covering the cost of production for the cooperative or the farms. We have a market outside of Fairtrade which is $2.08, this is more than Fairtrade. We sell 75% to the Fairtrade market].[141]

The cost of becoming certified for small producers compared to benefit

The cost function of certification presents problems for producers and is compounded when the amount of money circulating within the certification organisations, identified by wages paid to certification employees[142], is inconsistent with the producer experience. The RA certified plantation approach is more expensive for cooperatives in comparison to Fairtrade, as every farm is certified separately, rather than at the cooperative level. While a producer group

---

[140] Ibid.
[141] Cooperative manager, 25 February, 2009.
[142] Previous cooperative manager, coffee farmers and cooperative member, 12 January, 2009.

standard was developing in 2009, "[Era] más caro certificar muchas granjas, ya que Rainforest está acostumbrado a certificar las plantaciones. Esto hace que sea más caro" [it [was] more expensive to certify a lot of farms, as Rainforest is accustomed to certifying plantations. This makes it more expensive].[143] The issue of cost of production also extends to regional competition:

> El aumento de los costos de producción para nosotros también trae problemas de competencia en la región, una persona de Alemania nos llama y dice, 'Comprare comercio justo, pero en Nicaragua lo venden por 97 centavos y usted está vendiendo por $1.73, ¿verdad?' No paga la seguridad social, hay muchos factores y tengo todo el derecho a cobrar más porque hay costos que no podemos evitar.
>
> [The higher costs of production for us also bring problems of competition in the region, a person from Germany rings and says, 'I will buy Fairtrade but in Nicaragua they will sell it for 97 cents, and you are selling for $1.73, right?' Nicaragua does not pay social security, there are many factors and I have every right to charge more because there are costs that we cannot avoid].[144]

Fairtrade offers producer participation and voice through the organisational process and support to ensure international trade dynamics are informally regulated by Fairtrade.

Producer voice in Fairtrade organisational processes

The ability to effectively participate and influence fairtrade standards and processes also resulted in a loss for producers. Fairtrade seeks to support producers through producer services and relations, liaison officers, producer certification funds (for new entrants), providing information and training for producers, coordination of global Fairtrade strategy and promoting trade justice through the Fair Trade Advocacy Office. The Fairtrade standards and approach dictate interest and approach to the lobbying message. Fairtrade, alongside WFTO Network of European World Shops (NEWS) and European Fair Trade Association (EFTA) monitors European and International trade and development policies and ensures "a consistent dialogue between the Fairtrade movement and political decision makers, funded by the Fair trade movement." Whose voice this Office represents is a finer detail. The opportunity for producer involvement in the Fairtrade organisational process offered a glimmer of hope that such concerns related to minimum price would be effectively addressed in a timely manner. It would only be so where such involvement was effective and

---

[143] Ibid.
[144] International marketing manager, 11 May, 2009.

where an increase in price would not jeopardise Fairtrade operations. It seems having a producer's voice heard in the Fairtrade system has been a challenge for active producer groups.[145, 146, 147]

The challenge of adequately involving producer groups for Fairtrade

For Costa Rican fairtrade certified coffee producer groups the challenge to project their voices and develop their decision-making capabilities within the system remains. Some producer groups have successfully negotiated disputes with clients through the Fairtrade system. Fairtrade's dependence on major market players for mainstream market access is a result of a financial relationship where MNCs have, 'provide[d] most of the cash for their operating budgets' (Earley in Hutchens 2007). Fairtrade is ultimately reliant on funding from roasters, and producer cooperatives are reliant on Fairtrade to access markets. The dynamic created implies an indirect reliance of producers on buyers with Fairtrade standards becoming something of an ineffective mediating mechanism. Larger corporations will often become certified as suits strategic ambitions, producer groups might not because of financial constraints. This situation is similar for any certification which must be paid for by the producer.

RA and Fairtrade develop standards at an international level, and this can jeopardize stated intentions by denying producer inclusion and participation. Subsequently the development of collective capabilities and appropriateness of standards is limited. Producers can choose to participate in the Fairtrade system, there was not however sufficient scope for effective or influential participation or for adjusting standards to local conditions and capabilities. While SAN develops local indicators, they did not include coffee in Costa Rica in 2009, nor do they seek to include farm managers in organisational procedures. In addition, the approach to implementation and regulation was not proving effective or appropriate for the small producer group, local context.

Hired labour standards

Hired labour standards can present cultural considerations in any given context (Vogt 2019b). The coffee industry in Costa Rica relies significantly on migrant labour, particularly for harvest. The labour standards for RA and Fairtrade were also therefore an area for attention when considering sustainability outcomes. The Fairtrade hired labour standard did not adequately require compliance by small producers through their organisation or directly and failed to address

---

[145] Cooperative Manager, 11 May 2009.
[146] Cooperative Manager, 31 March 2009.
[147] International Marketing Manager, 11 May, 2009.

common issues facing seasonal workers on small coffee farms. The hired labour criteria, part of the SAN standard, was quite detailed, however, some community level adaptions were necessary. Migrant workers will continue to present issues for consideration and action within a sustainability consideration. They currently expose a divide between what the state requires; what the certifications require, and what businesses and farmers are realistically capable of providing, particularly when taking the mobility of these workers into consideration.

Formalised land title

Sustainability certifications by intention and standard operation work to improve sustainability in legally viable business; producer, trader, roaster or retailer (where relevant). From in-country perspectives the requirement that farmers hold formal title was an identified problem and barrier to being certified. Holding formal land title does not necessarily solve a poverty issue, although it might in some situations. In certain countries, formal land title might be unrealistic for numerous reasons including how the government manages and permits these titles. In Costa Rica it was observed as an existing point of contention for coffee farmers already presenting barriers to benefiting from environmental policies related to reforestation on farm, and now to being certified.

Certifications: labels and market-based reputation

Educating consumers through labelling and branding to become more aware of how their products are sourced and traded is not an invaluable activity (Vogt 2019b). It could be considered an initial process in shifting consumer opinion and behaviour which is and, particularly in the early 2000s, was, necessary. To manage the need for business-based incentive, positive association with these sustainability logos for brand salience or equity was often considered an argument for use. The positive association was only substantiated where consumers believed that what the label represented worked. What sustainability certifications are capable of and intending can often be overestimated, with expectations, set through marketing, reaching further than what is realistically possible. While cooperatives play a significant role in reducing the length of the sourcing chain Fairtrade certification was not a guarantee of protection against the significant challenges experienced in the coffee industry, particularly for coffee farmers that were already struggling for a variety of reasons. Environmental and socially sustainable farming practices were considered due to several factors, some external to certification systems. They include the high cost of chemicals, the environmental conscience of the nation, human rights and environmental activist organisations, national research centres, international university exchanges, multi-sectoral partnerships and government programs.

The alignment of intention compared to outcome varied for RA and FLO across different topics in 2009 and was overall inconsistent due to contextually inappropriate standards, or ineffective implementation. Certainly, significant misalignment between intentions of each certification and outcomes were observed, with more emphasis on sustainable business for a few stakeholders rather than sustainability. In 2009, implementing 'sustainable' standards was often unrealistic for producer groups due to financial or resource constraints. Within this situation, certifications often receive criticism for leaving the more disadvantaged producer groups out of certified markets. While these challenges are unresolved and misaligned intentions to outcomes continue, the actual purpose of the certifications and what they are, amongst all sustainability efforts and mechanisms is certainly questioned in Costa Rica. Shadows of doubt developed by 2009, and questions as to who was benefiting did emerge in interviews. It will therefore be important to clearly communicate what each certification is seeking to achieve and better ensure appropriate standards and effective implementation to allow a label and market based reputation to also mean something positive in producer communities and countries.

Quantified summary of key topics against poverty reduction indicators

To complement the consideration of positive outcomes, a quantified summary of how relevant topics identified through fieldwork and as presented in this section associate with poverty reduction indicators is presented in table 8. Key topics identified through triangulation of information collected through fieldwork and complementary literature informed headings provided in chapter 6–13. Several of these topics and subheadings were selected as relevant to poverty reduction indicators. They are organised in table 8 in the first column. Poverty reduction indicators were selected based on Townsend (1980) and Sen (1999) considerations and definitions of multi-dimensional poverty, explained in chapter 2. They include capability to achieve the functioning they choose; social and community relations; health; social security; assets; infrastructure, water, roads etc.; participation in decision making; empowerment; earning power. Where a subheading through chapters 6–13 is included in the quantified summary, the relevant indicator is noted below the subheading.

Poverty reduction performance are numbered at 50 positives, and 29 negatives. The ratings are not certification or alternative effort specific by this count but are listed as such in the table. The influence of an increasing number of certifications was most commonly identified as negatively rated. There are however additional considerations moving forward, including how the benefit of access to more markets might counteract the required juggle of certifications

Table 8: Accumulated poverty reduction indicators and outcomes by identified issue.

	1	2	3	4	5	6	7	8	9
	Capability to achieve the functionings they choose	Social and Community Relations	Health	Social Security	Assets	Infrastructure: water, roads etc.	Participation in decision making	Empowerment	Earning power
Subtler Advantages									
Redistributing national power dynamics	Positive	Positive					Positive	Positive	Positive
Orientation in International market							Positive	Positive	Positive
Access to credit	Positive (FI[149])								
The 'cost' of certifications									
FI minimum price[1]		Positive					Negative[2]	Negative	Negative (FI) Positive (RA)
FI Premium[3]	Positive	Positive	Positive		Positive	Positive	Positive	Positive	Negative
Accumulate: FI premium compensating for minimum price	Positive						Positive		Positive

Summative discussion

Standards	FI	RA					
Approach by each certification	Positive	Positive				Positive	Positive
						Positive	
Inappropriate standards							
Water management & RA	Negative (RA)	Negative (RA)		Negative (RA)	Negative (RA)	Negative (RA)	
FI minimum price	Negative (FI)						Negative
Labour standards	Positive (RA) Positive (FI)	Positive (RA)	Positive (RA)	Positive (RA)		Positive (RA)	Positive (RA)\ Negative (FI)
Transparency and Independent Monitoring							Negative (FI)

Continued

[149] Fairtrade International (FI).

Table 8: Continued

	1	2	3	4	5	6	7	8	9
	Capability to achieve the functionings they choose	Social and Community Relations	Health	Social Security	Assets	Infrastructure: water, roads etc.	Participation in decision making	Empowerment	Earning power
Increasing number of certifications									
Top down approach	Negative (RA in one circumstance, and FI)						Negative (FI)	Negative (FI)	Negative (FI)
Satisfaction with FI	Negative	Negative						Negative	Negative
Recent changes		Positive	Positive			Positive			
Support for implementation	Positive (Government and CAN)						Negative (FI)	Negative (FI) Positive (Government) Positive (CAN)	
Rationale for interpreting reinforced international supply chain dynamics	Negative	Negative					Negative	Negative	Negative

Alternatives	1	2	3	4	5	6	7	8	9
Locally developed standards	Positive	Positive					Positive	Positive	
Vertical integration of supply chain		Positive	Positive		Positive		Positive	Positive	Positive
Locally developed standards partnered with vertical integration and direct trade	Positive	Positive	Positive	Positive	Positive	Positive	Positive	Positive	Positive

1. *Indicators may become irrelevant where the minimum price doesn't cover cost of production; and the premium is then used to supplement income. This would move the indicator to 9 as positive; but the underlying cause for one indicator satisfied rather than multiple is the same certification.*

2. *Between farmer/cooperative and certification; and between buyer and farmer/cooperative.*

3. *Dependent on how premium is spent. Important to note that where the minimum price does not cover cost of production or allow a profit, the premium can be used to supplement farmer income directly. This will remove all associated positive indicators and outcomes apart from reinforcing indicator 1 & 7. It offers improved earning power but does not ensure adequate earning power.*

compared to being certified to only one scheme. It is likely and expected that several other topics could be taken from these chapters and from future considerations and considered against these poverty reduction indicators. It is also suggested that a similar range of indicators for sustainability, such as those available from the SDGs could also be used to consider and rate key topics identified through these interviews, and future considerations related to sustainability certifications in Costa Rica

A whim of the market

RA and Fairtrade certifications must be paid for by the producer organisation or business, and licensing to sell a product with the certification label carries a fee. The upfront costs of Fairtrade and RA has prevented some cooperatives in Costa Rica from experiencing a positive financial return. The limited benefit in this sense is more influential when the intended increase in price through certified market sales is not realised. The appropriateness of standards and their actual sustainability is an additional concern. The financial side of certifications represent frustration for producer groups, while the certifications appear to be more influenced by stakeholders in the international market. An increase in sustainability labels also evidences preference for buyer market requirements or benefiting from certification effort rather than a coordination for the benefit of producing communities or countries. Amongst the variable benefits and disadvantages of being certified by one certification label, the demand for different certifications only increases complication and variability in benefit compared to disadvantage.

In Costa Rica, several cooperatives were becoming certified by more than one standard to access different certified markets. The resulting juggle and resource expense to implement and effectively monitor implementation of several international standards of variable effectiveness or appropriateness was identified through interview comments. As a newly emerging trend in 2009 the internal amalgamation of standards for a producer group and merging of some certifications present opportunities for producer groups and organisations dedicated to certified markets. It is not however considered an appropriate situation for all producer groups, and most likely only appropriate where the producer group has adequate resources and/or a stable footing in and experience with the international market.

The accumulating cost of certification and keeping up with the demand for different certifications was leading to the common observation that certifications are "puramente un capricho del Mercado y del consumidor" [purely the whim of the market and the consumer].[149] "Hay una preocupación de que las certificaciones se han convertido en un gran negocio que generan puestos de

---

[149] Cooperative manager, 11 May, 2009.

trabajo bien pagados por su personal" [There is a concern that the certifications have turned into a big business that generate well paid jobs for their staff].[150] The opinion was complemented by the international marketing manager of Coope Agri:

> Las certificaciones se han convertido en un gran negocio y en este gran negocio la persona que se beneficia menos es el productor. Tenemos que pagar dinero por la inspección, por la membresía, y por cada exportación que hacemos. Lo mismo sucede con Rainforest, con todas las certificaciones. Por ejemplo, con productos orgánicos, si usted tiene Maya-cert para venir e inspeccionar, usted paga por el transporte desde Guatemala.
>
> [The certifications have all turned into a big business and in this big business the person who benefits the least is the producer. We must pay money for the inspection, for membership, and for every export that we do, the same thing happens with Rainforest, with all certifications. For example, with organic, if you have Maya-cert to come and inspect, you pay for transport from Guatemala].[427]

The idea that sustainability certifications are simply a whim of the market does then introduce or question whether it is only improvements required or a restructure of inter-organisational approach.

Reinforcing international trade dynamics

How sustainability certifications influence and contribute to existing international trade dynamics must also be considered, chapter 12. As a market based sustainability effort, susceptibility to international trade dynamics is highly possible. The intra market location of sustainability certifications and a need to increase market share and sales continues as an important objective despite variable evidence of consistent outcomes in Costa Rica. The situation can determine or influence how certifications include producers in organisational processes, including standard development, and how they support or improve a producer groups' negotiating ability versus keeping buyers involved and maintaining or increasing certified market sales. Fairtrade most intends to balance these dynamics in favour of producers, whereas RA seeks to achieve improved sustainability through a distanced but thoroughly guided certifying approach. While an example from only one country, the misaligned outcomes were observed across cooperatives and communities and were significant. There is reason to question what the sustainability certification movement is and how

---

[150] Previous cooperative manager, coffee farmers and cooperative member, 12 January, 2009.

to better organise the standard development, implementation and monitoring aspects of the sustainability certification effort (Vogt 2019f).

The role of the 'developed' world: from Green Revolution to a Sustainable Revolution?

The strength of sustainable development in the Costa Rican coffee industry since the 1990s is a contrast to the paradigm of change implemented through the green revolution. The way in which this change is introduced and the process that is involved relates to international influence, as Figueres alluded in his remark, "we resent the presence of speculators who assert that their motive in investing money abroad is to foster the development of our countries" (in Martz 1959, 243). The frustration felt toward previous and current influences from the West, or the developed world was evident in 2009, related to sustainability and the intensive farming paradigms introduced:

> Las certificaciones son solo un negocio, un negocio multimillonario que sigue tomando dinero del productor. En la mayoría, el productor siempre ha sido ambiental. ¿Quién no está consciente del medio ambiente? La gente del mundo desarrollado, nos dieron toda la basura, los agroquímicos de la revolución verde y nos fuimos con ella. Nos hicieron envenenar nuestra tierra para no protegerla. Así que hoy necesitamos invertirlo, ellos piden estas certificaciones porque lo piden en Europa y Estados Unidos y ahora quieren que seamos los limpiadores del mundo. Eso está bien, pero como hemos tenido que pagar, tienen que pagar; Oxigeno vale mucho dinero, al igual que el agua.
>
> [The certifications are just a business, a multi-million-dollar business that keeps taking money from the producer. In the majority, the producer has always been environmental. Who is not environmentally conscious? The people of the developed world, they gave us all the rubbish, the agrochemicals from the green revolution and we went with it. They made us poison our land not protect it. So today we need to reverse it, they ask for these certifications because they ask for it in Europe and the US and now, they want us to be the cleaners of the world. That is fine, but as we have had to pay, they must pay; oxygen is worth a lot of money, as is water].[151]

An increased reach of sustainability certifications in Costa Rica could be considered a positive contribution to overall sustainability. However, where processes and outcomes are in fact misaligned with intentions this cannot be

---

[151] Cooperative manager, 20 February, 2009.

considered the case. Categorising feelings that sustainability certifications reinforce frustration and feelings of hypocrisy in the producer country as inevitable is for further consideration. The importance of understanding the positive outcomes and pressure points for change; and allowing some room for mistakes but also ensuring reduced replication of already negative experiences from international influence is a significant consideration.

Positive outcomes and pressure points for influence

Environmental policy is considered a driving force for the countries leadership in tropical conservation in Central America (Steinberg 2001, 49). Steinberg (2001) seeks to explore pressure points between environmental activism and its influence on the development and content of environmental policy and practice in Costa Rica. The green revolution which reached Costa Rica in the 1950s was an economically driven pressure point with significantly negative influence on the environment. Certifications, activist organisations and policy and/or legislation can be understood as pressure points influencing sustainable development and poverty reduction through trade. The varying influences highlight a need to consider not only a certifications' influence but then their role alongside or within existing and similarly intended efforts. As a market incentive, complementing organic and sustainability production techniques, they are a different type of pressure for change to an activist organisation or state law.

Certifications can fail to effectively address or contribute to poverty reduction and development as freedom in Sen's terms (1999), see table 1 and 2. The driving motivation behind certifications and the conduct they codify appears most determined by the preferences of international institutions, and business orientation. This is one aspect of the double 'loss' for producing countries explained briefly in the previous section. The second is the issue of comparative poverty within supply chains where the "relatively poor in a rich community can prevent a person from achieving relative 'functionings'" (Evans 2002, 58).

It is necessary to understand and evaluate against accurate intentions, and then consider how the sustainability certification process can improve. Where effective, they certainly represent opportunity to apply positive pressure toward improved sustainability in production, sourcing and trade within the scope that they inherently work. Sustainability certifications are not however a solution for every situation. Opportunity for advancing nationally required practice through policy and law exists through less and more obvious influential flows, they also provide an opportunity for locally adapted, contextually appropriate standards, at a level that policy and law might not.

Summary

A sustainability reputation should only be as strong as the standards that lay the foundation for their claims. The intra market location of sustainability certifications, contrasted with a sustainability intention, can create an ultimate tension between market and in-producer community interest that addresses environmental, societal and economic aspects of sustainability. While benefits of RA and Fairtrade were evident in Costa Rica, perspectives also revealed several significant disadvantages and evidence of greenwashing.

The fieldwork observations and interviews also revealed alternatives as examples of Fairtrade certified contracts, or national or nationally based international programmes. These alternatives are presented in the following section. They might complement existing certification efforts, classify the best situations for certifications or simply override or supersede certifications as they currently operate. An improved understanding of alternatives can limit that uncertified markets result in harmful practices for environment and society.

Opportunities for Improvement

The fieldwork findings, as a series of perspectives and opinions reveal variability in advantages and disadvantages experienced through the certification process. While discussions and interview questions were intended to collect information related to sustainability certifications only, suggestions and observations of complementary and alternative efforts in each community offering similar or superior support and sustainability outcomes were not uncommon. The following chapter provides an overview of these observations and opinions related to alternatives to and complements for sustainability certifications.

CHAPTER 14

Alternatives to and complements for sustainability certifications in Costa Rica

Introduction

A logo is often the only way to know if a product is sourced and traded sustainably. Sustainability certification labels were, at the time of initial fieldwork, the most prominent indicator for sustainable products. In Costa Rica, as a producing and consuming country, several efforts were ongoing alongside labelled products providing considerations and discussions related to how these certification efforts were influencing Costa Rica coffee communities. The opinions and perspectives expressed across coffee farming communities visited demonstrate variance in benefits and disadvantages of sustainability certifications, RA and Fairtrade, which are economic, social and environmentally based.

With research questions primarily related to sustainability certifications, perspectives and information regarding alternative approaches were collected and considered as a secondary consideration. Where improvements on sustainability certifications are sought, these secondary considerations from Costa Rica can provide examples for future considerations. Examples of complements and alternatives to sustainability certifications include, programs for premium investment which strengthen outcomes related to education; certified direct trade compared certified conventional international trade arrangements; locally developed standards; vertical integration of the supply chain; reduced compliance costs through complementary or alternative programs; limiting international certification schemes to specific situations.

Structured education programs for premium investment

The Fairtrade premium can be allocated to social or environmental projects for the local community, or to support commercial production. The cooperative

---

How to cite this book chapter:
Vogt, M. 2019. *Variance in Approach Toward a 'Sustainable' Coffee Industry in Costa Rica: Perspectives from Within; Lessons and Insights.* Pp. 169–182. London: Ubiquity Press. DOI: https://doi.org/10.5334/bce.p. License: CC-BY 4.0

committee determines how the premium is allocated. As the minimum fairtrade price received in Costa Rica did not cover costs in 2009, and by 2015 had not increased to a level that would allow costs to be covered[152], the Fairtrade premium was, in most cases, allocated to supplement incomes. Where used for community development projects, developing community infrastructure were often favoured such as a football field which provided long-term benefits through continued use. Additional institutional efforts sought to further such support or community infrastructure as a complementary effort which could receive some funds from the premium. The limited income provisioned by the fairtrade price often meant that funds allocated for education purposes would also be limited. The Children of the Field Foundation *(Fundación Hijos del Campo)*, provides education programs for the children of Coocafe members. It offers specific support related to education in rural areas and had in 2009 recently started funding university education for children of the coffee fields. At the request of funding bodies to become more financially sustainable, this foundation now functions as a guarantor for government loans available for university students, with the vision of producing future leaders of the country. This is seen to be financially and politically beneficial, and sustainable for the coffee industry and coffee farming communities:

> Nuestra fundación es para los hombres que tomaran decisiones, pero importantes decisiones en política, economía y sociedad para los países en desarrollo. Para promover a la gente de los países centroamericanos, no de las grandes metrópolis. El desarrollo de muchos profesionales implica una visión muy reducida para el país, para el modelo de vida y para nosotros. Es muy importante que nuestra gente de Hijos del Campo tenga la oportunidad de formarse bien para tomar decisiones especialmente en política pública. En el siglo XIX los hijos de los productores de café fueron en los mismos barcos que tomaron café a Europa para estudiar en Inglaterra o Francia. Cuando regresarían eran grandes hombres de negocios o gente con mucha influencia política. Ahora como la producción y los ingresos del café ha caído tanto que ni siquiera pueden enviar a sus hijos a la escuela o la universidad en este país. Así que decidimos que era necesario tener un programa agresivo y visionario que comenzaría a generar hombres y mujeres, quienes con el trasfondo del campo podrían ser los tomadores de decisiones de mañana.
>
> [[Our Foundation] is for the men who would make decisions, important decisions in politics, economics, and society for developing countries. To promote people from Central American countries, not from the grand metropolises. Development of many professionals often diminishes vision for the country, for the model of life and so for us. It is very important that our people from *Hijos del Campo* have an oppor-

---

[152] Cooperative manager, 11 March, 2009; Cooperative manager, 25 February, 2009; International marketing manager, 11 May, 2009.

tunity to be well prepared for making decisions, especially in public politics. In the 19th Century the children of coffee farmers went on the same boats that took coffee to Europe to study in England or France. When they returned, they were great businessmen or people with a lot of political influence. Now, as production and income from coffee has dropped so much, they cannot even send their children to school or college in this country. We decided it was necessary to have an aggressive and visionary program that would start to develop men and women 'from the field' who could be the decision makers of tomorrow].[153]

Hijos del Campo programs provide a more sustainable approach for allocation of the Fairtrade social premium encouraging long term growth in representative decision making for the future. In 2019 there are 2598 beneficiaries, of which 2019 are high school students, 579 University students, and 240 schools (Coocafe 2019). Whether the Fairtrade premium would eventually be allocated to such a program was, as mentioned, often determined by how the minimum price covers the cost of production, and how technical production processes require further development. Establishing a cooperative programmed fund is complementary to the intentions of the Fairtrade premium.

Certifying direct trade compared to international sourcing chains

The financial expense compared to benefit, and barriers to becoming certified has led to a preference for non-certified market channels in Costa Rica. Farmers who were members of a regional cooperative indicated that they sold their beans to a private buyer rather than through the certified market channel of the cooperative, as price and payment arrangements were more beneficial.[154] The word of mouth opportunity amongst producer groups could result in such preferences increasing. Only a small proportion of all certified Costa Rican coffee was sold through certified market channels, meaning that the remaining certified coffee was sold through noncertified conventional markets. As supply is still above demand for certified coffee such preference will not result in an undersupply of certified coffee but will influence the conditions within which farm certified coffee, is traded. Whether this is a relevant consideration for RA certified coffee plantations is influenced by RAs approach to sustainable trade. The trend in Costa Rica certainly indicates preference for direct trade arrangements from small farmers.

Direct trade from producer community to roaster and retailer was the original intention of Fairtrade. Certifying existing sourcing chains and business provides an opportunity to increase sales of certified produce. It might not

---

[153] Director *Hijos del Campo y Café Forestal* 20 February 2009.
[154] Coffee farmers, Los Angeles de Páramo, 13 April, 2009.

however address the challenges already presented for producer groups by being or becoming certified. As there are few large traders in the coffee industry, working with MNCs and more complicated sourcing chains became, and will remain, necessary. To increase sales and market access to certified products, Fairtrade became something different by certifying existing sourcing chains and businesses through labelling and official certification processes. As the challenges compared to benefit of being certified became more obvious, including limited certified market purchases, producer organisations in Costa Rica have slowly found more direct noncertified market channels through which they can sell their coffee to local or international markets. The benefits of certifications compared to direct trade is an important consideration.

Direct trade is often preferred without certification due to simplicity in access, and reduced administrative and resource requirements of certifications, maintaining ability for farmers to obtain a higher coffee price. While there is opportunity for direct buyers to influence environmental and social standards it will be based on varying levels of expertise. Environmental and social practice requirements are not however often consistent or standardised and there are no trade protocols within the direct trade market providing opportunity for oversight and inconsistency.

While direct trade appears most aligned with the original intentions of Fairtrade, there is significant opportunity to overlook all producer interests due to heterogeneous stakeholder groups within a producer country. Farming techniques used might not be considered at all with all attention going to direct trade arrangements. This will become a country specific consideration. Direct trade can however use certifications to demonstrate sustainability, this may or may not reduce the financial benefit provided.

National law and already existing programs with similar intentions may influence practices as a parallel complement to direct trade and as an alternative to certified direct trade arrangements. Capacity building in terms of best practice in sustainable farming, shade trees, regionally specific, conservation of soils, waste management and water treatment is necessary as consistent.

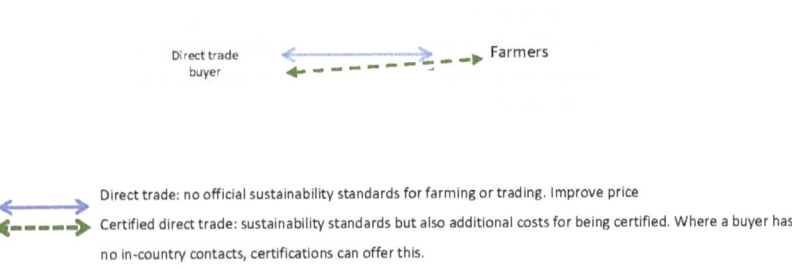

Figure 18: Basic comparison: direct trade and certifications.

Sustainability certifications do not necessarily offer the most sustainable solution, and certainly require improvement. They can however be effective for direct trade and international sourcing chains. Certified direct trade channels offer more formal farming practice, social conditions and environmental protection guidance compared to non-certified direct trade. Certified international sourcing chains can also provide an opportunity for an increase in sales of certified products. Ensuring flexibility in efforts, particularly for local contexts is necessary for more complicated sourcing chains as well as direct trade arrangements.

Examples of Fairtrade certified and directly traded coffee in Costa Rica

There were few examples in 2009 of certified direct trade arrangements. The first example was in Monteverde, where one of the first fair and direct trade arrangements was ongoing. The second example, in Agua Buena, Costa Rica is a more developed business model which includes certification and advances sustainability intentions through direct in-community exchange and interaction, certified direct trade and vertical integration of the supply chain. It was the result of an internationally funded in-community programme effort called the Community Agroecology Network (CAN). The two examples demonstrate certified coffee sourced from Costa Rican cooperatives directly traded according to and beyond Fairtrade standards, they offered a significantly superior price to farmers while trading certified coffee. "Vendemos a un cliente Fairtade Montana, esta es una relación comercial directa y compran nuestro café a un precio alto $2.57. Este precio solo sube; No disminuye" [We sell to a Fairtrade client, Montana, this is a direct trade relationship and they buy our coffee at a high price $2.57. This price only goes up; it does not decrease].[155]

> Aparte del Mercado de la certificación, tenemos un socio comercial que permite la negociación en el Mercado convencional. Estamos vendiendo café directamente a los Estados Unidos, a través de Internet y utilizando el servicio postal a través de CAN.
>
> [Aside from the certification market, we have a trading partner that allows negotiation in the conventional market. We are selling coffee direct to the United States, through the internet and using the postal service through CAN].[156]

A clear and appreciated benefit of the Monteverde Montana trade arrangement example was the consistency, stability and quality of the trade arrangement.

---

[155] Cooperative manager, 11 March, 2009.
[156] Cooperative manager, 20 February, 2009.

It had lasted over twenty years paying above the minimum price allocated by Fairtrade, and above conventional market rates, while sourcing from certified farms. While the cooperative in Monteverde is no longer operational, changing to an association compliant to several standards (Vogt 2019c), the original trade arrangement with a Fairtrade certified buyer in Montana was ongoing in 2014. In Agua Buena, CAN intended to improve agri-ecological practices through long-term student placements and specific studies on individual farms. They generated income for the community of the cooperative through student exchanges, and vertical integration of local coffee production paired with direct trade. Local community members were also involved in international education exchanges. CAN in Agua Buena, although no longer operational as the cooperative closed, remains relevant to the discussion of alternatives and complements for sustainability certifications. The CAN approach was identified as superior to Fairtrade according to the cooperative perspective, the alternative model was at no cost, and the price paid to farmers was significantly better through CAN than Fairtrade certified markets. Longevity of such efforts is however also important as a sustainability indicator. These are therefore examples of how direct trade for small-scale markets can include sustainability standard compliance and occasionally more advanced and progressive sustainability efforts.

While longevity of an approach is an important consideration, opportunity for learning from and replicating adapted versions of the CAN in Agua Buena approach exist. The direct trade, and in-community organisation, sourcing and trading arrangements do not need to remain exclusive to small scale markets. Adaptions in other communities and countries could complement, improve, possibly provide an alternative to sustainability certifications for producers who remain outside certified practices and markets, or for producers or traders left dissatisfied with certified markets and certification efforts, or who seek differentiated sustainability offering for the market.

Learning from experimental precedents in Costa Rica

The CAN example in Agua Buena as an experimental precedent, demonstrates opportunity for future applicability through three key aspects or offerings. These offerings assist to ease difficulties experienced with becoming certified, or further progress ideas of sustainable trade. The first, reducing the cost of compliance; the second, vertical integration of the sourcing chain, and the third, commencing locally developed standards.

Reducing the cost of compliance

Complying with sustainability certification standards presents a significant resource investment which can be out of reach for many coffee farmers and cooperatives. Where combined with the administrative costs of being certified alongside limited income benefit through certified market sales and arrangements, any opportunity to reduce compliance costs appears necessary. This is particularly so where alternative direct trade markets which require limited environmental and social practices are becoming more popular, emerging as a viable alternative.

CAN in Agua Buena provided an example of in-community, low cost to community, assistance program for future learning in this area. Where the coffee industry develops further, such in-community infrastructure could become a normal example of coffee farming community that MNCs source certified coffee from. The CAN program has since disappeared in Agua Buena. The community perception of coffee farming and historic experience reduced interest in coffee farming and the local cooperative collapsed for the second time in 2013. The region of Agua Buena was not always considered physically suitable for coffee growing as an additional consideration. While the benefits of what was implemented are still evident, long term and stable projects that continue to deliver for the community and move with community structure and changes are preferred. An essential to achieving such outcomes also rely on compliance with local policy and legislative requirements to ensure longevity. In Monteverde, assistance was sought from government departments ensuring compliance with national standards as well as the certification standards. The trade arrangement while consistently beneficial according to coffee price offered did not address the cost of implementing changed practices toward compliance.

Vertical integration of the sourcing chain

A sourcing chain can be considered horizontal including various stakeholders, figure 5, the numerous value-added attributes to transform a natural resource to a shelved and consumed product is a vertical process, figure 18. Currently, it is quite common to find the product reaching 'vertical height' via a buyer and in a consuming country, rather than in a producing country. The two examples of certified direct trade for small-scale markets in Costa Rica include vertical integration which increases source chain processes occurring in the producer country. Within the coffee industry this will include preparing the green bean for roasting through direct access to a mill on farm or by community and roasting in country rather than exporting green coffee beans. Roasted rather than green beans are then sold directly to local and international markets. Montana would occasionally source roasted coffee, and CAN would only sell roasted coffee online direct from Aqua Buena.

A representative of the environmental foundation of Coocafe, Café Forestal explained how vertical integration had become part of a national strategy: "Nuestro objetivo es plantar e industrializar café, agregar valor a nuestro café – tenemos que hacerlo – no tenemos otra opción (vuelta de hoja) – tenemos que hacerlo para que haya huevos para el futuro" [Our objective is to plant and industrialise coffee, add value to our coffee – we must do this – we do not have another option (*vuelta de hoja*) – we have to do it so that there are eggs for the future].[157] The domestic market in Costa Rica was a source of opportunity and *Café Forestal* has its own line of coffee produced by Coocafe members for sale on the domestic market and overseas.

To complement vertically integrated sourcing chains, nearly every member cooperative of Coocafe also offered a coffee tour, a part of which is the opportunity to buy the roasted coffee and/or drink a coffee in the cooperative's own café, encouraging sale of roasted coffee in Costa Rica. As with direct trade arrangements, local alternatives such as vertical integration complementary to direct trade arrangements must not contradict the environmental and social advances already achieved.

An increased presence of *beneficio* or mill in each community to localise the processing from berries to beans introduces additional considerations that may fall within locally developed standards. One small community visited for this study had invested to construct their own *beneficio* and small business to trade coffee. On inspection of the *beneficio* located next to the river, and the town's only source of drinking water, lakes for treating the processing water were missing. Their absence was dismissed with the idea that the field of grass would filter the contaminated water. This highlights the importance that either established standards or knowledge of state law and effective implementation can have on correct process. The difference between preventing the potential contamination of an entire community's waterway (Bailey et al. 1992, 129) and supply, and perhaps other communities' water supply[158] relies on knowledge of required processes.

The National Program for Sustainable Agricultural Production supported by MAG installed micro-mills, small *beneficios* directly on farms (OECD 2017,83) which would have reduced risk of the above-mentioned situation. Since the time of original fieldwork, micro-mills and in-country roasting had increased (Gyllensten 2017) and effective regulation is not yet evident (Vogt 2019c). This may also result in an increase of imported green beans for roasting blended origins for sale within country, see Figure 19.

Green bean imports are not significant compared to beans exported, see table 9, with 120 (000 50kg bags) imported compared to 1450 (000 50kg bags) exported.

---

[157] Director of *Hijos del Campo and Café Forestal*, 20 February, 2009.

[158] Personal reports and observations in Indonesia by an environmental activist group indicated the contamination of a communities' water supply was a result of a Brazilian owned coffee mill operating further upstream, the coffee cooperative using the mill was Fairtrade certified.

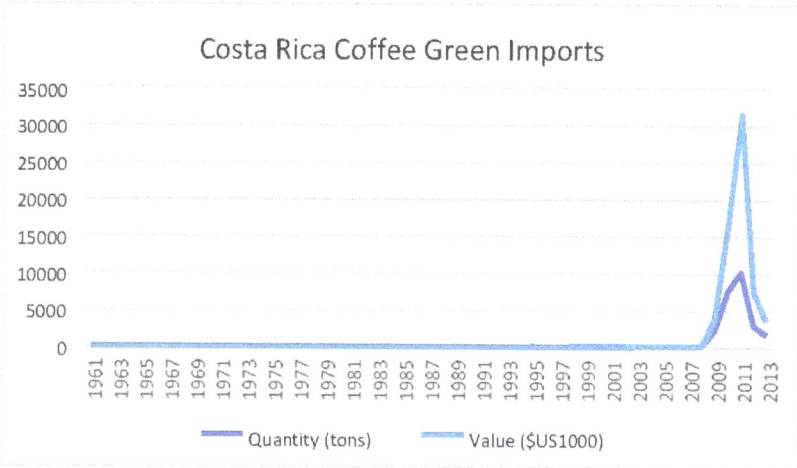

Figure 19: Costa Rican green coffee imports by quantity and value.
Data source: FAOStat 2019.

Trade arrangements will ultimately determine how vertical integration through sale and export of coffee roasted in the producer country will reach the producer, and their community, compared to national coffee industry institutions. While expanding market demand for roasted beans directly results in significantly higher revenues for producer communities and countries, it essentially cuts the foreign roaster out the coffee sourcing chain which might influence international trade and sales opportunities. A trader/buyer preference and association between cupping quality and time of roasting may also restrict market expansion and influence price for in-country roasted coffee.

Locally developed standards

A certification standard often depends on the philosophy of each certification body. Distance between what the certifications seek to achieve and what they are doing in the source country following the brand *protection* or positive association formula of CSR is of concern. Mimicking power relations within international coffee supply chains and discouraging control in decision making from the producer side of the supply chain is not considered a positive outcome. Locally developed standards, and country and regionally specific certification programs where effectively and independently monitored and implemented could replace or complement internationally developed standards. They can provide standards that are contextually appropriate increasing positive outcomes. The organisation that takes responsibility for developing standards locally and the approach taken for development will influence the

Table 9: Production, supply and demand data statistics.

Coffee, Green Market Begin Year Costa Rica	2014/2015 Oct 2014		2015/2016 Oct 2015		2016/2017 Oct 2016	
	USDA Official	New Post	USDA Official	New Post	USDA Official	New Post
Area Planted	98	98	98	84	0	84
Area Harvested	93	93	93	80	0	80
Bearing Trees	360	360	360	340	0	340
Non-Bearing Trees	70	70	70	24	0	24
Total Tree Population	430	430	430	364	0	364
Beginning Stocks	130	130	10	124	0	103
Arabica Production	1400	1455	1350	1654	0	1700
Robusta Production	0	0	0	0	0	0
Other Production	0	0	0	0	0	0
Total Production	1400	1455	1350	1654	0	1700
Bean Imports	150	80	175	120	0	120
Roast & Ground Imports	12	0	15	0	0	0
Soluble Imports	32	0	30	0	0	0
Total Imports	194	80	220	120	0	120
Total Supply	1724	1665	1580	1898	0	1923
Bean Exports	1220	1161	1100	1410	0	1450
Rst-Grand Exp.	40	0	10	0	0	0
Soluble Exports	0	0	0	0	0	0
Total Exports	1260	1161	1110	1410	0	1450
Rst. Ground Dom. Consum.	429	375	445	380	0	385
Soluble Dom. Cons.	25	5	25	5	0	5
Domestic Consumption	454	380	470	385	0	390
Ending Stocks	10	124	0	103	0	83
Total Distribution	1724	1665	1580	1898	0	1923

Data source: USDA Foreign Agriculture Service 2016.

outcomes. Opportunity for decentralisation of power through locally developed standards is considered reasonable motivation.

CAN in Agua Buena encouraged locally developed standards and appeared more capable of allowing for the contextual detail required to ensure positive outcomes compared to Fairtrade at the time of fieldwork, 2009. While CAN was not able to maintain a presence in Agua Buena, further work to encourage local standards could follow this approach, or a Participatory Guarantee System (PGS) approach (Vogt 2019b) and seek to diversify farming activities and increase prominence of diversified shade trees and other market valued crops on farms (Vogt & Englund 2019). This may also eventually involve a scaling down of yield by quantity production focus and decrease intensification, instead increasing shaded systems and potentially quality of yield. Social security systems also differ by country, leading to varying situations in relation to required standards, costs and existing practices for farmers and labourers. Costa Rica demonstrated some movement toward establishing government run certification standards and programs as considered by CIMS (2006) for Coocafe. A further move away from the structure of centralised power that exists within the certification systems is recommended. Reaching the scale of presence and market value of international certifications, RA, Fairtrade and other sustainable coffee certifications will ensure success in this approach. The independence of international sustainability certifications does however provide a differentiation not available from a national government program or an in-community programme. How the difference influences effective sustainability outcomes could be studied further.

Limiting international certification schemes to specific situations

The original intention of Fairtrade was to develop a direct channel of trade from producer to consumer (WFTO 2019). The reality of this objective within the structure and location of certification operations relative to supply chains, standard setting and regulatory function have left certifications away from a direct trade situation and integrated with MNCs. This is not necessarily a negative situation but does distance emerging operations from initial intentions. Certification schemes demonstrate benefit at varying degrees however the disadvantage or inconsistent benefit encourages revision of existing efforts. It has been suggested that Coocafe may 'no longer [be] in need of preferential terms on offer' (Leutchford 2006, 148), as a large consortium of several smaller cooperatives. Suggesting that any superiority offered by Fairtrade is most needed or most beneficial for least developed cooperatives. Neither situation has been proven however an idea that some cooperatives are not as 'in need' certainly is possible. In this situation, an idea for absolute implementation and benefit of certifications could become limited to those 'most in need' or those who would most benefit, which are two different things. The difficulty with this idea is the actual role certifications take and whether they, in fact, offer realistic benefit for smaller cooperatives, which is yet to be adequately proven (Vos et al. 2019; Vogt 2019c, 2019d). The idea of certifications being an appropriate assistance or 'aid' (Vogt 2019d) for smaller cooperatives only, might be where misunderstanding begins. The commercial approach of certifications could be more appropriate for organised and well-established cooperatives. Positioning certifications as NGOs, with or without social justice intentions, and the origins of Max Havelaar easily provides opportunity for such interpretations.

Fairtrade's involvement in the past has been just what was intended; it developed capacity to the point that perhaps the Fairtrade system is no longer needed for some coffee farming organisations in Costa Rica. They have developed past the initial need and are able to achieve better prices than the Fairtrade price with the networks and trade partners established through certified markets. In other situations, maintaining compliance with a certification could provide additional benefit through sustainability standards, implementation support, monitoring processes and certified market opportunities. It does however seem that suggesting sustainability certifications as an absolute solution for all coffee farmers is problematic. Limiting involvement to specific situations could be a beneficial way forward, particularly where alternative or complementary approaches and systems have already proven more appropriate. In other situations, complementary programs could ensure benefits from involvement in certifications are optimised.

Summary

The resulting perceptions and identified outcomes of certification efforts in Costa Rica clearly demonstrate areas for improvement. Understanding the role such certifications play within efforts of similar intention stimulate thought on how their role might improve in the future. Their strengths and abilities to improve outcomes, and similarly, how to reduce the disadvantages their current role is creating can be better understood. The Costa Rican context demonstrates that cost of production can influence economic outcomes of certification, particularly in the case of Fairtrade.

The suggested alternatives and complementary mechanisms seek to strengthen existing benefits or intentions of certifications as identified in country or as a synthesis of existing effective efforts with the certification efforts. Direct trade is an approach to trading coffee that allows for specialty coffee markets, higher prices paid for coffee and a direct trade relationship between roasters and producers. This was the initial intention of Fairtrade. The direct trade model does not however introduce standards for practice and roasters do not necessarily have the expertise to advise in this area. There is therefore the issue of farming practices encouraged through direct trade channels which are not addressed.

There were varying experimental programs and efforts found in Costa Rica at the time of research integrated with certification efforts. While one, CAN is no longer operating in Costa Rica it lasted for approximately ten years and set a precedent, demonstrating the benefit of local standard development agreed on at a community level with foreign postgraduate students who also provided a monitoring of implementation service, vertical integration of the sourcing chain by selling in-producer community roasted coffee and direct trade via online sales. It was not, at that time, considered scalable but did consistently pay above the Fairtrade minimum price. Most importantly it provided a more accurate indication of the work required to be compliant. Lessons can be learnt, and additional benefit achieved in other communities which are compliant to any sustainability certification standard or integrated to national approaches where reasons for cessation of their activities in Agua Buena are proactively addressed. Selecting strengths of any approach could assist to lower the cost of compliance and increase sale price.

The Monteverde Montana arrangement offered a certified vertically integrated sourcing model without in-community standard development and implementation monitoring activities. The coffee was sourced from FairTrade certified coffee farms in Monteverde and the trade arrangement had lasted over twenty years. It continues despite the cooperative model of the community shifting to an association compliant to numerous sustainability standards. The Montana Monteverde trade arrangement did therefore demonstrate longevity while the CAN approach in Agua Buena, while lasting ten years did not continue. It is suggested that more than one of the alternative recommendations will succeed in improving outcomes for small coffee farmers and their communities' long term. A combination can improve on the CAN effort in Agua Buena, perhaps ensure longevity of support and relationships provided as the additional example of the Montana Monteverde arrangement achieved.

The benefits of certification programs are clear, they do however vary. To recommend that certifications no longer be a chosen method for sustainability intentions would remove the subtler important advantages and disregard complementary efforts as a progressive process. It is therefore suggested that certifications are suitable in specific situations, contexts and countries, and that they can be complemented and strengthened by in-country capacity building. Structured education programs to emphasise benefit of the Fairtrade premium is one example. Standards as used by certifications are internationally created and administered. Producer involvement while intended is not occurring in implementation. Standards are a key influencer via a certification effort for sustainability practices and eventually poverty reduction. Locally developed standards may be more appropriate and create improved outcomes. Whether managed via a CAN like model or through Participatory Guarantee System

(PGS) approach (Vogt 2019b), locally administered and regulated standards may represent a financial saving, a more sustainable and culturally appropriate standard and improved environmental outcomes.

Strength in trading arrangement which adapts to and allows for the most sustainable practices appears a reliable situation to ensure longevity amongst continually changing circumstances, in producer community and within the international trade context. It is also necessary to ensure adequate sustainability mechanisms and support to facilitate such adaptability through changing circumstances.

Conclusion

CHAPTER 15

Summarising comments and recent developments

Introduction

Coffee has consistent cultural and social significance in Costa Rica (Cooperative manager, 31 March 2009; Cooperative manager, 12 February 2009; Cooperative manager, 4 February 2009; Cooperative manager, 20 February 2009; Cooperative manager, 11 March 2009; Director Hijos del campo, Café Forestal, 20 February 2009) while economic value has varied. In comparison to the largest agricultural industries of pineapples and bananas which are in the majority foreign owned and plantation sized, the coffee industry is the only one dominated by small farm holdings owned by Costa Ricans. Uniting a large but declining number of small farm holders, the land use structure has allowed a shared experience not only in the culture of coffee farming but also with the international market. The international coffee industry is a contrast of poverty, dependency and simultaneously great wealth dependent on location in, and structure of, the sourcing chain. While coffee prices often remain 'quiet' for end consumers, farmers and producers in the *bean belt* ride the wave of price fluctuations and market cycles. Maintaining a social and cultural value through the centuries, coffee is no longer the bean of economic promise it was at the time of independence in Costa Rica.

Coffee has been a source of cultural and social unity, and shared experiences but also a source of environmental, social and economic insecurity not only for farmers but also for farm labourers, most of whom are seasonal and highly mobile migrant populations (Cardoso 1986, 209; Bolanos et al. 2008). Responses to challenges have varied across the country by coffee growing community. Sen's considerations of poverty stay in the realm of capability and functioning,

---

How to cite this book chapter:
Vogt, M. 2019. *Variance in Approach Toward a 'Sustainable' Coffee Industry in Costa Rica: Perspectives from Within; Lessons and Insights.* Pp. 185–194. London: Ubiquity Press. DOI: https://doi.org/10.5334/bce.q. License: CC-BY 4.0

leading to freedom by the elimination of oppression, improved community relations and access to education, health and social security provisions.

The capabilities approach broadens definitions of poverty to allow not only "opulence, utilities, primary goods or rights but functionings (doings and beings) – [as] a measure that encompasses these other units of evaluation" (Comin 2001, 4). A person's capability to achieve the functionings they choose will determine that "person's freedom – the real opportunities – to have well-being" (Sen 1992, 40). Where corporations through international trade proved to increase poverty and disregard sustainability, sustainability certifications emerged within the international coffee industry as one of many CSR efforts. Coffee farming practices and trade can significantly influence the environment, conservation efforts and community, including health.

The outcomes associated with certifications in the Costa Rican coffee industry are proving positive and negative, varying across the country. Each certification is distinct by intention and organisational structure and approach. The distinction between objectives of each certification introduces a theoretical and philosophical consideration, a different facet for perspectives and outcomes in country.

Quantified summary according to poverty reduction indicators

The quantified summary compares key topics of the monograph against poverty reduction indicators, table 8. The poverty reduction consideration is slightly more specific to sustainability and the summary serves as an additional and simplified layer for understanding findings and should not distract from discursively presented opinions that are more difficult to quantify. These discursive findings still provide a detailed understanding of the situation. More positive poverty reduction[159] outcomes were identified compared to negative according to the quantified summary. These outcomes are not limited to certifications and are based on the alternatives identified through fieldwork, shown as a distinct category.

Recognising in-country frustration with international sustainability certification process

The coffee industry has been through certain trends, following international supply and demand, and paradigm cycles. Farming practices and dimensions

---

[159] A similar range of indicators for sustainability, such as those available from the SDGs could be used to consider and rate key topics identified against sustainability outcomes.

of land use have shifted due to such cycles. The green revolution has successfully demonstrated the negative environmental and health impacts of intensified coffee farming. The 'negative' influence of the green revolution has subsequently resulted in a reverse shift in practices by necessity; contributing toward more sustainable practices and poverty reduction. Observing such an occurrence provides scope for understanding the role and influence of the 'developed' world. A system based on economic gains and agricultural intensification has proven unsuccessful and extreme to the point of forcing a contrary trend of food shortages and economic difficulty. Such paradigm cycles from a producer country perspective can be perceived as foreign interference, particularly where foreign presence and activity is understood, at some level, as unified and negative. As the stakes are arguably higher for a producer country, foreign intentions to rectify situations 'they' ultimately created through education and an economic expense to the producing country does generate frustration and disrespect. That is not however the only response to or perception of such efforts.

The difference between RA and Fairtrade in Costa Rica

It is difficult to conclude with a statement about how Fairtrade and RA comparatively satisfy sustainability outcomes as the philosophical understanding and approach of sustainability, including prioritized land holding sizes, organisational structure and approach, standard criteria, and the number of stakeholders involved is different. The difference in standards is an important observation, alongside the intended involvement of producers in organisational processes and trade practices including negotiation between producers and buyers. The different approach and intentions of RA and Fairtrade; and other certifications mean that poverty reduction efforts result distinct. At base, RA and Fairtrade represented very different sustainability approaches to the coffee industry in 2009, and still do. The major difference was the size of farm holding prioritised for certification, RA clearly certified plantation farms most despite the small producer group standard, and Fairtrade only certified small farmers organised into a cooperative. Given coffee farming landscapes are often a combination of larger and small land holdings, the difference could be considered necessary as certifying larger land holdings compared to small land holdings is an extremely different process, with different sustainability considerations and needs. It is important to recognise that the difference between small farm holdings and plantations is not only by number of people involved in managing the farm but also by the explicit and implicit roles and responsibilities; capabilities and capacity for risk taking. There is also difference between a small farm and a producer group of small farmers.

Hired labour standard considerations are different for a plantation compared to a small farm which influences the difference between Fairtrade and RA hired labour standards. RA for does not state or intend to be involved in facilitating negotiations between a producer and buyer, Fairtrade seeks to encourage agreements between producers and buyers at the producers' discretion. Fairtrade also seeks to consistently encourage certified producer participation in organisational processes.

Overview of achieved intentions

RA appears to be achieving most intentions for plantations more than for small producer groups. The plantation preference is a significant environmental and social consideration, and one that may see RA criticised before seeking to measure or gauge perspectives in a producer country. On the other hand, plantations tend to associate with high yield, monoculture and intensified farming and large land use proportions by hectares. SAN standards may therefore assist to improve areas where environmental influence is the most negative. Fairtrade developed with a socially orientated priority, certifying small farm holding groups who have different privileges and advantages compared to plantation farms. The Fairtrade organisational structure is different to RA and in practice appears more complex by process as it attempts to involve the producer groups in standard setting and organisational processes increasing the number of stakeholder interests to consider. Fairtrade also addresses the price paid to farmers and producers by setting a price, and was initially controversial idea within free trade discourse. How successful the minimum Fairtrade price is, is country dependent. In Costa Rica it is a clear cause for complaint but was, in the past, an achieved intention.

Identified benefits

Intended benefits of RA and Fairtrade often associated with variable disadvantages. RA achievements for labour standards, ensuring a superior price is paid and overall standard implementation appears strong for plantations. Access to certified international markets is clearly identified and valued as a benefit. Support from Fairtrade to involve producers in organizational processes and their intention to promote farmer group interest through trade terms, while not always doing so successfully, was appreciated by small producer groups. The minimum price paid through Fairtrade certified markets proved beneficial only during phases of the international coffee industry, and market price fluctuations. The price premium, where allocated to social community projects, was also appreciated but often allocated to price paid for coffee.

RA was not, in 2009, achieving the same level of influence for small producer groups and so benefits were limited for these farmers. There were almost no complaints about RA from certified plantations and possible benefit from RA and Fairtrade included standard detail and how it complements and possibly advances legal requirements. Particular standards provided detail to legal requirements while allowing for local contexts. Producer participation and the minimum price demonstrate how intended benefits can become complicated in implementation. The associated benefit is useful to consider over time.

Producer participation

Fairtrade's intended involvement of producer groups in negotiation of trade contracts and agreements, or in standard development it is not resulting as intended. There appeared to be limited scope for producer involvement or input for negotiation within the certification process and organisation; despite being an intended activity. There was also little demonstration of Fairtrade assisting negotiations between buyers and producers. While there is no obligation to favour producers, there could be recognition of a need to manage existing power dynamics through international trade. Instead there was only the choice to not trade with a buyer where circumstances for negotiation were not satisfying the producer groups' interests. In this way, social and community relations are encouraged but not to the extent of achieving chosen function for producers.

Price and poverty reduction

Economic benefits are not central to poverty reduction intentions, but they are recognised as a significant element or dimension. Stability in income is a relevant poverty reduction intention and indicator and ensuring a stable price amongst a volatile market, and that costs are covered are equally important as poverty reduction outcomes.

The most alarming finding related to Fairtrade involvement in the Costa Rican coffee industry may be that the key intention of the certification, to provide a minimum and fair price for farmer cooperatives and their members is not consistently beneficial over time. The cost of production versus the market price for coffee was identified as a cause for concern and financial loss across cooperatives in Costa Rica. Where the market price for coffee is well above the Fairtrade minimum price and the cost of production is not covered; Fairtrade was locking certified producers via contractual trade agreements with the cooperative into an avoidable financial loss. Interviews indicate that several of the current disadvantages of the Fairtrade system are related to the minimum price and override that which most interviewees consider Fairtrade's positive influence:

> Ha sido un año difícil para nosotros desde 2004 hemos estado perdiendo dinero con el café. Así que en realidad Fairtrade no tiene un impacto. En su época, en 1983/1985 cuando nuestro contacto Fairtrade vino a Cerro Azul para ser honesto había una gran diferencia entre lo que se pagaba el mercado convencional y lo que se pagaba a través del mercado de Fairtrade.
>
> [It has been a difficult year for us, since 2004 we have been losing money from coffee. So, in reality Fairtrade does not have an impact. In its time, in 1983/1985 when our Fairtrade contact came to Cerro Azul, to be honest there was a big difference between what was paid conventional and what was paid through the Fairtrade market].[160]

For plantation managers, RA was consistently revered for achieving high market prices. RA does not set a minimum price, instead intending to achieve a higher market price through certified markets. This was reported as successful by all interviewed RA certified plantations. The approach may not however necessarily generate success in a context of small farm holding producer groups. While RA is identified as beneficial by plantation managers and administrators, it was not organised to provide benefit to small farmers or cooperatives in 2009.

Considering the benefit of certifications over time

Appreciation of what the certification systems are encouraging, and of the concept of sustainable development introduced through the market[161, 162] in Costa Rica is underpinned by frustration across Fairtrade certified cooperatives. It is not only a secure and fair price, and international networks that will ensure business survival and success. The difference in prosperity between member cooperatives of Coocafe is indicative of the varying security that Fairtrade certification represents; it is not a guarantee of business survival and is not uniform. This is complementary to the fact that each coffee farming region in Costa Rica while sharing a common history with the coffee industry holds distinct experiences, successes, outcomes from and responses to coffee crises of the past. The emphasis on Fairtrade standard implementation was only beginning in 2009, and as such the environmental and social benefits were not widely occurring or easily identified by cooperative representatives. The price paid through Fairtrade certified channels before 2001 was higher than conventional market prices on average. Since that time and despite an increase in the minimum price in 2011, it was not higher remaining below the average price for *Arabica* coffee over the past 5 years. Information from interviews conducted in 2009

---

[160] Cooperative manager, 13 April 2009.
[161] Administrator of certification programs, 25 February, 2009.
[162] Cooperative manager, 11 March, 2009.

indicated satisfaction with improved and more thorough RA and Fairtrade certification standards and processes, the plantation and ownership structure are considered to influence this opinion. The cost of implementing existing and new standards versus the benefit influenced these opinions.

Sustainability standards and legal requirements

The difference between legal requirements and certification standard requirements are an opportunity to consider how one might influence the other. As internationally developed standards, the certifications might be more progressive or ambitious than legally required practices. There is then opportunity for the law to integrate these more detailed requirements to policy and law. The RA recycling criteria and the hired labour standard of RA and Fairtrade provide examples.

The RA certified coffee plantation were already recycling as required by SAN standards in 2009 before waste management legislation of 2010 was passed. The Integrated Waste Management Bill (GIR) became law in a unanimous vote (Ben-Haddej et al. 2010–2011). Costa Rica had not signed the ILO convention for migrant workers in 2009 and according to national law, when workers are illegal or without visa their rights are not officially recognised. Some bilateral agreements which complement regulatory effort for migrant labour populations (Martin 2011). There are cultural considerations (Vogt 2019b) related to migrant labour for coffee farms, and certifications, to the extent that the standards are adequately implemented, provide and encourage the opportunity for cultural adaptions and to recognise these workers, ensuring their rights to education, healthcare and adequate working conditions are provided. The Fairtrade hired labour criteria and standards uphold ILO conventions through its hired labour standard. Applicability of this standard is however limited to a specific number of workers. RA upholds only a few ILO conventions through the SAN standard but does so in detail with all labourers covered by the criteria.

Demand for multiple certifications

The role of multiple certifications in the Costa Rican coffee industry follows a similar consolidation of positives and negatives. The top-down approach evident within certification efforts appears to reflect the need for international market demand with implications for producer organisations. These implications include demands on administrative resources alongside the requirement to implement all standards and organise audits. Were certification influence completely positive such a situation could be beneficial for sustainability and poverty reduction outcomes. Benefits of certification programs were however identified in interviews as occasionally contradictory and to involve downfalls.

With increasing numbers of certifications and minimal explicit coordination at the certification, certified producer group or farm level, variance in such outcomes would only maintain. Multiplying such variable influence through an increasing number of certifications does not therefore seem a positive outcome unless the certified producer group or plantation is well equipped by experience and resources to manage the requirements.

Summary

The influence of RA and Fairtrade in the Costa Rican coffee industry, in 2009 and to date, was and is not straight forward as positive. Alternative efforts in Costa Rica demonstrate a depth of positive outcomes particularly regarding realistic expectations related to implementation. The philosophical understanding of sustainability is different for each certification. Outcomes must therefore be evaluated against the specific sustainability intentions of each certification rather than against all sustainability intentions. Sustainability certifications for the Costa Rican coffee industry are not a definite or absolute solution for sustainable production, sourcing and trade challenges. Their contribution over time has however been important for producer communities. They have allowed functionings in and access to the international markets that were not previously possible, particularly for Fairtrade certified small farmers and their cooperatives. The less obvious influence of such market access within the producer country for redistributing national power dynamics is recognised. However, the depth of these functionings appear limited according to their participation in certification processes and support provided for negotiations between traders and producers. Fairtrade was also failing to cover costs through the minimum price offered in Costa Rica. RA certification consistently offered a superior market price through certified markets for plantations, but not for producer groups. Access to certified international markets was necessary but not to conventional markets for the certified plantations. Adequate compliance monitoring, particularly against the SAN hired labour criteria was falling short in some situations. Improvement in the Fairtrade and RA approach is in part occurring through more stringent standards and monitoring processes which might result in barriers to being compliant and certified. Sustainability certifications might only be useful in specific situations rather than being treated as a uniform sustainability solution for all products that are traded internationally. Or as something that all producers should strive toward to achieve sustainability and market access.

Several alternatives found in Costa Rican coffee communities provide examples of complementary efforts improving upon sustainability certification efforts. Two examples demonstrated improved sustainability outcomes compared to Fairtrade certified conventional sourcing chains in Costa Rica.

These alternatives involve either long term in-community involvement or long term and specialised trade arrangements that are favorable for producer communities and countries. For the second example, the trade arrangement complies with Fairtrade standards that require discretion of the producer rather than the buyer, and then goes beyond these requirements including (1) encouraging locally developed standards (2) in-community educational support for implementation and monitoring of implementation at minimal cost to farmers and producers, and (3) vertical integration of the supply chain which provides a level of benefit for all involved in the producer community which is recommended. The examples of alternatives have demonstrated depth of operations and consistency over time but have not always withstood local requirements or situations. As they currently exist, they can complement sustainability certification efforts and become examples of ways to adjust sustainability certification processes to local contexts. Improvement within the alternatives presented are possible and can occur when used in other coffee farming communities. Further developments have seen preference for direct trade arrangements with reduced priority for certification or cooperatives.

While popularity for these certifications might be declining or changing form, they have influenced sustainable practices in the Costa Rican coffee industry. The direct experience with international markets has in many cases formalized understanding of required sustainable practice from an international perspective and allowed an in-producer community critique of standards which has in some cases informed preference for locally developed and nationally administered standards. The recently emerged and preferred standards now being used demonstrate changes over time and historic influence of a long-term process that is perfecting what sustainable production, sourcing and trade of coffee looks like.

Recent developments

Since follow up fieldwork in 2014, several developments have been observed including a merge between RA and UTZ Kapeh in 2018. It is early days to consider how this might influence the findings in this book but is expected to relate most to chapter 10 and the need to juggle sustainability certifications.

Further information about developments and research specific to Costa Rica and coffee is provided in a summary chapter (Vogt 2019d). Highlights from this chapter include:

- Decreased use of sustainability certifications observed for coffee in Costa Rica.
- An increase in use of micro mill associations.

- How Fairtrade certified cooperatives consider water use in the processing of coffee berries.
- Considerations for non-certified coffee farming and processing, and for non-certified direct trade.

A list of recommended reading is included after the bibliography, many of the references are included in the cited chapter, Vogt 2019d.

Epilogue

Coffee: Whose Sustainability?

Introduction

Adams and Ghaly (2006) discuss expanding 'sustainable development' to include interdependence and fairness. Poverty reduction discourse and definitions are relevant here and complementary to sustainable development within these terms. There are a range of stakeholders involved in the international coffee industry, and sustainability for one stakeholder may not be considered sustainable for another. Working to make the industry more sustainable does therefore require consideration of difference between stakeholders and the dependence dynamic between stakeholders across the international coffee industry. This dynamic often results in minimal sustainability outcomes due to a yield quantity priority. Highly volatile international market prices and alarming food security issues call into question the prioritisation of coffee farming for land use, particularly if it results in or if there are national food shortages (Cardoso 1986, 209). In addition, the impact of coffee farming on biodiversity is often disproportional to the land dedicated to the activity globally (Donald 2004), environmental considerations are therefore also significant.

The importance of "a moral (coffee) economy" (Goodman 2004) which aims to achieve improvements in conditions for farm labourers, coffee farmers, the environment and the industry, is a useful beginning. Often such a moral economy manifests as state law and regulation alongside voluntary systems of regulation through certifications and/or direct trade relationships aiming to allow significantly larger revenues reach farmers. The growing popularity of specialty coffee and a strong demand for coffee quality (Pendergast 1999; Thomsen 2010) fueled and supported by marketing and popular culture trends that are slowly becoming international mass culture have, arguably, stimulated interest in a moral economy. While sustainable coffee certifications seek to improve

---

How to cite this book chapter:
Vogt, M. 2019. *Variance in Approach Toward a 'Sustainable' Coffee Industry in Costa Rica: Perspectives from Within; Lessons and Insights.* Pp. 197–201. London: Ubiquity Press. DOI: https://doi.org/10.5334/bce.r. License: CC-BY 4.0

sustainability outcomes, complementary to a moral economy, an alternative framing may assist. Instead of asking if our coffee is sustainable, it may be useful to ask if coffee farming, as it currently exists, is sustainable. Encouraging coffee production and the necessary transport for it to arrive to the consumer does not seem sustainable. Coffee grown and traded in a 'sustainable' way therefore seems a contradiction according to the geographic divide between farmers and many consumers, and in the context of peak oil and global targets to reduce carbon emissions.

Finding a sustainable balance across stakeholders of a cash crop commodity does therefore require a consideration social and cultural significance of coffee, and the economic benefit; and what would be involved in reducing intensive coffee farming.

Social and cultural significance of coffee in Costa Rica

Most coffee is farmed between the tropic of Cancer and Capricorn. This region of coffee cultivation is called the coffee belt. The 'culture' of coffee is deeply entrenched throughout the world and social significance of coffee consumption is a unifying aspect throughout the world, within or outside the coffee belt. It offers a common opportunity for people to stop and rest, and in this instance, it functions with the same social qualities of food, albeit with an additional buzz. Coffee brings people together. Weinberg and Bealer (2001, 197) bring attention to the Café Society[163], relevant to outside the coffee belt. Within the coffee belt farmers' reliance on coffee for income, their connection to coffee as a historically cultural and social activity and the consumers' reliance as a stimulant cannot be denied. In Costa Rica there is an emotional and historic connection to coffee that fuels the small farmer owned coffee industry.

The culture of coffee in Costa Rica unites a large group of smallholder and smaller group of plantation farmers through a common routine, skill and knowledge set and way of life. It has been pivotal in shaping Costa Rican culture and economy. It is uncommon to meet a Tico (Costa Rican) who does not have, know, or is related to someone" quien tiene café" (who cultivates coffee) and the presence of coffee in the minds and hearts of the Costa Rican mentality cannot be denied.

While the ICO recognised dangerously low profit margins for coffee farmers at a global scale in 2016 (ICO 2016), which may be addressed though diversification of farm and landscape profiles (Vogt & Englund 2019), the value of coffee is beyond economic in Costa Rica. A comment made consistently in the interviews conducted with cooperatives was that: El café no es la actividad

---

[163] Using examples of popular culture turned mass culture American television series such as Friends demonstrating the significance of the coffee shop as somewhere to hang out and chat.

económico más importante de nuestra cooperativa, pero es increíblemente importante como actividad social para los miembros de nuestra comunidad [Coffee is not the most important economic activity for our cooperative, but it is incredibly important as a social activity for our members][164]

The manager of one of the first Fairtrade certified cooperatives with a direct trade relationship, and a founding cooperative of Coocafe, Coopecerroazul, explained that despite being Fairtrade certified it was, at that time, one of the most financially and infrastructurally depressed of Coocafe's' members. This has influenced the perceived and/or observed significance of Fairtrade for cooperatives but also emphasized that the role of coffee farming in the community was not economic:

> Nuestra cooperativa no puede confiar en el café para obtener un ingreso. Fairtrade no ha logrado hacer un impacto que nos permita confiar en el café. El 85% de nuestros beneficios proceden de otras actividades de nuestra cooperativa. Estos departamentos son los que sustentan la cooperativa.
>
> [Our cooperative cannot rely on coffee for an income. Fairtrade has not succeeded in making an impact to allow us to rely on coffee. 85% of our profits come from our cooperatives' other activities. These departments are what sustain the cooperative].[165]

Despite an intention for high yield per hectare production, often compromised by prominent pest or disease and climatic shifts, all coffee cooperatives interviewed in 2009 were multi-service relying on additional activities to remain financially viable. "Nuestra cooperativa tiene otras actividades, un supermercado, una gasolinera, un almacén de productos agrícolas y un mecánico" [Our cooperative has other activities, a supermarket, service station, warehouse for agricultural products and a mechanic].[166] "El 85% de nuestro beneficio se genera a partir de nuestras dos ferreterías, vendemos fertilizantes y otros herbicidas para el cultivo del café y naranjas, estas áreas de negocios sostienen nuestra cooperativa" [85% of our profit is generated from our two hardware stores, we sell fertilisers and other herbicides for coffee and orange cultivation and farming, these business areas sustain our cooperative].[167]

---

[164] Cooperative manager, 31 March, 2009; Cooperative manager, 12 February, 2009; Cooperative manager, 4 February, 2009; Cooperative manager, 20 February 2009; Cooperative manager, 11 March, 2009; Director *Hijos del Campo, Café Forestal*, 20 February, 2009.
[165] Cooperative manager, 13 April, 2009.
[166] Cooperative Manager, 12 February 2009.
[167] Cooperative Manager, 13 April, 2009.

Reducing intensive coffee farming

Increasing biodiverse coffee systems appears to make sustainability sense. Where allowed to occur, the environmentally damaging practices associated with more intensive coffee farming would no longer be necessary with benefits for society, including health benefits. Converting intensive coffee farms to biodiverse coffee farms would result in a gradual reduction in coffee crop density, with varying options for complementary farm design and crop diversification (Vogt 2019d; Vogt & Englund 2019), requiring significant adjustments in producing communities (Vogt 2019d) while also representing a cultural shift in consumer countries. Reduced coffee crop density will influence yield quantity but can also provide opportunity for improved yield quality. Valuing coffee quality allows continued, low crop density diversified coffee farms for more farmers rather than removing coffee crops and farms. The social and cultural significance for a larger proportion of coffee farmers maintains, while also providing the opportunity for improved environmental and maintained economic outcomes. Where quality of yield is prioritised and the market values yield quality via price paid, risk of or incentive to intensify crop density is less likely. The influence of farm and landscape composition and configuration requires a coffee industry that is interested in the quality of coffee instead of quantity harvested. More biodiverse coffee systems provide an opportunity to integrate and produce diverse crops and plants alongside coffee. Industry demands that include diverse produce from the same agricultural systems or landscapes (Vogt & Englund 2019), can support reduced coffee crop density and supply while maintaining economic benefit for coffee farming landscapes.

Summary

In the context of the international coffee industry, sustainability is perspective, and stakeholder experience and interest based, often resulting in some contradiction. How the coffee industry operates and certainly, intensive coffee farming through increased crop density does not uniformly encourage sustainability nor all dimensions of poverty reduction. The idea of reduced coffee supply often leads to discussion dominated by implications for consumers. Alternatives for end consumers may include buying locally grown coffee or substituting coffee with other beverages. The implication for coffee farming communities is however more important to consider. Reducing coffee supply does not have to mean a decrease in coffee farming, but it will result in changed farming techniques that include biodiversity (Vogt 2019d). Moving to an absolute halt in coffee consumption would disregard the cultural and social significance of coffee, and the continuing reliance on coffee that many farmers in developing countries have.

The WCED definition of sustainability emphasises the need to focus on the world's poor, to whom, 'overwhelming priority should be given.' Alternatives to farming coffee in the coffee belt, where the world's 'poor' populate the international coffee industry, may include diversification of farm and landscape profiles (Vogt & Englund 2019) where markets of equal or greater value are present and accessible. Food sovereignty, most important for small producer communities but also relevant for plantations could also be assured. Ensuring an increase in biodiverse coffee farms will influence coffee supply and should precede reduced demand from consuming countries. An integrated industry and producing country effort for coffee yield quality over quantity through farm and landscape composition and configuration of diversified profiles might assist to avoid positive association with intensive coffee farming despite negative environmental implications. Yield by quality allows scope for diversified agri-systems in contrast to monocultures. How the industry values yield quality above quantity is a necessary consideration.

The changes that have occurred in the Costa Rican coffee industry in the last fifty years, more specifically in the last fifteen years, have been the result of more than certification standards and demand. Where the influence of certifications becomes more significant or where they seek to become more influential, they could perhaps consider their role in encouraging diversification of produce sourced (Vogt & Englund 2019) rather than certifying only one crop. They might also begin to encourage diversified farm and landscape profiles through standard criteria. How sustainability certifications like Fairtrade and RA might complement farm and landscape diversification is therefore certainly for future consideration.

Bibliography

Acuña, V.H. 1978. Historia económica del tabaco en Costa Rica: época colonia. *Anuario de Estudios Centroamericanos, 4,* 279392.
Acuña, V.H. 1986. Patrones del conflicto social en la economía cafetalera costarricense (1900- 1948). *Revista de Ciencias Sociales,* pp. 31.
Acuña, V.H. 1987. La ideología de los pequeños y medianos productores cafetaleros costarricenses (1900–1961). *Revista de Historia,* pp. 16.
Adams, M.A. & Ghaly, A.E. 2006. An integral framework for sustainability assessment in agro- industries: application to the Costa Rican coffee industry. *The International Journal of Sustainable Development and World Ecology 13,* 1–20.
Akiyama, T. & Varangis, P.N. 1990. The Impact of the International Coffee Agreement on Producing Countries. *The World Bank Economic Review 4* (2), 157–73.
Alfaro, C.M. 1980. Historia de Costa Rica. Editorial Costa Rica. 16th Ed. San José.
Alvarez, G., Pilbeam, C. & Wilding, R. 2015. Nestle Mespresso AAA sustainable quality program: an investigation into the governance dynamics in a multi-stakeholder supply chain network. *Supply Chain Management: An International Journal 5* (2), 165–82.
Amanor, K.S. 2013. Global resource grabs, agribusiness concentration and the smallholder: two West African case studies. In White B., Borres Jr. S.M., Hall

R., Scoones I., Wolford W. (eds). The New Enclosures: Critical Perspectives on Corporate Land Deals. Routledge New York, London., Chapter 5.

Arce, V.J.C., Raudales, R., Trubey, R., King, D.I., Chandler, R.B., Chandler, C.C. 2009. Measuring and Managing the Environmental Cost of Coffee Production in Latin America. *Conservation and Society* 7 (2), 141–4.

Avelino, J., Cabut, S., Barboza, B. & Barquero, M. 2007. Topography and Crop Management are key factors for the development of the American Leaf Spot epidemic on coffee in Costa Rica. *Phyopathology* 97 (12), 1532–42.

Avelino, J., Ten-hoopen, G.M. & Declerck, F. 2011. Ecological mechanisms for pest and disease control in coffee and cacao agroecosystems of the Neotropics. In Ecosystems Services from Agriculture and Agroforestry Measurement and Payment. Routledge, pp. 91–117.

Babbar, L.I. & Zak, D.R. 1995. Nitrogen loss from coffee agroecosystems in Costa Rica: Leaching and Denitrification in the Presence and Absence of Shade Trees. *Journal of Environmental Quality* 24 (2), 227–33.

Bacci, M.L. 2006. Los estragos de la conquista. *Barcelona: Crítica*, 22.

Bailey, H., Sallee, B. & Garcia, S. 1992. Project de traitement des eaux residuaires d'usines de preparacion du café par voie humuide. Café, Cacao, *The Paris* Vol. XXXVI 2 (129).

Banco Central de Costa Rica. 2016. Cuenta de Bosques: Documento de Trabajo. Area de Estadisticas Ambientales. Departamento de Estadistica Macroeconomica. Division Económica. May 30.

Ben-Haddej, D., Buchenen, A., Owen, A. & Shakan, G. 2010–2011. Managing Costa Rica's Waster: recommendations for a Municipal Solid Waste Management Plan. Worcester Polytechnic Institute. Available from https://web/wpi/edu/Pubs/E-project/Available/E-project-121310-16192/unrestricted.

Bentley, J.W. & Baker, P.S. 2000. The Colombian Coffee Growers' Federation: Organised, successful smallholder farmers for 70 years. Agricultural Research and Extension Network. Network Paper 100. Available from https://www.odi.org/sites/odi.org.uk/files/odi-assets/publications-opinion-files/5126.pdf.

Beyene, A., Kebede, Y.K., Addis, T., Assefa, F. 2011. The impact of traditional coffee processing on river water quality in Ethiopia and the urgency of adopting sound environmental practices. *Environmental Monitoring and Assessment* 184 (11), 7053–63.

Black Coffee. 2007. Documentary. Mongrel Media.

Bolanos, L., Partanen, T., Berrocal, M., Alvarez, B. & Cordoba, L. 2008. Determinants of health in seasonal migrants: coffee harvesters in Los Santos Costa Rica. *International Journal of Occupational Environmental Health* 14 (2), 129–37.

Botey, A.M. 2005. Costa Rica entre guerras, 1914–1940. (San José: Editorial de la Universidad de Costa Rica), pp. 52.

4C Association 2019. Resources: Annual Reports. Available from https://www.globalcoffeeplatform.org/resources/p3.

Cáceres, R. 2000. *Negros, mulatos, esclavos y libertos en la Costa Rica del siglo XVII* (México: IPGH). Cardoso, C.F.S. 1986. Central America: The Liberal era c. 1870–1930. In Bethell L. (ed). The Cambridge History of Latin America – Part II Central America and the Caribbean c. 1870 to 1930. Cambridge University Press.

Carriere, J. 1991. The crisis in Costa Rica: An ecological perspective. In Goodman D., Redclift M. Environment and Development in Latin America: The politics of sustainability. New York Manchester University Press.

Cerda, R., Avelino, J., Gary, C., Tixier, P., Lechevallier, E. & Alinne, C. 2017. Primary and Secondary Yield Losses Caused by Pests and Diseases: Assessment and Modeling in Coffee. *PloS ONE 12* (1), e0169133. https://doi.org/10.1371/journal.pone.0169133.

Charrier, A. & Berthaud, J. 1985, Botanical Classification of Coffee, in Clifford M.H. & Wilson K.C. *Coffee: Botany, Biochemistry and Production of Beans and Beverage*, AVI Publishing, Westport, Connecticut, pp. 14.

Chaverri, A., Vaughan, C. & Poveda, L.J. 1976. Informe de la gira efectuada al Macizo de Chirripo a raiz del fuego ocurrido en marzo de 1976. *Revista Costa Rica 11*, 243–79.

Chirwa, E.W., Dorward, A. & Kydd, J. 2007. Reforming the Smallholder Coffee Sector in Malawi: A

Case Study of Smallholder Commercialisation. *Future Agricultures Consortium Report.*

CIMS 2006. Sustainable Market Intelligence Centre. Available from https://www.cims-la.com.

Comin, F. 2001. Operationalising Sen's capability approach. Paper prepared for the conference Justice and Poverty, examining Sen's capability approach. Cambridge UK.

Coocafe. 2019. Foundations. Available from www.coocafe.com/foundations/?lang=en.

Dahl, R. 2010. Green washing: do you know what you are buying? *Environmental Health Perspectives 118* (6), A246–52.

Daviron, B. & Ponte, S. 2005. The coffee paradox: global markets, commodity trade and the elusive promise of development. Zed Books New York.

de Burca, G. 2005. Democratising transnational governance: Lessons from the EU experience. Presented at the law faculty, Columbia University, pp. 10–11.

Del Monte. 2006. Pineapples. Available from https://freshdelmonte.com/our-products/whole-produce/pineapples.

Donald, F. 2004. Biodiversity Impacts of some agricultural commodity production systems. *Conservation Biology 18* (1), 17–38.

Dunn, K. 2010. Interviewing. In I. Hay (ed.) Qualitative Research in Human Geography 3rd Edition, Oxford University Press, pp. 101–38.

Ecolabel Index. 2018. All Ecolabels. Available at http://www.ecolabelindex.com.

Edelman, M. 2005. Campesinos contra la globalización. Movimientos sociales rurales en Costa Rica. San José: Editorial de la Universidad de Costa Rica.

Evans, P. 2002. Collective Capabilities, Culture, and Amartya Sen's Development a Freedom Studies. *Comparative International Development 37* (2), 54–60.

Fairtrade. 2009. Fairtrade Leading the Way: Fairtrade Labelling Organisations International. Fairtrade Annual Report (2008–2009). Available from https://sellocomerciojusto.org.

Fairtrade Foundation. 2019. Social and Annual Reports (2004–2009). Available from https://www.fairtrade.org.uk.

Fairtrade International. 2019a. Fairtrade Trader Standard. https://www.fairtrade.net/fileadmin/user_upload/content/2009/standards/TS_EN.pdf.

Fairtrade International. 2019b. Fairtrade Standard for Small-scale Producer Organisations. Available from https://fairtrade/net/fileadmin/user_upload/content/2009/standards/SPO_EN.pdf.

Fairtrade International. 2019c. Fairtrade Standard for Hired Labour 2014 (due for review this year). Available from https://www.fairtrade/net/fileadmin/user_upload/content/2009/standards/document.

FAOStat. 2019. Coffee. Available from www.fao.org/faostat/en/#search/coffee.

FLANZ and Oxfam Australia. 2010. Tackling Poverty through Trade: How Australians Buying Fairtrade Benefits Producers in Developing Countries. www.oxfam.org.au/wp-content/uploads/site-media/pdf/oaus-tacking povertyfairtrade-0409.pdf.

FLO (Fairtrade Labelling Organisations International). 2009. Generic Fairtrade Standards for Small Producer Organisations. Available from https://dol.gov/ilab/issues/child- labour/consultativegroup/statement5.pdf

FLOCert. 2015. Quality Manual: explanatory document. Available from https://www.FairtradeInternationalcert.net/wp-content/uploads/2017/08/QualityManual_en.pdf.

Fonseca, E. 1994. *Economía y sociedad en Centroamérica. 1540–1680*. En R. Carmack (ed.). *Historia General de Centroamérica, tomo II*. San José: FLACSO).

Fonseca, E., Alvarenga, P. & Solórzano, J.C. 2001. Costa Rica en el siglo XVIII. San José: editorial de la Universidad de Costa Rica.

Freire, P. 1972. Pedagogy of the oppressed. Herder and Herder, New York.

Fundación Neotropica. 1988. Desarrollo Socioeconomico y el Ambiente Natural de Costa Rica. Situación Actual y Perspectivas. Editorial Heliconia. San Jose. Costa Rica.

Garcia, J.F. & Lemos, M.C. 2006. Growing sustainability: A case study on the use of sustainable agricultural practices for adapting to the coffee crisis in Agua Buena, Coto Brus, Costa Rica. Master of Science Thesis, University of Michigan.

Gathara, S. & Borgemeister, C. 2013. Climate change or urbanization? Impacts on a traditional coffee production system in East Africa over the last 80 years. *PLoS ONE 8* (1), e5815.

Giovannucci, D. & Ponte, S. 2005. Standards as a new form of social contract? Sustainability initiatives in the coffee industry. *Food Policy 30*, 284–301.

Giovanucci, D., Pierrot, J. & Kasterine, A. 2010. Trends in the Trade of Certified Coffee. Munich Personal RePEc Archive Available from http://mpra.ub.uni-muechen.de/27551/.

Gliessman, S.R. 2007. Agroecology: The Ecology of Sustainable Food Systems. CRC Press Boca Raton, London, New York.

Gresser, C. & Tickell, S. 2002. Mugged: Poverty in our coffee cup. Oxfam Campaign Report. Available from https://policy-practice.oxfam.org.uk/publications/mugged-poverty-in-our-coffee-cup.org

Gudmundson, L. 2010. Costa Rica antes del café. sociedad y economía en vísperas del boom exportador. San José: EUNED.

Gudmundson, L. 2010. La Costa Rica cafetalera en contexto comparado. Available from Centro de Informacion y Referencia sobre Centroamérica y el Caribe (CIRCA), pp. 11–23.

Gunnerod, A. & Hasse, F. 2016. The micro mill revolution. Bachelor thesis in logistics. Available from https://gupea.ub.gu.se/bitstream/2077/46767/1/gupea_2077_46767_1.pdf.

Hall, C. 1985. Costa Rica, A geographical interpretation in Historical Perspective. Boulder CO. Westview.

Hallam, D. 2003. Falling Commodity vi Prices and Industry Resources: Some lessons from the International Coffee Crisis. Commodity Market Review 2003–2004. FAO, Rome. Available from http://www.fao.org/docrep/006/y511e/y5117e03.htm#fnB13.

Happy Planet Index. 2019. Available from www.happyplanetindex.org.

Hopfensitz, A. & Miquel-Florensa, J. 2017. Mill ownership and farmer's cooperative behaviour: the case of Costa Rica coffee farmers. *Journal of Institutional Economics 13* (3): 623–48.

Honey, M. 1994. Hostile Acts. U.S. policy in Costa Rica in the 1980's. University Press of Floridad.

HDR (Human Development Report). 2016. Country Fact Sheets. Available from http://hdrstats.undp.org/en/countries/country_fact_sheets/cty_fs_SLV.html.

Hutchens, A. 2007. Entrepreneurship, power and defiance: the globalisation of the fair trade movement. Unpublished dissertation.

Icafe (Instituto del Café de Costa Rica). 2019. Estructura del Sector. www.icafe.cr/nuestro- cafe/estructure-del-sector.

ICE Coffee Futures. 2019. Coffee Cs Futures. Available from https://www.theic.com/products/15/Coffee-C-Futures.

ICO (International Coffee Organisation) Statistics. 2008. Cofee prices. Available from http://www.ico.org/coffee_prices.asp

ICO. 2010. Historical Data on the Global Coffee Trade. Available from www.ico.org/new_historical/asp.
ICO. 2013. Prices. Available from http://www.ico.org/prices/po.htm.
ICO. 2016. Assessing the economic sustainability of coffee growing. International Coffee Council, 19–23 September. Available from www.ico.org/documents/cy2015-16/icc-117-6e-economic-sustainability.pdf
ICO. 2017. Assessing the economic sustainability of coffee growing. International Coffee Council. viewed March 2017 http://www.ico.org/documents/cy2015-16/icc-117-6e-economic-sustainability.pdf.
ICO. 2017a. Daily prices. Available from www.ico.org/coffee_prices.asp.
ICO 2017b. Price paid to growers in exporting countries in US cents/lb. Available from www.ico.org/historical/1990%20onwards/PDF/3a-prices-growers.pdf.
ICO. 2018. 'Country Data on the Global Coffee Trade. #CoffeeTradeStats – country infographics' Available, <http://www.ico.org/profiles_e.asp>.
ICO. 2019. Coffee Market Report March 2019. Available from www.ico.org/documents/cy2018-19/cmr-0319-e.pdf.
IFAD (International Fund for Agriculture). 2006. IFAD Strategic Framework 2007–2010: enabling the rural poor to overcome poverty. EB 2006/89/R.2/Rev.1. Available from https://webapps.ifad.org/members/eb/89/docs/EB-2006-89-R-@-Rev-1.pdf.
IFAD. 2010. IFAD Rural Poverty Report 2010. Available from https://ifad.org/en/web/knowledge/publication/asset/39184963.
IFAD. 2010. IFAD Annual Report 2010.
IFAD. 2013. Smallholders, food security, and the environment. IFAD and UNEP. Available from https://www.ifad.org/documents/38714170/39135645/smallholders-reports.pdf/133e88903-0204- 4e7d-a780-bca847933f2e.
Igami, M. 2015. Market Power in International Commodity Trade: The Case of Coffee. *Journal of Industrial Economics* 63 (2), 225–48.
ILO (International Labour Organisation). 2010. Report of the Committee of Experts on the Application of Conventions and Recommendations.
INEC (Instituto Nacional de Estadísticas y Censos). 2000. Censos 2000. Available from www.inec.go.cr INEC. 2006. Censos Cafetalero. Available from www.inec.go.cr/censos/censos-cafetalero.
INEC. 2010. Poblacion. Available from http://www.inec.go.cr/Web/Home/pagPrincipal.aspx.
INEC. 2011. Censos 2011. Available from www.inec.go.cr/censos/censos-2011.
IOM (International Organisation for Migration). 2010. World Migration Report 2010: the future of migration: building capacities for change. Available from https://publications.iom.int/system/files/pdf/wmr_2010_english.pdf.
ITC (International Trade Centre). 2011. The Coffee Exporter's Guide: third edition. Geneva. Available from http://www.intracen.org.

ITUC (International Trade Union Confederation). 2008. Costa Rica helping migrants organise. Union View. December. Available from https://www.ituc-csi.org/IMG/pdf/VS_Costa_Rica_EN.pdf.

Jaramillo, J., Setamou, M., Muchugu, E., Chabi-Olayr, A., Jaramillo, A., Mukabana, J., Maina, J., Kanbur, R., Calvo, C.M., Das Gupta, M., Grrotaert, C., Kwakwa, V. & Lustig, N. 2000. World Development Report 2000/01: attacking poverty. Report Number 22684. Washington D.C: World Bank Group.

Karungi, J., Nambi, N., Ijala, A.R., Jonsson, M., Kyamanywa, S. & Okbom, B. 2015. Relating shading levels and distance from natural vegetation with hemipteran pests and predators occurrence on coffee. *Journal of Applied Entomology 139* (9), 678.

Kastaneda, A., Doan, D., Newhouse, D., Nguyen, M.C., Uematsu, H. & Azavedo, J.P. 2016. Who are the poor in the Developing World? Policy Research Working Paper No. 7844. World Bank. Washington DC. ©World Bank. Available from https://openknowledge.worldbank.org/handle/10986/25161.

Kennedy, J. & King, L. 2014. The political economy of farmers suicides in India. Indebted cash-crop farmers with marginal landholdings explain state-level variation in suicide rates. *Global Health* 10 (16).

Kramer, M. & Kania, J. 2006. Changing the Game: Leading Corporations Switch from Defense to Offense in Solving Global Problems. *Stanford Social Innovation Review 4* (1), 22–9.

Labour Rights. 2009. Response to Rainforest Alliance. International Labour Rights Forum and Organic Consumers Association. Available from https://labourrights.org/sites/default/files/publications-and-resources/Rainforest Alliance.

Leclair, M.S. 2002. Fighting the Tide: Alternative Trade Organisations in the Era of Global Free Trade. *World Development 30* (6), 949–58.

Leefmans, S. 1926. The coffee berry borer, S. hampei. I. Life history and ecology. *Meded. Inst. Plantezieken 57*, 61–7.

Le Pelley, R.H. 1968. Pest of Coffee. Tropical Science Series, Longmans, Green and Co., London. Le Pelley, R.H. 1973. Coffee Insects. Annual. *Review of Entomology 18*, 121–42.

León, J. 2002. Evolución del comercio exterior y de transporte marítimo de Costa Rica (1821–1900).

San José: Editorial de la Universidad de Costa Rica.

Leonard, T.M. (ed). 2012. Encyclopedia of US-Latin American Relations. CQ Press, California. Leutchford, P. 2006. Brokering Fair Trade: relations between coffee cooperatives and alternative trade organisations – a view from Costa Rica. In Lewis D., Mossse D. (eds.) *Development Brokers and Translators: The Ethnography of Aid and Agencies*. Kumarian Press, pp.127–48.

Lewin, B., Giovannucci, D. & Varangis, P. 2004. *Coffee markets: New paradigms in global supply and demand*, Agriculture and Development Discussion Paper 3, World Bank, Washington, DC.

Lopez, M. 2012. *The Incorporation of Nicaraguan Temporary Migrants into Costa Rica's Healthcare System: An Opportunity for Social Equity*. Electronic Thesis and Dissertations, 502.

Ludi, E. & Bird, K. 2007. Understanding Poverty. Brief No 1. Poverty-wellbeing. net. Available from www.poverty-wellbeing.net.

Luis, F. & Sibaja, L.F. 1982. Los indígenas de Nicoya bajo el dominio español, 1522–1560. *Estudios Sociales en Centroamérica*, pp. 32.

Luong, H.V. 2003. *Postwar Vietnam: dynamics of a transforming society*. ISEAS, Singapore.

Lyutov, N. 2010. New Sources and New Actors of International Labour Law. *Issues of Business and Law 2*, 95–103. Doi: 10.2478/v10088–010-0009–6.

Madrigal, E. 2007. La élite colonia de Costa Rica de cara a las instituciones de poder monárquico, 1600–1718. *Reflexiones 86* (2), 181–89.

Mahoney, J. 2001. Radical, reformist and aborted liberalism: origins of national regimes in Central America. *Journal of Latin American Studies 37* (2).

Martin, I. 2011. Bilateral Labour Agreements in Practice: Issues and Challenges. Background note presented as an external consultant for the IOM at the international workshop 'Information needs in support of bilateral labour agreements. Bogota, 22–23 June 2011.

Martz, J.D. 1959. Central America, The Crisis and the Challenge. Chapel Hill: University of North Carolina Press, pp. 242–43.

Mauri, C. 2002. Environmental law enforcement and compliance in Central America. Sixth international conference on environmental compliance and enforcement. INECE. April 15–19. San Jose, Costa Rica, pp. 21.

Mazza, J. & Sohnen, E. 2010. On the other side of the Fence: Changing Dynamics of Migration in the Americas. Migration Information Source, May. Available from https://www.scribd.com/document/131032916/Mazza-J-and-Sohnen-E-On-the-Other-side-of-the-fence-changing-dynamics-of-migration-in-the-americas.com.

Mchumo, A. 2007. Quoted in meeting reported on in APO 2008. The Common Fund Joins UN Secretary-General's Call for Global Action on Commodities and Development. Available from https://appablog.wordpress.com/2008/04/24/the-common-fund-joins-un-secretary-general's-call-for-global-action-on-commodities-and-development/ (Mchumo reported on the Global Initiative on Commodities (GIC) at one of the official pre-UNCTAD XII events. Information about UNCTAD available from https://unctad.org/en/pages/MeetingsArchive.aspx?meetingid=13044)

Mitchell, M.T. & Pentzer, S. 2008. Costa Rica: A Global Studies Handbook. ABC CLIO, Santa Barbara, California.

MIT. 2017. Costa Rica Exports. Available. http://atlas.media.mit.edu/en/profile/country/cri

Molina, I. 2003. Costa Rica (1800–1850). El legado colonial y la génesis del capitalismo. San José: editorial de la Universidad de Costa Rica.

Molina, I. 2005. Del legado colonial al modelo agroexportador. Costa Rica (1821–1914). San José: Editorial de la Universidad de Costa Rica.
Molina, I. 2008. Costarricense por dicha. Identidad nacional y cambio cultural en Costa Rica durante los siglos XIX y XX. San José: Editorial de la Universidad de Costa Rica.
Montero, A. 2014. Una aproximación a los cambios en el paisaje en el Valle Central de Costa Rica (1821–1900). *HALAC 3*, 2, 294.
Moore, D. & Prior, C. 1988. Present status of biological control of the coffee berry borer Hypothenemus hampei. *Pests and Diseases 3*, 1119–24.
Multatuli, S. 1982. Max Havelaar: Or the Coffee. Auctions of the Dutch Trading Company. University of Massachusetts Press.
Murray, D. L., Raynolds, L. & Taylor, P.L. 2003. The Future of Fair Trade of Coffee: Dilemmas Facing Latin America's Small-scale Producers. *Development in Practice 16* (2), 179–92.
Museos Banco Central de Costa Rica. 2019. Museo de Numismática. Exhibición permanente. Available from https://museodelbancocentral.org/en/exhibitions/currentexhibitions/the-numismatica-museum.org.
Nakajima, K. 2008. Shaping Global Partnerships. Presented at the Forum on Global Citizenship. YMCA Asia Youth Center, Tokyo Japan on behalf of Fairtrade Label Japan. Available from https://slideplayer.com/slide/10861253.
Naranjo, C. 1997. La modernización de la caficultura costarricense 1890–1950. Tesis de Maestría en Historia. Universidad de Costa Rica, pp. 94–104.
National Geographic. 1999. The Coffee Belt. Website no longer available.
NotiCen. 2006. No longer Available online. See OECD/ILO. 2018. How immigrants contribute to Costa
Rica's Economy. OECD Publishing, Paris. https://dx.doi.orf/10.1787/9789264303850-en.
O'Brien, T.G. & Kinnaird, M.F. 2003. 'Caffeine and conservation'. *Science 300* (5619), 587.
OECD. 2009. Costa Rica. Available from www.oecd.org/countries.costarica/44535774/pdf, 229
OECD. 2015. Costa Rica. Available from https://atlas.media.mit.edu/en/profile/country/cri/.
OECD. 2017. Agricultural Policies in Costa Rica. OECD Publishing, Paris. Available from http://dx.doi.org/10.1787/9789264269125-en
Osorio, N. 2002. The Global Coffee Crisis: A threat to sustainable development. ICO, <http://www.ico.org/documents/globalcrisise.pdf.
Osorio, N. 2004. Lessons from the world coffee crisis. International Coffee Organisation. 18 June. Available from www.ico.org/documents/ed1922e.pdf.
Paige, J.M. 1997. Coffee and Power: revolution and the rise of democracy in Central America. Harvard University Press.

Pendergast, M. 1999. The history of coffee and how it transformed our world. Basic Books, New York.
Pendergast, M. 2001. Uncommon grounds – the history of coffee and how it transformed our world. London, Texere.
Pendergast, M. 2009. Coffee second only to oil? Is coffee really the second largest commodity? Mark Pendergast investigates and finds some startling results. *Tea and Coffee Trade Journal 181* (4), 38–41.
Pendergast, M. 2010. Uncommon grounds – the history of coffee and how it transformed out world. Basic Books, New York. (first published 1999).
Pérez, H. 1981. Economía política del café, 1850–1959. *Avances de Investigación 5*.
Pierrot, J., Giovanucci D. & Kasterine A. 2010. Trends in the Trade of Certified Coffees. International Trade Centre Technical Paper. Available from https://ssrn.com/abstract=1736842.
Ponte, S. 2001. The 'Latte Revolution'? Winners and Losers in the Re-structuring of the Global Coffee Marketing Chain. CDR Working Paper 01.3 Centre for Development Research, Copenhagen Denmark. Available from https://pdfs.semanticsscholar.org/cf15/d6695139339ec04af142692de867ca99f411.
Ponte, S. 2004. Standards and Sustainability in the Coffee Sector: a global value chain approach. United Nations Conference on Trade and Development and the International Institute for Sustainable Development. Available from http://www.iisd.org.
Pumarino, L., Sileshi, G.W., Gripenberg, S., Kaartinen, R., Barrios, E., Muchane, M.N., Midega, C. & Jonsson, M. 2015. Effects of agroforestry on pest, disease and weed control: a meta-analysis. *Basic and Applied Ecology 16* (7), 573–82.
Quinteros, E., Ribo, A., Mejia, R., Lopez, A., Belteton, W., Comandri, A., Orantes, C.M., Pleites, E.B., Hernandez, C.E. & Lopez, D.L. 2017. Heavy metals and pesticide exposure from agricultural activities and former agrochemical factory in a Salvadoran rural community. *Environmental Science and Pollution Research 24* (2), 1662–76.
Quirós, C. 2001. La era de la encomienda. San José: Editorial de la Universidad de Costa Rica.
Quirós, C. & Solórzano, J.C. 2006. Costa Rica en el siglo XVI. Descubrimiento y conquista. San José: Editorial de la Universidad de Costa Rica.
RA (Rainforest Alliance). 2016a. Raising the Bar on Sustainability Standards. Press Release, September 20. Available from https://rainforest-alliance-org/press-releases/2017-san-standard-released.org.
RA. 2016b. Requirements and Guidelines for Use of the Rainforest Alliance Trademarks. Available from https://rainforest-alliance.org/business/wp-content/uploads/2018/07/rainforest-alliance-marks-guide.pdf.
RA. 2019. Certified product Nespresso. Available from https://www.rainforest-alliance.org/find-certified/nespresso.

RA/SAN (Rainforest Alliance/Standard Agricultural Network). 2019. Annual Reports. Available from https://www.rainforest-alliance.org/about. Information sourced from 2009 Annual Report. Ransom 1997.

Ravallion, M. 2016. Economics of poverty: History, measurement and policy. New York: Oxford University Press.

Raynolds, L. Murray, D. & Taylor, P. 2003. One Cup at a Time: Fair Trade and Poverty Alleviation in Latin America. Fair Trade Research Group, Colorado.

Raynolds, L. Murray, D. & Wilkinson, J. 2007. Fair Trade: The Challenges of Transforming Globalisation. Routledge.

Raw, A. & Free, J.B. 1977. The pollination of coffee (Coffea arabica L.) by honeybees. Plant Protection Division, Ministry of Agriculture, Kingston, Jamaica, pp. 365–69.

Remarque, E.M. 1929. All quiet on the western front. Propylaen Verlag. Little, Brown and Company. Rice, R. & Ward, J. 1996. Coffee, conservation and commerce in the Western Hemisphere. White paper 2. Smithsonian Migratory Bird Centre. Washington D.C.

Ronchi, L. 2002. The impact of fair trade on producers and their organisations: a case study of COOCAFE in Costa Rica. Working Paper 11. Poverty Research Unit at Sussex. Available from https://core.ac.uk/download/pdf/6301547.pdf.

Rovira, J. 2000. *Estado y política económica en Costa Rica (1948–1970)*. San José: Editorial de la Universidad de Costa Rica.

Salazar, O. 2003. *El apogeo de la república liberal en Costa Rica, 1870–1914*. San José: Editorial de la Universidad de Costa Rica.

Samper, M. 1989. "Historia agraria y desarrollo y desarrollo agroexportador: tendencias en los estudios sobre el periodo 1830–1850," *Revista de Historia* 19, 114.

Samper, M. 2000. Derivaciones de la modernización e intensificación cafetalera. In Samper M., Naranjo, C. & Sfez, P. (eds.) *Entre la tradición y el cambio: Evolución tecnológica de la caficultura costarricense*. SEE S.A.

SAN (Sustainable Agriculture Network). 2019. Available from https://www.sustainableagriculture.eco.

Sanchez-Azofeifa, G.A. 1996. Assessing land use/cover change in Costa Rica. UNH Scholars Repository. University of New Hampshire.

Saoud, et al. 2003. The Coffee Route from Yemen to London 10th – 17th Centuries. Available from www.muslimheritage.com/article/coffee-route.

Seligson, M.S. 1977. Prestige amongst Peasants: A Multidimensional Analysis of Preference Data. *American Journal of Sociology* 83, 632–52.

Sen, A. 1990. Objectivity and Position: Assessment of Health and well-being. Seminar of the Centre for Population Studies at Harvard University

Sen, A. 1992. Inequality Reexamined. New York: Harvard University Press.

Sen, A. 1999a. Choice, Welfare and Measurement. Cambridge, London: Harvard University Press.

Sen, A. 1999b. Development as Freedom. New York. Anchor Books.
Sen, A. & Dreze, J. 1999. The Amartya Sen and Jean Dreze Omnibus: (comprising) Poverty and Famines; Hunger and Public Action; and India: Economic Development and Social Opportunity. Oxford University Press.
Sen, A. 2002. Rationality and Freedom. Cambridge, London: The Belknap Press of Harvard University Press.
Shaw, D. & Black, I. 2010. Market based political action: a path to sustainable development? *Sustainable Development 18* (6), 385–97.
Snider, A., Gutierrez, I., Sibelet, N. & Faure, G. 2017. Small farmer cooperatives and voluntary coffee certifications: Rewarding progressive farmers of engendering widespread change in Costa Rica? *Food Policy 69*, 231–42.
State of the Nation Project. 2001. Binational Study: Th state of migration flows between Costa Rica and Nicaragua: analysis of the economic and social implications for both countries. Prepared for IOM. Available from https://publications.iom.int/system/files/pdf/binationa_study_cr-nic.pdf
Solórzano, J.C. 2008. La sociedad colonial. San José: Editorial de la Universidad de Costa Rica, pp. 14–15. Steinberg, P.F. 2001. Environmental leadership in developing countries: transnational relations and biodiversity policy in Costa Rica and Bolivia. The MIT Press. Cambridge, Massachusetts; London England.
Stone, S. 1982. *La dinastía de los conquistadores.* San José: EDUCA.
Terazono, E. 2013. Coffee slides on strong Colombia supplies. Agricultural Commodities, Financial Times, November 7. Available from https://www.ft.com/content/d76c4b04-46ff-11e3-9c1b-00144feabdc0.com.
Trauben, J. 2009. Fair Expectations: Rainforest Alliance, V. Fairtrade. Available from https://www.organicconsumers.ord/news/fair=expectations-rain forest-alliance-v-fairtrade Torres-Rivas, E. 2011. *Revoluciones sin cambios revolucionarios. Ensayos sobre la crisis en Centroamérica.* Guatemala: F y G Editores.
Trolliet, F., Vogt M. & Kleinschroth F. 2019. How does FSC certification of forest management benefit conservation of biodiversity? In Vogt, M. (ed). *Sustainability certifications in the agricultural and natural resource sector: outcomes for society and environment.* Earthscan studies in natural resource management. Routledge New York, London.
UN (United Nations). 2018. About the Sustainable Development Goals. Available from https://www.un.org/sustainabledevelopment/sustainable-development-goals.org.
UN. 2019. Goal 1: Eradiate Extreme Poverty & Hunger. Target 1.A: Halve, between 1990 and 2015, the proportion of people whose income is less than $1.25 a day. Available from https://www.un.org/milleniumgoals/poverty.shtml.
UNHCR (the United Nations Refugee Agency). 2014. Submission by the United Nations High Commissioner for Refugees for the Office of the High Commissioner for Human Rights' Compilation Report – Universal Periodic Review: Costa Rica. 19th UPR Sessions.

UN Millennium Project. 2005. Investing in development: a practical plan to achieve the Millennium Development Goals. United Nations. New York.

UTZ Certified. 2009. UTZ Annual Reports. Available from https://utz.org/attachment_id=4711.

Van Den Berghe, F. 2006. Good Coffee, Bad Governance: Flo's Legitimacy. Human Rights and Global Justice Working Paper No. 12. Available from SSRN: https://ssren.com/abstract=1399352.

Vargas, L.P. 2003. Modelo desarrollista y de industrialización sustitutiva. San José: Editorial de la Universidad de Costa Rica.

Vargas, L.P. 2003. La estrategia de liberalización económica (1980–2000). San José: Editorial de la Universidad de Costa Rica.

Vega, F.E., Posada, F. & Infante, F. 2006. Coffee Insects: Ecology and Control. In Encyclopedia of Pest Management, Taylor and Francis, pp. 1–4.

Ventura, F. 2007. Examining the Rainforest Alliance's Agricultural Certification Robustness. Graduate School of International Relations and Pacific Studies, University of California, San Diego.

Víctor H. Acuña "Patrones del conflicto social en la economía cafetalera costarricense (1900–1948)," *Revista de Ciencias Sociales*, no. 31 (1986), 114.

Vogelpohl, T. & Verbandt, D. 2019. Biofuel sustainability certifications in the EU: democratically legitimate and socio-environmentally effective? In Vogt, M (ed.) (2019). *Sustainability certifications in the agricultural and natural resource sector: outcomes for society and environment*. Earthscan studies in natural resource management. Routledge New York, London.

Vogt, M. 2019a. Sustainability certifications and their unique position of influence. In Vogt, M. (ed.) *Sustainability certifications in the agricultural and natural resource sector: outcomes for society and environment*. Earthscan studies in natural resource management. Routledge New York, London, chapter 1.

Vogt, M. 2019b. Sustainability certifications: cultural implications, flows and synergies. In Vogt, M. (ed.) (2019) *Sustainability certifications in the agricultural and natural resource sector: outcomes for society and environment*. Earthscan studies in natural resource management. Routledge New York, London, chapter 2.

Vogt, M. 2019c. Juggling sustainability certifications in the Costa Rican coffee industry. In Vogt, M. (ed.) (2019) *Sustainability certifications in the agricultural and natural resource sector: outcomes for society and environment*. Earthscan studies in natural resource management. Routledge New York, London, chapter 11.

Vogt, M. 2019d. Comparing and seeking complementarity between four farm design. *Global Ecology and Conservation 17*, e00520.

Vogt, M. (ed.) 2019e. Sustainability certifications in the agricultural and natural resource sector: outcomes for society and environment. Earthscan studies in natural resource management. Routledge New York, London.

Vogt, M. 2019f. Collating correlations, conclusion, recommendations and ideas for future research, evaluation and practice. In Vogt, M. (ed.) (2019) *Sustainability certifications in the agricultural and natural resource sector: outcomes for society and environment.* Earthscan studies in natural resource management. Routledge New York, London.

Vogt, M. & Englund, O. 2019. Biodiversity outcomes associated with sustainability certifications: contextualising understanding and expectations and allowing for ambitious intentions. In Vogt, M. (ed.) (2019). *Sustainability certifications in the agricultural and natural resource sector: outcomes for society and environment.* Earthscan studies in natural resource management. Routledge New York, London, Chapter 3.

Vos, J., Van omen, P. & Mena-Vasconez, P. 2019. To certify or not to certify flower production practices in Ecuador. In Vogt, M. (ed.) (2019). *Sustainability certifications in the agricultural and natural resource sector: outcomes for society and environment.* Earthscan studies in natural resource management. Routledge New York, London.

Waller, J.M., Bigger, M. & Hillocks, R.J. 2007. Coffee pests, disease and their management. CAB International.

Watts, M. 2005. Culture, development and global neo-liberalism pp. 31. Available from http://globetrotter.berkeley.edu/bwep/greengovernance/papers/Watts_CultureDevelopment.pdf WCED (World Commission on Environment and Development). 1987. Our Common Future: Brundtland Report. Oxford University Press, pp. 383.

Weinberg, B.A., Bealer, B.K. 2001. The World of Caffeine: The science and culture of the world's most popular drug. Taylor & Francis.

WFTO [World Fair Trade Organisation]. 2019. History of Fair Trade: 60 years of fair trade: a brief history of the fair trade movement. Available from https://wfto.com/about-us/history-wfto/history-fair-trade.

Winson, A. 1989. Coffee and Democracy in Costa Rica. Springer, Political Science.

World Bank. 2017. World Bank Development Indicators. Available from http://data.worldbank.org/country/costa-rica.

WFTO (World Fair Trade Organisation). 2019. History of Fair Trade. Available from https://www.wfto.com/about-us/history-wfto/history-fair-trade.com.

Workman, D. 2019. Costa Rica's Top 10 Exports. Available from www.worldstopexports.com/costa-ricas-top-10-exports.

Wrigley, E.A. 1988. Continuity, chance, and change. The character of the Industrial Revolution in England. Cambridge University Press, New York, pp. 146.

Recommended Reading for Recent Developments

Babin, N. 2015. Coffee crisis, fair trade, and agroecological transformation impacts on land-use change in Costa Rica. *Agroecology and Sustainable Food Systems 29* (1), 99–129.

Bacon, C. Mendez, E. Gliessman, S. Goodman, D. & Fox, J. (eds.) 2008. Confronting the Coffee Crisis: Fair Trade, Sustainable Livelihoods, and Ecosystems in Mexico and Central America. MIT Press.

Barham, B.L., Callenes, M., Gitter, S., Lewis, J. & Weber, J. 2011. Fair trade/organic coffee, rural livelihoods, and the 'agrarian question': southern Mexican coffee families in transition. *World Development 39* (1), 134–45.

Buckingham, K. & Hanson, C. 2010. The Restoration Diagnostic, Case Example: Costa Rica. World Resources Institute. wri.org.

Costa Rica. 1961. Ley 2762 del 21/06/1961: Ley sobre régimen de relaciones entre productores, beneficiadores y exportadores de café. Costa Rica, Asamblea Legislativa de la Republica de Costa Rica.

Costa Rica. 2010. Ley 8839 del 8/12/2010. Decreta: Ley para la gestión integral de residuos. Asamblea Legislativa de la Republica de Costa Rica. *La Gaceta 135*. www.ucr.ac.cr/medios/documentos/2015/LEY-8839.pdf.

Danse, M. & Wolters, T. 2003. Sustainable coffee in the mainstream: the case of the SUSCOF Consortium in Costa Rica. *GMI 43*, 37–51.

De Neve, G., Luetchford, P., Pratt, J. & Wood, D.C. (eds.) 2008. Hidden Hands in the Market: Ethnographies of Fair Trade, Ethical Consumption and Corporate Social Responsibility. Emerald.

Diaz, D. 2015. Costa Rica: How quality pays for coffee farmers. responAbility Investments Ag. Zurich. Fairtrade International 2018. www.fairtrade.net/.

Gyllensten, B. 2017. Micro Mills, Specialty Coffee and Relationships: Following the Supply Chain from Costa Rica to Norway. Thesis. Reprosentralen, University of Oslo.

Hanson, L., Terstappen, V., Bacon, C.M., Leung, J., Ganem-Cuenca, A., Flores, S.R.D. & Rojas, M.A.M. 2012. Gender, health, and Fairtrade: insights from a research-action programme in Nicaragua. *Development in Practice 22* (2), 164–79.

ICA. 2007. International Coffee Agreement 2007. www.ico.org/ica2007.asp.

Icafe. 2015. El café sostenible de Costa Rica. www.icafe.cr/nuestro-cafe/proceso-de-liquidacion/. Icafe. 2018. Estructura del sector. www.icafe.cr/nuestro-cafe/estructura-del-sector/.

ICO (International Coffee Organisation). 2018. Developing a Sustainable Coffee Economy. www.ico.org/sustaindev_e.asp.

Luetchford, P. 2008. Fair Trade and a Global Commodity: Coffee in Costa Rica. Pluto Press.

MAG (Ministerio de Agricultura y Ganadería de Costa Rica). 1988. Decreto 18135 MAG: Prohibición para sembrar la variedad de café denominado Coffea Canephora Robusta. *La Gaceta 106* (25), 3 June.

MAG. 1989. Decreto 19302 MAG: Autoriza al Instituto del Café de Costa Rica y al Ministerio de Agricultura y Ganaderia para eliminar las siembras existentes de la especie denominada Coffea Canephora 'Robusta'. *La Gaceta 229* (6–7), 4 December.

Martz, J.D. 1959. Central America: The Crisis and Challenge. University of North Carolina Press. Mitchell, M.T. & Pentzer, S. 2008. Costa Rica: A Global Studies Handbook. ABC-CLIO.

Potts, J., Lynch, M., Wilkings, A., Huppe, G., Cunningham, M. & Voora, V. 2014. The State of Sustainability Initiatives Review. International Institute for Sustainable Development, Winnipeg.

Rainforest Alliance. 2018. www.rainforest-alliance.org/approach.

Rovira Mas, J. 1982. Estado y política económica en Costa Rica 1948–1970. Editorial de la Universidad de Costa Rica.

Ruben, R. & Zuniga, G. 2010. How standards compete: comparative impact of coffee certification schemes in northern Nicaragua. *International Journal of Supply Chain Management 16* (2): 98–109. Smith, J. 2008. The search for sustainable markets: the promise and failure of fair trade. *Culture and Agriculture 29* (2), 88–99.

SSI Review. 2014. Coffee Market. Chapter 8. Available from www.iisd.org/pdf/2014/ssi_2014_chapter_8.pdf.

Vogt, M. 2011. *Tico Time: The Influence of Coffee Certifications on Sustainable Development and Poverty Reduction in Costa Rica: A Discussion with Coffee Farmers and Cooperative Managers.* PhD. Flinders University, Faculty of Social and Behavioural Sciences.

Wollni, M. & Zeller, M. 2006. *Do farmers benefit from participating in specialty markets and cooperatives? The case of coffee marketing in Costa Rica.* Contributed paper prepared for presentation at the International Association of Agricultural Economics Conference, Gold Coast, Australia, 12–18 August.

Glossary

Beneficiado	Coffee processors
Beneficio	Coffee mill in Costa Rica
Chacras	Farm
Ejidos	An area of communal land used for agriculture
Encomenderos	An entrusted person
Habilitation	Advanced financing
Hacienda	An estate in the form of Roman villa, common in the colonies of the Spanish empire.
Indios	Costa Rican indigenous, referred to through the paper as first nations
Mestizos	A person of mixed race: usually of Spanish and Indigenous descent
Mulatto	A person of mixed 'white' and 'black' ancestry; of one white and one black parent, or mulatto parents
Petacas	A bag in which a product is transported
Pueblos de Indios	Communities of Costa Rican indigenous, First Nation people exploited for labour
Reino	A commune or municipality

Appendix A: Themes for fieldwork discussion and interviews

Employees of Certification Bodies
Perceived benefits of certifications in a sustainable development framework; Role and process in Costa Rica; Difference in approach to other certifications; Areas in Costa Rican coffee production that could still be improved

Labourers
All labourers
Working arrangements (work status (casual, contract), hours worked, rate of pay, length of work 'contract', access to health care, sick pay), knowledge of certification and required processes for farm, opportunities to be involved in local unions, NGOs, and level of involvement in those bodies, political knowledge and involvement Activities in off-season, for ongoing workers observed difference in working conditions over years

Migrant labourers
Reasons for moving to Costa Rica; Working arrangements (potential for disparity) Living with family or alone; Visa status

Women labourers
Working arrangements (potential for disparity)

Small family run farm owners – members of cooperatives or certified farms
Key issues facing small coffee farm holders; If applicable, choosing between certifications 3 Interaction with certification body; Level of participation in Cooperative Model – attendance to meetings; Difference in farm activities, economic and social situation before and after certification involvement; Key perceived benefits of certification and membership of cooperative 6 Resulting feelings of association; Potential improvements to standards of certification or contract conditions

Personal benefits, financial and social of certification and cooperative membership 9 Fairtrade price premium versus financial assistance from public sector

Farms employed by larger local roaster without certification
Contract/employment conditions; Key environmental and social standard clauses to be upheld Knowledge of certifications, current employer or contractors' standards, State law and government role; Preference toward current employer and certification or cooperative; Observed difference over time – economic and social from work relationship with un-certified roaster;

For both groups
Migrating family members, options for selling land versus maintaining; Options for crop diversification Women's role, involvement in farm work and in the household

Managers of Cooperatives
Working with certification bodies; Working with cooperative structure, managing membership, political activity of cooperative; Opinions and knowledge of Central American Free Trade Agreement and maintaining lands; Decisions for community development projects; Difference before and after certification (income, lifestyle, crop diversification, stability, health care, education)

Plans to move past certification; Areas of improvement of certification; Fairtrade premium versus public financial assistance

Socially and environmentally responsible Coffee Exporters (non-certified)
Opinions on certification; Standards (environmental and social) adhered to, monitoring system, changes over last 5 years; Opinions on CAFTA; Plans for business expansion

Employees of Certification Bodies
Perceived benefits of certifications, difference in approach and opinions of other certifications; Areas to be improved

Local NGO
Key issues facing local community related to coffee farming; Impacts of varying certifications and business activities on community development and environment

Academics
Certifications and environment, trade and community development; Government role in regulating coffee industry

Government
Policy related to standards of certifications; State regulation of coffee industry

www.ingramcontent.com/pod-product-compliance
Lightning Source LLC
Chambersburg PA
CBHW061254230426
43665CB00027B/2944